CW00959235

Understanding
PETER WEISS

UNDERSTANDING MODERN EUROPEAN and LATIN AMERICAN LITERATURE

James Hardin, *Series Editor*

ADVISORY BOARD

George C. Schoolfield
Yale University

Charles Porter
Yale University

Theodore Ziolkowski
Princeton University

Roberto González-Echevarría
Yale University

Michael Winkler
Rice University

Sara Castro-Klarén
The Johns Hopkins University

Understanding Günter Grass
by Alan Frank Keele

Understanding Elias Canetti
by Richard H. Lawson

Understanding Graciliano Ramos
by Celso Lemos de Oliveira

Understanding Thomas Bernhard
by Stephen D. Dowden

Understanding Gabriel García Márquez
by Kathleen McNerney

Understanding Heinrich Böll
by Robert C. Conard

Understanding Claude Simon
by Ralph Sarkonak

Understanding Céline
by Philip H. Solomon

Understanding Mario Vargas Llosa
by Sara Castro-Klarén

Understanding Gerhart Hauptmann
by Warren R. Maurer

Understanding Samuel Beckett
by Alan Astro

Understanding José Donoso
by Sharon Magnarelli

Understanding Jean-Paul Sartre
by Philip R. Wood

Understanding Milan Kundera
by Fred Misurella

Understanding Albert Camus
by David R. Ellison

Understanding Italo Calvino
by Beno Weiss

Understanding Max Frisch
by Wulf Koepke

Understanding Franz Werfel
by Hans Wagener

Understanding Erich Maria Remarque
by Hans Wagener

Understanding Peter Weiss
by Robert Cohen

Understanding

Peter Weiss

by
Robert Cohen

University of South Carolina Press

Copyright © 1993 University of South Carolina

Published in Columbia, South Carolina, by the
University of South Carolina Press

Manufactured in the United States of America

Library of Congress Cataloging-in-Publication Data

Cohen, Robert, 1941 Apr. 13–
    Understanding Peter Weiss / by Robert Cohen.
        p.   cm. — (Understanding modern European and Latin American
    literature)
    "This monograph was written in German . . . and translated by Martha
    Humphreys"—P.
    Includes bibliographical references and index.
    ISBN 0–87249–898–0 (acid-free paper)
    1. Weiss, Peter, 1916–   —Criticism and interpretation.
    I. Title.   II. Series.
    PT2685.E5Z63   1993   93–17439
    832′ .914—dc20

Without Jenna Osiason I neither could have
nor would have written this book.
It is dedicated to her.

CONTENTS

CONTENTS

EDITOR'S PREFACE

*U*nderstanding Modern European and Latin American Literature has been planned as a series of guides for undergraduate and graduate students and nonacademic readers. Like its companion series, Understanding Contemporary American Literature, the aim of the books is to provide an introduction to the life and writings of prominent modern authors and to explicate their most important works.

Modern literature makes special demands, and this is particularly true of foreign literature, in which the reader must contend not only with unfamiliar, often arcane artistic conventions and philosophical concepts, but also with the handicap of reading the literature in translation. It is a truism that the nuances of one language can be rendered in another only imperfectly (and this problem is especially acute in fiction), but the fact that the works of European and Latin American writers are situated in a historical and cultural setting quite different from our own can be as great a hindrance to the understanding of these works as the linguistic barrier. For this reason, the UMELL series will emphasize the sociological and historical background of the writers treated. The peculiar philosophical and cultural traditions of a given culture may be particularly important for an understanding of certain authors, and these will be taken up in the introductory chapter and also in the discussion of those works to which this informant is relevant. Beyond this, the books will treat the specifically literary aspects of the author under discussion and attempt to explain the complexities of contemporary literature lucidly. The books are conceived as introductions to the authors covered, not as comprehensive analyses. Nor do they provide detailed summaries of plot since they are meant to be used in conjunction with the books they treat, not as a substitute for the study of the original works. The purpose of the books is to provide information and judicious literary assessment of the major works in the most compact, readable form. It is our hope that the UMELL series will help to increase our knowledge and understanding of the European and Latin American cultures and will serve to make the literature of those cultures more accessible.

Professor Cohen's thoughtful, expert analysis of the works of Peter Weiss—some of which are little-known in the English-speaking world—is in my view an especially valuable contribution to the UMELL series. It explicates a view of the world largely foreign to American eyes, and does so in a closely reasoned, lucid manner that is the goal of all the books in this series. It is not only the best book in English about Weiss, it is the most readable in any language.

J. H.

ACKNOWLEDGMENTS

This monograph was written in German for the University of South Carolina Press series, *Understanding Contemporary European and Latin American Literature,* and translated by Martha Humphreys. Martha died after she finished the translation, and her enormous efforts are remembered here.

Many thanks to Volkmar Sander, chairperson of the German department at New York University, where I spent the two years it took to write this book as a visiting scholar.

Thanks also to my colleagues and friends Margret Herzfeld-Sander and Konstanze Streese, both of New York University, for critically reading parts of the manuscript.

Special thanks to my editor, James Hardin, University of South Carolina, and to my friends Michael Winkler, Rice University, and Manfred Haiduk, professor emeritus of Rostock University, who read the complete manuscript and whose comments led me to reevaluate and improve many passages.

ABBREVIATIONS

W orks cited in the text have been abbreviated as follows. The full citations for these editions are in the Bibliography.

G/R:

Rainer Gerlach and Matthias Richter, *Peter Weiss im Gespräch* (Interviews with Peter Weiss).

Marat/Sade:

Peter Weiss, *The Persecution and Assassination of Jean-Paul Marat as Performed by the Inmates of the Asylum of Charenton under the Direction of the Marquis de Sade.*

N I/:

Peter Weiss, *Notizbücher 1960–1971* (Notebooks 1960–1971).

N II/:

Peter Weiss, *Notizbücher 1971–1980* (Notebooks 1971–1980).

Viet Nam Discourse:

Peter Weiss, *Discourse on the Progress of the Prolonged War of Liberation in Viet Nam and the Events Leading up to It as Illustration of the Necessity for Armed Resistance against Oppression and on the Attempts of the United States of America to Destroy the Foundations of Revolution.*

I/ II/ III/:

Peter Weiss, *Die Ästhetik des Widerstands* (The Aesthetics of Resistance). Roman numerals refer to volume number, arabic numerals to page number. (The pagination is the same in all Suhrkamp editions.)

CHRONOLOGY

1916   Born November 8, in Nowawes (today Potsdam/Babelsberg) near Berlin.

1919   Moves to the harbor city of Bremen, Grünenstrasse 23.

1920   Birth of his sister Irene.

1922   Birth of his sister Margit.

1923   Moves to Marcusallee 45, in the patrician section of Bremen. Attendance at *Volksschule* (elementary school), followed by the gymnasium.

1924   Birth of brother Alexander.

1928   Summer in Tübingen with relatives of his mother, the Autenrieths, descendants of the physician of the same name who had once treated the poet Friedrich Hölderlin.

1929   Moves to Berlin. Attends the Heinrich-von-Kleist Gymnasium in Berlin-Schmargendorf.

1932   First drawing instruction; then attends Eugen Spiro's painting class for several months.

1933   In the wake of the seizure of power by the Nazis, Weiss is transferred from the gymnasium to the Rackow-Handelsschule (trade school) in Berlin.

1934   First large-scale paintings. Earliest texts. In early August his sister Margit killed in an automobile accident.

1935   March: the family goes into exile in Chislehurst, near London. Weiss works in his father's office and attends the Polytechnic School of Photography.

1936   First exhibition in a storeroom in Little Kinnerton Street, London.

1936–37   Moves to Varnsdorf in Bohemia (Sudetenland), Czechoslovakia, where his father assumes management of a textile factory.

1937   In addition to painting, literary efforts continue. Spends the summer in the Ticino (Italian part of Switzerland), near the admired German writer Hermann Hesse. Through Hesse's mediation, Weiss comes into contact in Prague with Max Barth, whose recommendation leads to Weiss's acceptance in Willy Novak's painting class at the Prague Art Academy. He meets Endre Nemes, Robert Jungk, Peter Kien, and Lucie Weisberger.

1938   Winter 1937–38: attends the Prague Art Academy. Paintings reflect influence of Bosch and Brueghel. Recipient of an award from the academy in the spring. With friends Robert Jungk and Hermann Levin Goldschmidt, he again visits Hesse in the Ticino in September. Following the occupation of the Sudetenland by the German army (1 October), his parents emigrate to Sweden. Peter Weiss remains in Switzerland.

1939   Writes and illustrates "Traktat von der ausgestorbenen Welt" (Treatise about the Died-Out World). Early 1939: travels through Berlin to Alingsås, in western Sweden, where his father takes over the renovation and management of the Silfa textile factory. Until 1942 Weiss works in his father's office and in the factory, designing patterns for fabrics.

1940   Reunion with friends Max Barth and Endre Nemes, now exiles in Sweden; acquaintance with socialist physician and psychiatrist Max Hodann.

1941   March: first exhibition in Sweden, in Stockholm's *Mässhallen*. April to August: psychoanalysis with Dr. Iwan Bratt in Alingsås.

1942   Lives with the painter and sculptress Helga Henschen. Spends the summer as a farm worker.

1943   February–March: works as a lumberjack in northern Sweden. Returns in the spring to Alingsås to earn his living. First contacts with young Swedish writers—including Stig Dagerman—from the "Fyrtiotalisterna" group. Marries Helga Henschen in November.

1944   Moves to Stockholm for good. January–April: participates in the exhibition "Konstnärer i landsflykt" (Artists in Exile) in Stockholm and Göteborg. June: birth of daughter Randi-Maria. Writes his first Swedish language book, *Från ö till ö* (*Von Insel zu Insel;* From Island to Island).

1945 April: exhibition in Gummesons Konsthall, Stockholm.

1946 Exhibition in the Louis Hahne Art Gallery, Stockholm. November 8, acquires Swedish citizenship.

1947 Spends summer in Berlin as correspondent for *Stockholms Tidningen;* eight reports are published. In conjunction with this journalistic work, Weiss writes the prose text *De Besegrade* (*Die Besiegten;* The Vanquished). *Från ö till ö* is published by Bonnier, Stockholm.

1948 *De Besegrade* published by Bonnier. The prose text "Der Vogelfreie" (The Outlaw) is rejected by the German publisher Peter Suhrkamp.

1949 "Der Vogelfreie" is privately published in a Swedish version as *Dokument I*. Brief marriage with Carlota Dethorey, birth of son Paul. Writes the radio play *Rotundan* (*Der Turm; The Tower*).

1950 Starting late 1949 (until 1952), psychoanalysis with Lajos Székely, a student of Freud. Swedish stage premiere of *Rotundan*.

1951 Writes the prose text *Duellen* (*Das Duell;* The Duel).

1952 Writes the micro-novel *Der Schatten des Körpers des Kutschers* (*The Shadow of the Coachman's Body*) and the play *Die Versicherung* (The Insurance). Becomes member of Swedish Experimental Film Studio (later, Work Group for Film). Lives with the artist Gunilla Palmstierna. Begins directing experimental films. Teaches painting and, later, film at the Stockholm People's University (until the mid-1950s).

1953 The prose text *Duellen* privately published in Stockholm with pen-and-ink drawings by Weiss. Main work is the production and direction of experimental films.

1956 Collection of Weiss's Swedish language essays and criticisms on film published under the title *Avantgardefilm*. Makes his only experimental film in color, *The Studio of Dr. Faust*. First documentary film, about the homeless in Stockholm.

1957 Illustrations (collages) to *A Thousand and One Nights*. Continues work as a documentary filmmaker.

1958   Directs his only (experimental) feature film *Hägringen (Der Verschollene)*. December: Weiss's mother dies.

1959   March: his father dies. Start of work on *Abschied von den Eltern (Leavetaking)*. West German literary critic Walter Höllerer places the manuscript *The Shadow of the Coachman's Body* with the prestigious Suhrkamp publishing house, where it is published. Suhrkamp becomes the publisher for all Weiss's works.

1960   Works on an exploitation film about Swedish girls in Paris, then distances himself from the final version. In the south of France he writes the short prose text "Der Grosse Traum des Briefträgers Cheval" (The Postman Cheval's Big Dream). From August to November he directs one more documentary film.

1961   *Leavetaking* is published with eleven collages by Weiss. Works on the novel *Fluchtpunkt (Vanishing Point)*. Translates into German August Strindberg's *Miss Julie*.

1962   *Vanishing Point* is published. Translates Strindberg's *A Dream Play*. May 27: gives a speech, "Gegen die Gesetze der Normalität" (Against the Laws of Normality), in conjunction with the Strindberg Festival at the Schiller Theater in West Berlin. Late October: First participation at a meeting of the West German Writers' group Gruppe 47, in West Berlin.

1963   Writes the street ballad-like play *Nacht mit Gästen (Night with Guests)*. Awarded the Charles Veillon Prize by the Swiss city of Lausanne for *Vanishing Point*. Starts work on *Marat/Sade*. Writes the prose fragment *Das Gespräch der drei Gehenden (Conversation of the Three Wayfarers)*. November 16: premiere of *Night with Guests* at the workshop of the Schiller Theater, West Berlin. Translation of Strindberg's *Dream Play* is published. Weiss's paintings are shown at Galerie Springer in West Berlin.

1964   January: marries Gunilla Palmstierna, his important collaborator of long standing, a set and costume designer. April 29: premiere of *Marat/Sade* at the Schiller Theater, West Berlin. Weiss is asked to assume direction of the new film academy in West Berlin, but he eventually rejects the offer. Occasional presence at the Auschwitz trial in Frankfurt am Main. December 13: visits the Auschwitz concentration camp.

1965 Awarded the Lessing Prize by the city of Hamburg, and a literature prize by the Swedish labor movement. March 26: premiere of *Marat/Sade* in Rostock, GDR. Start of important collaboration with the GDR director Hanns Anselm Perten and his staff. Publication of the essay "10 Arbeitspunkte eines Autors in der geteilten Welt" (An Author's Ten Working Points in the Divided World). The short prose texts "Meine Ortschaft" ("My Place") (about Weiss's visit to Auschwitz), as well as "Vorübung zum dreiteiligen Drama divina commedia" (Preliminary Study for the Three-Part Divine Comedy Drama) are published. October 19: simultaneous premieres of the Auschwitz play *Die Ermittlung* (*The Investigation*) on sixteen stages in West and East Germany. December 28: in an open letter Weiss defends the East German songwriter Wolf Biermann, who had been vehemently attacked in the GDR.

1966 Awarded the Heinrich-Mann Prize by the Academy of Arts, East Berlin. Filming of *Marat/Sade* by Peter Brook in England. First public expression of support for the People's Republic of Vietnam at a Gruppe 47 meeting at Princeton University. April 25: gives a speech in English at Princeton University, "I Come Out of My Hiding Place." Dispute with Hans Magnus Enzensberger about the Third World in the July issue of the West German cultural journal *Kursbuch*.

1967 Awarded the Carl Albert Anderson Prize (Stockholm culture prize). January 26: premiere of *Gesang vom lusitanischen Popanz* (*Song of the Lusitanian Bogey*) at Scala Theater, Stockholm. October 6: German premiere at the Schaubühne am Halleschen Ufer, West Berlin. April: participation at the first Russell Tribunal on the Vietnam War in Stockholm. In his essay "Der Sieg, der sich selbst bedroht" (The Victory that Endangers Itself) Weiss protests Israel's policy after the Six-Day War. July–August: travels to Cuba with Gunilla Palmstierna-Weiss. Late November: participates in the continuation of the Russell Tribunal, in the Danish town of Roskilde. December 2: German premiere of the play *The Tower* at the Theater am Belvedere, Vienna. December 19: GDR premiere of *Song of the Lusitanian Bogey,* in Rostock.

1968 March 20: premiere of *Viet Nam Diskurs* (*Viet Nam Discourse*), Städtische Bühnen of Frankfurt am Main. March 31: GDR premiere in Rostock. May 16: premiere of *Wie dem Herrn Mockinpott das Leiden ausgetrieben wird* (*How Mr. Mockinpott Was Cured of His Sufferings*) at the Landestheater in Hanover. May 15–June 21: travels to North Vietnam with Gunilla Palmstierna-Weiss. Subsequently, "Notizen zum kulturellen Leben der Demokratischen Republik Viet Nam" (Notes Concerning the Cultural Life of the Democratic Republic of Vietnam) are published. Publicly protests against the Soviet invasion of Czechoslovakia. Joins the Swedish Communist Party (VPK).

1969   Works on *Trotzki im Exil* (*Trotsky in Exile*).

1970   January 20: premiere of *Trotsky in Exile* at the Schauspielhaus in Düsseldorf. As a result, relations with the GDR reach a low point. Starts work on *Hölderlin*. June 8: heart attack. Work on the prose text "Rekonvaleszenz."

1971   April 8: German language premiere of *Die Versicherung*, Städtische Bühnen, Essen. September 18: premiere of *Hölderlin*, Würtembergisches Landestheater, Stuttgart. Early November: Weiss is refused entry into the GDR from Berlin. Late November: a meeting with East German cultural representatives leads to improved relations.

1972   The prose text *Duellen*, written in Swedish in 1951, is published in German under the title *Das Duell* (The Duel) by Suhrkamp. First notes for *Die Ästhetik des Widerstands* (*The Aesthetics of Resistance*). In the ensuing months and years numerous discussions, extensive research, and travel in conjunction with the novel. November 16: birth of daughter Nadja.

1973   June 16: GDR premiere of *Hölderlin* in Rostock.

1974   At Ingmar Bergman's suggestion, dramatization of Kafka's novel *Der Prozess* (*The Trial*). Bergman rejects Weiss's dramatization. Weiss travels to the Soviet Union and participates in the writers' congress in Moscow; visit to Volgograd (formerly Stalingrad).

1975   May 28: premiere of *Der Prozess* (The Trial) in Bremen. Publication of the first volume of *Die Ästhetik des Widerstands*.

1976   Exhibition: "Peter Weiss—Paintings, Collages, Drawings, 1933–66," in Sodertälje, Sweden; subsequently shown in Rostock, East Berlin, Munich, Paris, and Zurich. November 27:

GDR premiere of *How Mr. Mockinpott Was Cured of His Sufferings* in Rostock.

1977   Protest against the exclusion of the Czechoslovakian writer Pavel Kohout at the international writers' meeting in the Bulgarian capital, Sofia. The protest is ineffective; Weiss cancels his planned participation.

1978   Thomas Dehler Prize. Publication of the second volume of *Die Ästhetik des Widerstands.*

1979   Work on the third volume of *Die Ästhetik des Widerstands.*

1980   Exhibition, "Der Maler Peter Weiss," in the Bochum Museum. The 1948 prose text "Der Vogelfreie" is published in German by Suhrkamp as *Der Fremde* (The Foreigner), under the pseudonym Sinclair. Work on *Die Ästhetik des Widerstands* is concluded.

1981   Work on *Der neue Prozess* (The New Trial). October 1981: Awarded the Literature Prize by the city of Cologne. Publication of the third volume of *Die Ästhetik des Widerstands* and *Notizbücher 1971–1980.*

1982   January: awarded literature prize of his childhood city, Bremen. March 12: Swedish language premiere of *Der neue Prozess* in Stockholm, directed by Peter Weiss. May 2: Rejection of the honorary doctorates offered him by Wilhelm Pieck University in Rostock and by Marburg University. May 10: Peter Weiss dies in Stockholm. Posthumously awarded the Georg Büchner Prize and the Swedish Theater Critics Prize. Publication of *Notizbücher 1960–1971.*

1991   November 8 (Weiss's seventy-fifth birthday): a commemorative plaque is placed on the house where Weiss was born in Potsdam/Babelsberg.

Understanding
PETER WEISS

INTRODUCTION

In the early 1960s the first record albums by the Beatles appeared in stores. The four young musicians from the Liverpool proletariat were creative, irreverent, and extravagant. They went on to change the way of life of an entire generation. Youth, creativity, irreverence, and extravagance were suddenly in demand, and where there is demand, business will follow. The new creativity—and those who marketed it—had an effect not only on music but also on art and literature. It was a time that thrived on the new and ever more extravagant. In 1964 a play opened in the Federal Republic of Germany that seemed to fit these criteria by its title alone: *The Persecution and Assassination of Jean-Paul Marat as Performed by the Inmates of the Asylum of Charenton under the Direction of the Marquis de Sade.*

The author of this literary coup de main, a work that was to attract attention far beyond the FRG, had until then been unknown to a wider public. He was, it turned out, no young genius trying to establish himself through irreverence and extravagance in the world of art and entertainment. The biographical information about him was confusing. Peter Weiss was almost fifty years old, and he was Swedish. Yet, curiously enough, he had written his play in German. For Weiss had been born and raised in Germany between the two world wars. After 1933 he and his family had had to leave the Nazi state.

It turned out that Peter Weiss had been a painter for many years and had also worked as a film director. It was only a short while before the play about Marat and Sade appeared on the stages of the world that he had abandoned painting and filmmaking in order to devote his time entirely to writing. All of which explained why he had, until then, been little known on the German literary scene. Now, however, his name became the proverbial household word, and his next play was awaited impatiently. It had a terse title, *The Investigation,* and it brought the topic of Auschwitz to the stage. A play with not a trace of extravagance, although, with plenty of irreverence, according to certain circles. Its author had become a communist. He considered that it was not enough to reveal the horrors of the camps and mourn the dead. One needed also to point out guilt and to name the perpetrators, some of whom had once again reached the highest political and economic positions in the FRG. Revealing their names on stage was not only irreverent, it was fraught with risk and was to expose the recently admired author of *Marat/Sade* to the hatred of those who did not appreciate this type of irreverence.

A difficult life.

And a difficult work.

"Abandon all hope ye who enter here." That is the message on the gate to hell through which Dante and Virgil enter the Inferno, in the third canto of the *Divina Commedia*. Dante's epic poem served as the focus around which Peter Weiss constructed his literary work. His intention was to write a *Divine Comedy* of the twentieth century. Out of the many years he spent on this project came some of his major works, from *The Investigation* to *The Aesthetics of Resistance*. The latter, a 1,000-page novel on which Weiss worked during the last ten years of his life, does come close to Dante's epic poem in several ways. It is increasingly considered as one of the great literary works of the century ("Jahrhundertbuch").[1] Nonetheless, there was not to be a new *Divine Comedy*. For one thing, Weiss's reading of Dante's poem hardly went beyond the *Inferno*, as he himself noted on occasion. He tried to explain his difficulty with Dante's text in terms of his lack of historical knowledge.[2] But there may have been other reasons why he endlessly lingered with the *Inferno*. After all, what experiences had there been in Weiss's life that might have made it easier for him to grasp the concept of the *Paradiso?* He lived in dark times, and this is expressed in his work. Whoever becomes involved with Weiss's oeuvre is always closer to hell than to paradise.

Weiss's work is filled with the awareness that this is "a world of bodies," as he has the Marquis de Sade say. His whole creative oeuvre, but particularly his literary work, contains numerous obsessive descriptions of tortures that are inflicted on the human body: during the French Revolution and the German restoration, in fascist Germany, in the Spanish Civil War, under Stalinism, in Angola, and in Vietnam. Located in the deepest circle of hell is a place Weiss once described in an essay titled "My Place" ("Meine Ortschaft"): Auschwitz.

And yet, readers of Peter Weiss's works need not abandon all hope. He himself did not—especially not after the early 1960s and his turn toward socialism and communism, wherein he found a basis for hope. He clung to it, despite his doubts and his many protests against the deformations of socialism in the communist countries. He believed that the world could be changed, that the debased and exploited masses—by which he increasingly meant the people of the Third World—could be redeemed from their fate. Repeatedly, he portrayed the longing of the oppressed for leaders, redeemer figures to guide them out of their misery. Over time these redeemer figures became more secular until finally the sober insight was arrived at that no redeemer would ever appear. The people "would have to empower themselves, would have to seize this broad and vibrant movement with which they would finally be able to sweep away the terrible pressure weighing them down," according to the mighty closing sentence of *The Aesthetics of Resistance.*

Today, it appears that in the last period of Weiss's life doubts about the forces and countries that still represented socialism in the early 1980s replaced earlier hopes. It is undeniably no longer a socialist but rather an anticapitalist position that informs his last work, *Der neue Prozess* (The New Trial). This is more than a nuance. Weiss's modification of his thinking preceded the political upheavals he did not live to see. Communism, prescribed from above and bureaucratically administered, had not been able to bring people that redemption for which Weiss and other millions had hoped.

The epoch of the October Revolution is over. But people will still have to learn to "empower themselves," to "seize this broad and vibrant movement."

NOTES

1. Wolfgang Fritz Haug and Kaspar Maase, "Vorwort," in Haug and Maase, eds., *Materialistische Kulturtheorie und Alltagskultur* (Berlin: Argument, 1980) 4.

2. See Peter Weiss, "Gespräch über Dante" (1965), in Weiss, *Rapporte* (1968) (Frankfurt/Main: Suhrkamp, 2d ed., 1981) 142–43.

CHAPTER ONE

A Life in a Time out of Joint:
Biographical Notes

Peter Weiss had a difficult life, which is not surprising, considering the historical events that formed and at times so deformed it as to make it virtually unlivable: two world wars, class struggles of the Weimar Republic and the victory of fascism, the cold war, rearmament, and a Third World that became increasingly impoverished while at the same time poverty also increased within the growing wealth of the "first world." The socialist revolution of 1917 was followed by its distortion to the point of unrecognizability and the long battle for its restoration. A battle which has since been lost. In the middle of the century there occurred an event unparalleled in the history of mankind: the production of millions of corpses, methodically carried out by means of an industrial process. All this had to be endured by a person born of Jewish ancestry in Germany in the year 1916, who defied all probability by staying alive until 1982.

A human being's life cannot be separated from the historical epoch in which it is lived—it is the product of its era, into which it simultaneously intervenes productively. This is especially true of Peter Weiss. The impact the era had on his life produced the impact that Weiss had on his era. Rather than simply accepting the deformation of his life by the course of historical events, he increasingly opposed them in his thinking and in his work. His life is so inextricably interwoven with the history of his epoch that it is impossible to isolate individual threads. The whole fabric must be examined.

The first historical fact in the early life of Peter Ulrich Weiss was the Great War of 1914–18. By the time of his birth on 8 November 1916 in Nowawes near Berlin (today known as Potsdam/Babelsberg), the slaughter had already been under way for more than two years. On the Western front the war had come to a standstill. For no reason or purpose, entire armies were being sacrificed at Verdun. In the East and South of Europe the fighting was spreading. The armaments business was booming. "Dividends are rising and proletarians are falling," wrote Rosa Luxemburg, whose thinking would someday become important for Peter Weiss.[1] There was widespread starvation not only in Berlin but in all of Germany during the *Kohlrübenwinter* (rutabaga winter) of 1916–17.

Eugen Weiss—a Hungarian textile merchant, Jewish, and a lieutenant in the Habsburg army—was wounded in July 1915 while stationed on the Eastern front. That same year he married Frieda Thierbach: a German Christian, who had been reared in Basel and the Alsace, a divorced mother with two sons, wealthy, and a former actress who had worked with the famous theater director Max Reinhardt. The marriage was solemnized in a Jewish ceremony. Peter Weiss, the first of four children, acquired the Austro-Hungarian nationality of his father. Hence the infant appeared to be clearly defined in the usual categories—birthplace, family status, citizenship, and religious affiliation. But just two years later, in late 1918, the antiquated structures in Europe were gone—with unforeseeable consequences for entire peoples, for individuals, and for young Peter Ulrich Weiss—his family status, his citizenship, and his religious affiliation. The Danube monarchy had ceased to exist; no longer was there such a thing as an Austro-Hungarian citizenship. The Hungarian birthplace of Eugen Weiss became part of the Republic of Czechoslovakia, constituted in the fall of 1918. With his father now a Czech citizen, two-year-old Peter Weiss became the citizen of a country he would not see until he was twenty years old, whose language he never spoke, and where he spent only a short period of his life. Peter Weiss was never a citizen of that country in which he grew up, whose language he spoke, and whose literature he enriched with two major works: the play about Marat and Sade and *Die Ästhetik des Widerstands* (*The Aesthetics of Resistance*).

Bremen on the coast of the North Sea is the city of Weiss's childhood. The Weiss family lived there from 1919 until 1929, at first in an apartment in Grünenstrasse, later in a house in the elegant Markusallee. Bremen was the only place that for Weiss retained a sense of belonging, of home; a place where his otherwise rootless life had formed roots. He always clung to these roots;[2] later, when his recollections of Bremen had paled, he reconstructed them through arduous research.[3] Bremen was synonymous with "industrial suburbs, factories, trains, boxcars, freight depots" (27),[4] as well as fairs and circuses, tricksters, clowns, artists, and traveling merchants. What Weiss saw, heard, felt, thought, and learned during his early years in the harbor city on the Weser River left its mark on all phases of his oeuvre as painter and writer.

Bremen was the place where his father, as co-owner of a textile company, came into wealth, and where Peter started to rebel against the emotional coldness of his upper middle-class family. The personal trauma of this childhood would later be re-created in the autobiographical story *Abschied von den Eltern* (*Leavetaking*).

But Bremen was also the place of traumatic historical events. In November 1918 civil war had broken out in Germany. On 10 January 1919 revolutionary workers and soldiers had formed a workers' government in Bremen. Three weeks later it was overthrown with much bloodshed. How much of these events can have registered with a small child? In *The Aesthetics of Resistance* a long passage deals with revolutionary events in the city of Weiss's childhood.[5]

The few somewhat tranquil years in the history of the Weimar Republic were coming to an end. The New York stock market crashed on 25 October 1929. Black Friday was followed by one of capitalism's large cyclical crises. Unemployment, starvation, and misery spread through Germany as well. Workers stepped up their battle for jobs and fair wages. Big business began to look for allies to oppose worker demands, and so the historical development of fascism was placed on the agenda. Eugen Weiss's business does not seem to have been adversely affected by these developments. The introverted man had always shied away from political involvement. Soon after his marriage he had converted to Protestantism, and his children had been baptized. There seemed to be no reason to be concerned about political developments.

In Berlin, where Eugen Weiss's textile firm had moved in 1929, the bourgeois existence of the young Peter Weiss took its course. His life was defined by school, literature, music, and the arts; for that is how those who would represent German culture were formed—through the exclusion of social reality. The works of Hermann Hesse, Thomas Mann, Franz Werfel, and Frank Wedekind formed a world apart from that other world in which Nazi storm troopers began to take over the streets. Several years later, there would be the coexistence of Goethe, Bach, and Auschwitz. At his childhood friend Uli Rothe's house young Peter Weiss was introduced to *The Three-Penny Opera* (1928) and the play, *The Rise and Fall of the City of Mahoganny* (1927), thus marking the start of Weiss's lifelong involvement with the work of Bertolt Brecht.[6] Also with Uli Rothe there were visits to the Pergamon Museum where the two adolescents studied the ancient temple frieze from Asia Minor which more than forty years later would become the subject of the opening passages of *The Aesthetics of Resistance*. And there was the study of painting, especially of the German expressionists Nolde, Feininger, Hofer, Schlemmer, Klee, and Dix. In 1932 Weiss attended a drawing course and a few months later a painting school.

The start of Peter Weiss's existence as a painter was at once promising, and completely unreal. It was no longer possible to exclude real life from the painting student's aesthetic existence. After 30 January 1933 power had been handed over to the fascists; the Reichskanzlerplatz was renamed the Adolf Hitler Platz. At school the Nazi salute was introduced. Peter Weiss was exempt from this regulation; his was not among the stiffly raised hands of the students at the Heinrich von Kleist Gymnasium. His nonbelonging had become visible.

The reason, however, why the student Peter Weiss was not allowed to give the Nazi salute had nothing to do with his being Jewish. Foreigners were not expected to make the Nazi salute and he was, after all, a Czech citizen. How should he have known that he was Jewish? Was he indeed, and according to whom? After all, he had been baptized. Also, according to traditional Jewish law, Jewishness is matrilineal, and Weiss's mother was a Christian. (But when had anti-Semites ever been interested in the Jews' own definition of Jewishness?) Besides, the young student *wanted* to raise his hand in the fascist salute like his schoolmates, like his "Aryan" half brothers. That Weiss's father was born a Jew must have been the family's best kept secret.[7] With Eugen Weiss the issue of his repressed Jewishness seems to have produced a trauma for which the overused term, Jewish self-hatred, seems appropriate. In any case, that is how one may interpret the episode in Weiss's fictionalized autobiography, in which the enraged father screams at the younger son, "You bloody Jewish lout, you bloody Jewish lout!"[8] Only later did Weiss realize that his Jewishness was his salvation, that it had prevented him from taking the route of becoming a Nazi murderer; an insight that remained with him for the rest of his life.[9] Nothing in this life was ever forgotten, least of all the suffering, the horror about oneself and the era.

The split that went through Germany went right through the Weiss family. The two half brothers, Arwed and Hans Thierbach, sons from their mother's first marriage, opted for the new Germany. One of them later became a high officer in the SS (N I/246, N II/670). In 1933, right after Hitler had come to power, the parents took the seventeen-year-old Peter out of the college preparatory school he had been attending and sent him to a trade school. This was clearly done with emigration in mind; the parents no longer harbored any illusions about staying in Germany. Then in 1934 came what Weiss would later call the "decisive experience" (18): the violent death of his twelve-year-old sister Margit in an automobile accident. Whatever feelings of love and warmth the emotionally crippled parents had managed to express had been directed toward this daughter. The older brother, Peter, too had transferred all his needs for love and tenderness to his sister Margit. This is movingly depicted in the incestuous relationship between the young narrator and his sister in *Leavetaking*. With Margit's death, the Weiss family began to disintegrate.

The fascist developments in Germany were hardly noticed; the departure from their homeland and the beginning of exile were no big events; the worst, after all, had already happened.

In the spring of 1935 the German Weiss family, using their Czech passports, emigrated to England where the father's business contacts enabled him to work as a manager of a textile factory. The family rented a house in Chislehurst, near London. The oldest son attended photography school, since—as the parents saw it—this was no time for a young person to become a painter. With photography, or so they hoped, he might someday be able to earn some money. In addition, the parents made the eighteen-year-old spend a good part of his days in the offices of the textile factory. In the evenings, however, he painted. In his room in the attic he led a life far removed from the world of his bourgeois family. Within the family this triggered week-long quarrels alternating with week-long silences. A Kafkaesque insect had settled into the attic room.

Life became unlivable. Peter Weiss, a penniless Bohemian in increasingly proletarian or, as he himself was later to say, "lumpen proletarian" conditions (22), fled to urban London to become a painter. A friend, Jacques Ayschmann, several years older than Weiss, briefly entered his life. Ayschmann was preparing to leave for Spain to join the fight against Generalissimo Franco (1892–1975), who had begun his war against the legitimate republican government. Ayschmann, who was to perish in Spain, is remembered not only in *Leavetaking* but also in *The Aesthetics of Resistance,* Weiss's "counterarchive" (Burkhardt Lindner) to traditional historiography, in which so many names of those who died fighting fascism are preserved. An exhibition of Peter Weiss's paintings was held in a storage room near Hyde Park. No one came; it didn't matter. In the absence of chairs, the young painter sat on the floor of the exhibition space with Ayschmann and Ruth Anker, a young Jewish emigrant. Weiss was overpowered by the feeling of a nascent work. It was, of this he was now sure, the beginning of his existence as a painter.[10]

But exile is discontinuity, interruption, and uprootedness. The Weiss family had been in England no more than two years when Eugen Weiss's business opportunities dried up. Another door opened in Czechoslovakia, in the north Bohemian town of Varnsdorf near the German border, in an area called Sudetenland by its German-speaking majority, who looked favorably on Hitler and the Nazis. Here the Czech citizen Eugen Weiss was able to take over the business management of a large weaving mill in the fall of 1936. Thus, at age twenty, Peter Weiss for the first time came to the country whose citizenship he had held since infancy. He was now an exile in his own country—such were the grotesque forms life could assume at the time. It was impossible to disregard the proximity of this new home to fascist Germany: flags bearing the swastika were waving above the streets of Varnsdorf in which the gangs of the Sudeten German fascist leader Konrad Henlein were marching. Nothing of this can be found in Peter Weiss's paintings of that time. He had again withdrawn into an attic room, painting and writing in complete isolation. The reality that so affected his existence increasingly eluded him. The sense of isolation became so great that the hermit in the attic took the least promising of all possible routes: he sent several of his texts and drawings to the world-famous author Hermann Hesse (1877–1962).[11] The polite author of *Steppenwolf* replied a short time later.

For a young man who had discarded all bourgeois values, it must have been an elective affinity. Since his school days Weiss had been reading Hesse's works, which were his "favorite books" (26). How could Hesse, whose works would achieve world fame for the second time among the "hippies"— social castoffs of the 1960s—not have affected Peter Weiss? This is especially true of the story about "Steppenwolf" Harry Haller, a novel dealing "with a life crisis, an artist's crisis, a social crisis" (Hans Mayer), which Hesse had provided with the motto "only for crazy people." This book had become an object of identification for Weiss that decades later still held him in its grip.[12] The "master," as Hesse was addressed in that first letter, had answered, had confirmed the young man's talent, and had advised him to continue with his drawings as well as with his literary studies and exercises. But Hesse had also warned against "indulging in romantic scenery," and had emphasized the importance of moving "from a romantic attitude towards a responsible poetic vocation."[13] More than this wise advice, the fact that his call for help had been answered at all—and by Hermann Hesse at that—gave the young Peter Weiss powerful encouragement. There followed an exchange of letters, and a few months later, in the summer of 1937, while a concentration camp was being built in Buchenwald near Weimar, the young man from Varnsdorf was en route, by train, by hitching rides, and on foot, to Montagnola in Switzerland's Ticino to the revered "master."

Weiss spent the summer in Montagnola. He frequently visited Hesse and discussed his work and his plans with him; Hesse gave him the names and addresses of friends in Prague who might be of help. In Hesse's presence, during meals, when making music, or when playing boccia, there may again have arisen something of a feeling of belonging. The sixty-year-old master, a helpful as well as an imposing man, became one of several father figures in

Weiss's life who took the place of a weak father. They include the silent film director Murnau, the publicist Max Barth, the painter Willi Novak, the physician Max Hodann and, in a different way, even Bertolt Brecht.[14]

Returning from Ticino, Weiss was detained at the Swiss border. A young man with an artist's portfolio traveling across the Alps where the Swiss were just starting to build their alpine fortifications against a possible Nazi attack was bound to arouse suspicion. The customs officials wanted to know precisely what was the subject of these drawings. The time when a young artist out of touch with historical reality could travel about Europe to acquire culture, the time when a young person could still become an artist, was rapidly coming to an end.

In the meantime, the young painter succeeded in being accepted at the Art Academy in Prague. Once again that led to vehement disputes with his parents; and once again the son was to be forced to work in his father's textile factory. Following Hesse's advice, Weiss now turned to Max Barth, the German socialist and publicist living in exile in Prague, who in turn recommended him to the painter Willi Novak, a committed antifascist and a teacher at the Prague Art Academy. A letter from Novak finally persuaded Weiss's parents to grant their son a trial year at the academy.

Endre Nemes, a painter who befriended Weiss during that period, recalls that the Art Academy student was an outsider, unable to speak Czech and unfamiliar with Czech history and culture. His paintings, influenced by the old Flemish masters, especially Brueghel the Elder (1525–69), were considered old-fashioned; artist groups in Prague were interested in the avant-garde, expressionism, surrealism, and dadaism. The young exile remained an outsider from fellow exiles as well, failing to notice the occasional presence in Prague of such exiled avant-garde artists as Raoul Hausmann and Oskar Kokoschka, John Heartfield, and even Brecht. Nemes noticed not a trace of political awareness in his young friend.[15] What Nemes recalls here—and Weiss's own recollections completely concur (28–29)—is the image of an extremely alienated existence. Only through a few people was Weiss's life connected with the reality of everyday life and historical events: through Barth, Novak, and Nemes, as well as through his friendship with the young student colleague, Peter Kien, and his fleeting acquaintance with a young woman named Lucie Weisberger. With these last two people, however, one is again reminded of the fragility of Weiss's existence, of the growing threats, and of the shortage of time. For Peter Kien and Lucie Weisberger time would soon run out. Weiss's last news of them—by which time he was in Sweden—was from the Theresienstadt concentration camp (32). (Their memory is preserved in *Leavetaking* and its sequel *Fluchtpunkt* [*Vanishing Point*].) After his insight into how close he had come during his gymnasium years to associating himself with the perpetrators, there was now also the recognition that only through a fragile chain of circumstances had he not become a victim. The horror about *both* possibilities never again left Weiss.

In addition to painting while at the academy, 1937–38, he continued his literary efforts. Weiss, still corresponding with Hesse, sent the master a story, "Chloe: Caspar Walthers nachgelassene Papiere" (Chloe: Caspar Walther's Posthumous Papers). In the summer of 1938 Weiss again traveled to the Italian part of Switzerland. This time he was accompanied by two friends his age, Robert Jungk (the future nuclear researcher and futurologist) and Hermann Levin Goldschmidt (who would remain in Zurich and become a philosopher), both of them Jews who had been forced into exile by fascist Germany. Once again Weiss lived near Hesse, whom he now met as an artist in his own right, an "accomplished painter" (29) who had received an award from the Prague Art Academy for two of his paintings. Once again Weiss was cordially received by Hesse and even given paid assignments: to copy by hand and illustrate two of Hesse's stories which Hesse presented to friends as gifts. Siegfried Unseld, Weiss's publisher, later bought them back and had them published.[16] Hesse also bought several of Weiss's paintings, enabling the young artist to earn a little money and to live from his artwork. That summer there was also the comfort of Ticino's southern climate, the beauty of nature (long since ruined by tourism), and a liberating relationship with a woman. For the first time since childhood Weiss's difficult life was free of threats and anxieties. He was twenty-two years old.

Hesse and Weiss never again shared such closeness. Historical events as well as Weiss's further development would prevent that. They remained in contact by letter, meeting again in the early 1960s, only to become aware of the distance that now existed between them (N I/61ff.). Later still, while working on *Hölderlin* during the fall of 1971, Weiss, now a Marxist, concluded that Hesse's late work, *The Glass Bead Game,* did not measure up to Weiss's own criteria (N I/854ff.). Also, Weiss had now become a "master" in his own right. In the 1,000 or so pages of *The Aesthetics of Resistance,* with its extended passages on literature, on Kafka, Brecht, and others, there was only one mention of Hesse which Weiss deleted in the final version (N II/920).

Weiss was still in Ticino when, in October 1938, the Nazis occupied the Czechoslovak Sudetenland. A few months earlier in March 1938 he had been able to ignore the German invasion of Austria. But now Varnsdorf came under fascist domination and the life of the Weiss family was directly threatened. His father left Czechoslovakia immediately. The owners of the textile factory he had been managing in Varnsdorf planned to set up a new factory in Sweden, and Eugen Weiss was again to take over the management. Frieda Weiss, who was not immediately threatened, remained in Varnsdorf with the two youngest children. While the SS paraded through the streets, she packed up the household—a desperate effort to at least preserve the material possessions of her family, which was disintegrating ever more under the blows of history. She destroyed several of her son's main works; large, gloomy paintings that she feared might attract the attention of the Gestapo. For a long time Peter Weiss would not be able to overcome the trauma of this destruction. From earliest childhood his development had been impeded by his cold, dominating mother, who had been responsible for his intermittently almost autistic state, who had time and again sabotaged his development as a painter. Her son's paintings had become the scapegoat for all her frustrations; they were the reason she and her family were unable to live the life of the upper bourgeoisie that was their due. By destroying the paintings she destroyed her son, who had been able to find himself and was connected with reality only through these paintings. That, more or less, was how Peter Weiss experienced this act of destruction which he was to describe twenty years later in *Leavetaking*.[17] It took another twenty years until he was able to do justice to his mother, until he was able to put himself in her place and to explain her destructive action from the historical events that had overwhelmed her and her family in Varnsdorf (31–32).

Weiss remained in Switzerland until early 1939. Then he traveled across Germany to Sweden, where he arrived on 18 January 1939.

Peter Weiss became Swedish. In 1946 he would obtain Swedish citizenship. Eventually, he would become fluent in the Swedish language in which he would write his first significant literary works. Sweden is where he lived for the rest of his life, where he had his family, and where he found a basis for his growing political commitment: by joining the Communist Party of Sweden (Vänsterpartiet Kommunisterna, VPK) in 1968. From Sweden he would involve himself in the support of the struggle of the Vietnamese people, and in the liberation movements in Angola, in Central America, and in South Africa. Here he would write all his important works. Here he would remain, despite repeated plans for a (temporary) move to the Federal Republic of Germany. Never, though, would there be a feeling of home. Sweden would remain exile, and exile would forever be experienced as "an affliction . . . that is incurable" (N II/728). Together with the Austrian lyricist Erich Fried (1921–88), Peter Weiss would be among the youngest writers to be exiled by the rise of fascism, and, like Fried, he would die in exile.

The textile factory that Eugen Weiss was to manage was still under construction in 1939 in the Swedish town of Alingsås, near Göteborg in the southwest of Sweden. For Weiss, the heightened sense of life in Ticino was followed by a "terrible fall back into all the old stuff" (33). Once again he had to join his father's business; once again there were the endless hours spent in the office and in the factory; and once again there was an attic-room existence. Attempts at breaking out were followed by humiliating returns to the parental bourgeois world. After all, what could an unknown twenty-three-year-old artist in a foreign country live on, especially in the year 1939? For Weiss, the "hermit, the proletarian," as he would later refer to himself (33), life once again became unlivable.

Important paintings nonetheless date from this era—this era during which Poland was crushed, Denmark and Norway were occupied, and the corpse of his childhood friend, Uli Rothe, wearing the uniform of the German aggressor, washed up on the Danish coast (20). There is no trace of these events in Peter Weiss's work of that time: his paintings from the years 1939 and 1940 have such titles as "Der Hausierer" (The Peddler), "Jahrmarktsleben" (At the Fair), "Jahrmarkt am Stadtrand" (Fair at the Outskirts of Town), and "Circus." It seems almost inconceivable that from this autistic existence in various attics in Chislehurst, Varnsdorf, and Alingsås there would emerge the author of plays about Marat and the French Revolution, about Trotsky and the Russian Revolution, as well as of one of the great novels of the century, whose topic is the history of the workers' movement and the resistance of the left to fascism.

Again the trip to one of his father figures became for Weiss a step toward self-liberation. Fleeing the German army, Max Barth—twenty years Weiss's senior and the friend who made it possible for the young painter to study at the Prague Art Academy—had escaped to Norway. Having remained in contact by writing letters, the two now met in Stockholm. The socialist and publicist, himself in difficult circumstances, once again aided the young man and encouraged him toward independent artistic work. Weiss moved to Stockholm and lived in the same boarding house as Barth and other exiles. It was a life under "extremely proletarian conditions" (34), close to the subsistence level, repeatedly interrupted by stays in Alingsås, and by factory work whenever it became necessary for Weiss to earn money to sustain his life in Stockholm. Part of his life was now Helga Henschen, a Swedish painter who became Weiss's first wife and with whom he had a daughter in 1944. All that is described in only slightly fictionalized form in *Vanishing Point*.

In March 1941 Weiss's first Swedish exhibition took place in the old Stockholm exhibition hall (Mässhallen) at Brunkebergsplatz where Nemes had just had a showing of his own work. The German army was now in Africa; two months later it would attack the Soviet Union. Weiss recalled his first contacts with Swedish art as a "collision" (34). Here, too, his paintings were considered out of step; here, too, he did not fit in. Sweden, spared from war because of its strong anticommunism and its tolerant attitude toward Nazi Germany, showed little sympathy for emigrants, especially Jewish emigrants. Weiss, Nemes, and Barth—exiles, Jews, and aliens—continued to live without success, without any recognition of their work, and without income.

In the winter of 1942–43 Weiss went to northern Sweden. While the *Wehrmacht* came to a standstill at Stalingrad and the Soviet army was fighting for its first big victory over Nazi Germany, he was working as a lumberjack in the Swedish forests. How did he perceive this experience at the time? For a long time Weiss was to see his own developmental history only from the perspective of an artistry outside of any social context. Life among the lumberjacks was perceived as a low point, an end of all hopes, and a self-destructive attempt to "deliver himself into banishment and damnation," as the author has the first-person narrator sum up his life among the lumberjacks in *Vanishing Point*. At the same time there is, in this strongly autobiographical novel, a productive view of this phase of the narrator's life. The description of the narrowness and apathy of the lumberjacks, who lacked everything that seemed meaningful to the elitist young painter, is followed by the simple admission that "they knew much that I didn't know."[18] In his later years Weiss became ever more appreciative of how much he had learned from these people. Having experienced early on the lives of scarcity of these workers, the author increasingly came to believe in the capacity of the working class, in spite of all obstacles, to make themselves into subjects of history (G/R 248). To his experience among the lumberjacks of northern Sweden, Weiss added the objectifying Marxist analysis. Thus were laid the foundations which one day would make possible the writing of *The Aesthetics of Resistance*.

Toward the end of the winter of 1942–43 Peter Weiss returned to Stockholm and married Helga Henschen. There was no longer any prospect for an existence as a painter. For a monthly fee he accepted assignments from his father's textile factory and designed fabric patterns, especially flowers. For each pattern a design had to be copied up to a dozen times and the copies sent to Alingsås. It was an unproductive, unlivable time, suffused by the feeling that everything was disintegrating, everything was fragmenting (37). At this point, it may be appropriate to recall that Weiss's fate was hardly worse than that of the majority of exiled German artists and writers who often were forced into equally harsh and debasing work in order to earn a livelihood: Günther Anders, the philosopher from Breslau, labored in the United States as a factory worker; the composer Paul Dessau worked at a chicken farm; and Brecht's wife, the great actress Helene Weigel, was reduced to the role of housewife. The difference was that these exiles had been able to complete their schooling and training, that they had had the opportunity to create a body of work and establish themselves prior to 1933. Many of them had taken a public stand against fascism and knew why they were forced to leave Germany. In contrast, Peter Weiss at the start of his exile was just eighteen years old. There had not been enough time to develop an identity and to define artistic or political positions. He had had no chance to develop a sense of self-worth. It was not he who had chosen exile but his parents. Thus he lacked everything that could have given him strength in the early years of exile.

Although little is made of this in Weiss's statements and autobiographical texts, there also seem to have been moments in which the young painter received public recognition. In January 1944 there was an exhibition of "Artists in Exile" where artists who had fled fascism showed their works and where Peter Weiss's paintings were praised.[19] That same year contacts with a group of young Swedish writers helped Weiss out of his isolation (36). Yet it is altogether believable that, between the extreme difficulties of earning a living and the lack of success with his painting, Weiss's existence seemed so bleak and hopeless that at times he "wasn't able to do anything at all" (37). He now had a child, he was divorced, and his efforts to establish himself on the Swedish art scene had failed. In early 1945, when Europe lay in ruins, the twenty-nine year-old Weiss also seemed to have reached bottom.

But there was no zero hour, just as there had been none in Germany at the war's end. The old endured while, slowly, the new began to emerge. In 1945 there was a retrospective showing of Weiss's works in Stockholm. His painting now began to change, reflecting the influence of that prewar avant-garde, especially surrealism, that he had earlier ignored in Prague. Among the surrealists it was less the painters than the writers (Paul Eluard) and film directors (Luis Buñuel) whose works became important for Weiss. There was also a new father figure, Max Hodann, a Jew and a socialist, a physician and psychiatrist, who in pre-Nazi Germany had written a highly praised book educating the working class about sexuality, contraceptive methods, and abortion, and who, as a doctor, had joined the ranks of the International Brigades in the Spanish Civil War. As with Hesse, Barth, and Novak, Hodann provided Weiss encouragement, awakening his interest in psychology and psychoanalysis, in Freud, Reich, and Jung. In the late 1940s Weiss underwent psychoanalysis with the Hungarian emigrant and former student of Freud, Lajos Székely—with little success, according to comments in his later years. Nonetheless, the analysis must have laid the groundwork for all the painful and unsparing insights into a traumatic childhood which would eventually be recreated in the two autobiographical novels, *Leavetaking* and *Vanishing Point*.

Weiss's friendship with Hodann also stirred his interest in political matters and led him toward the realization that social and historical contexts could be rationally understood. Hodann, however, did not live to see the political development of Peter Weiss. Increasingly repulsed by the Stalinist deformations of the communist movement, Hodann turned away from his longtime political allies even before the war had ended. His increasing contacts with representatives of Great Britain, rather than with the Soviet Union, further alienated him from his socialist comrades. Isolated, impoverished, suffering from severe asthma attacks, and no longer able to earn a living for himself and his family, Hodann committed suicide in 1947. The memory of this man, his greatness, his weaknesses, and his suffering are preserved in *The Aesthetics of Resistance*.[20]

The list of Weiss's dead friends and family grew longer: his sister Margit (run over by an automobile), Jacques Ayschmann (Spain), Uli Rothe (Denmark), Peter Kien (Auschwitz), Lucie Weisberger (Auschwitz), and Max Hodann (suicide). This is emphasized here because the central themes of suffering, torture, and horrible death in Weiss's work have been explained by some critics on the basis of their "individual psychological" roots. From such a perspective the torture and torment that is depicted, say, in *Marat/Sade* or in *The Investigation (Die Ermittlung)*, is explained as an unchanging anthropological fact about mankind.[21] That was hardly Weiss's intended meaning. Having increasingly become the chronicler of men's and women's suffering at the hands of their fellow men in the twentieth century, Weiss did not conceive of this as an eternal condition or as something inherent in human nature. The horrible death of persons close to him was the consequence of knowable social and historical conditions. And these conditions, having been created by human beings rather than by some metaphysical force, could therefore have been created differently. One can follow the development of such insights in Weiss's work, from *Leavetaking* to *Vanishing Point*, from *Marat/Sade* and *The Investigation*, to *The Aesthetics of Resistance*. Little is explained by maintaining that Weiss simply was "magically" attracted by the motifs of torment and torture (Bohrer). In order to increase our understanding of Weiss's life and work, it is entirely appropriate to use the methods of psychology, all the more so since the author himself allotted them much space in both his life and work. One should not, however, lose sight of the social and historical contexts within which Weiss's life and work evolved.

Peter Weiss's postwar development by no means followed a straight path. In the years when it seemed possible for him to become established on the Swedish art scene, when the end of Hiroshima and Nagasaki signaled the start of a new epoch, when Europe was being rebuilt and Germany was divided, and when the cold war entered its hot phase with the dispute over Berlin, Peter Weiss had started to write again: this time in Swedish. There was a volume of prose poems, *Från ö till ö*, 1947 (*Von Insel zu Insel* [From Island to Island]). A year later, after Weiss's first trip to postwar Germany (1947), there followed a series of reports for a Swedish newspaper, and, based on that material, a text on postwar Berlin, *De Besegrade*, 1948 (*Die Besiegten* [The Vanquished]). According to Gunilla Palmstierna-Weiss, Peter Weiss's widow, these Swedish texts constitute the writer's attempt to become assimilated, to "conquer by means of its language the society in which he was living."[22] But from the beginning there must have been doubt because at that time Weiss also began again to write in German. His experimental text, *Der Vogelfreie* (The Outlaw), was rejected by the publisher Peter Suhrkamp, whom Weiss had met on his trip to Germany. Weiss then translated it into Swedish, publishing it at his own expense in 1949 under the title *Dokument I*. In this confusion of languages Weiss wrote his manuscripts simultaneously in a Swedish and a German version; at times they were all "mixed up, German and Swedish together, sometimes even English" (40). In addition, in the 1950s he began his film work, although he also continued to paint. It was a period in which Peter Weiss no longer knew whether he was, or wanted to be, a painter or filmmaker or writer and, if a writer, in which language. He married for the second time (Carlota Dethorey, 1949), became a father for the second time (son Paul, 1949), and soon divorced again. During this period he taught painting and film at the adult evening school in Stockholm, and one of his plays, *The Tower* (*Der Turm*, 1949), was performed for the first time; he made the acquaintance of his life's companion and third wife, Gunilla Palmstierna (whom he married in 1964); he created experimental and documentary films; in 1952 he wrote a German-language text entitled *The Shadow of the Coachman's Body* (*Der Schatten des Körpers des Kutschers*), which at the time remained unpublished; he illustrated *A Thousand and One Nights;* and in the late 1950s he directed his first feature film, *Hägringen,* like most of his films, with far too few financial means. This period in Weiss's life conveys the image of someone whose life is a tangled confusion of diverse activities and who is unable to make a breakthrough in any of them. His identity as a painter, for which he had struggled for so long, began to blur. His film work also reached a dead end when he became entangled in the production of a quasi-pornographic film (according to the standards of the time) and realized, how, in the film business, creativity is a commodity whose use is decided by market forces (Brecht had gone through a similar experience with the film version of his *Three-Penny Opera*).

The cold war peaked in the 1950s. Soviet troops invaded Hungary in the fall of 1956 (the German Communist Party was banned in the Federal Republic that same year); in February 1956 Khrushchev, in an internal address, informed the Twentieth Party Congress of the Communist Party of the Soviet Union about the crimes of Stalinism. In the following years there would gradually emerge a "thaw" period, as it was termed after a novel by the Soviet writer Ilya Ehrenburg. In 1959 two first novels by West German writers were published that were considered an expression of a new epoch: Günter Grass's *The Tin Drum* (*Die Blechtrommel*) and Uwe Johnson's *Speculations about Jacob* (*Mutmassungen über Jakob*). In the German Democratic Republic that same year it was decided at the first Bitterfeld Conference that writers should be encouraged to recreate in their works the realities of daily life in a socialist country. This led, among other things, to a first novel called *The Divided Heaven* (*Der geteilte Himmel*), which established Christa Wolf's fame. Literature in both German nations had begun to involve itself in new ways with the present and the immediate past of Germany. That same year, 1959, excerpts from an avant-garde text that seemed equally out of step with literary developments in both East and West Germany appeared in *Akzente,* a West German literary journal. One year later the entire text was published by the prestigious Suhrkamp publishing house. Its title: *The Shadow of the Coachman's Body.* Peter Weiss's battle for his "existence as a writer" (43) had been won.

The film work was halted. Painting came to a standstill. Peter Weiss, almost forty-five years old, became a writer. With hindsight one might be tempted to say that his talent simply was in literature and not in painting (and even less in his film work). But one should also remember the extent to which Peter Weiss, the painter, had suffered since his earliest beginnings from his isolation and outsider status, as well as from his lack of success. It seems entirely possible that with success in painting comparable to that which he now achieved in literature, he would have continued to regard his writing only as a sideline. But the liberating effect of success, the public confirmation of his literary talent, must have been overwhelming. And so he now devoted himself entirely to writing.

NOTES

1. See Robert Cohen, *Versuche über Weiss' "Ästhetik des Widerstands"* (Bern: Peter Lang, 1989) 41–43.
2. See Peter Weiss, "Wurzeln," *die horen* 27, no. 126 (Summer 1982): 185–87.
3. See Karl Heinz Götze, "Der Ort der frühen Bilder. Peter Weiss und Bremen. Eine Spurensuche," in Hans Höller, ed., *Hinter jedem Wort die Gefahr des Verstummens. Sprachproblematik und literarische Tradition in der "Ästhetik des Widerstands" von Peter Weiss* (Stuttgart: Akademischer Verlag, 1988) 173–96.
4. The page numbers in parentheses refer to the extensive Weiss interview by Peter Roos; see Roos, "Der Kampf um meine Existenz als Maler. Peter Weiss im Gespräch mit Peter Roos" (Stockholm, 19 December 1979), in *Der Maler Peter Weiss* (Berlin: Frölich and Kaufmann, 1982) 11–43.
5. On the revolutionary events in Bremen and their portrayal in *The Aesthetics of Resistance*, see Michael Töteberg, "Späte Rückkehr nach Bremen. Peter Weiss und die Stadt seiner Kindheit," in *die horen* 27, no. 125 (Spring 1982): 113–22.
6. On Weiss and Brecht, see Cohen, "Annäherung und Distanz. Zu Weiss' Rezeption von Brechts literarischem Werk," in Cohen, *Versuche über Weiss' "Ästhetik des Widerstands"* 155–80.
7. According to Weiss's sister Irene Eklund, only when the family was in Varnsdorf were the children told that their father was Jewish. See Eklund, "Frieda Weiss, née Hummel—'A Life' " (1979), "Letter," and "Interview," in Åsa Eldh, *The Mother in the Work and Life of Peter Weiss* (Bern: Peter Lang, 1990) 184.
8. Peter Weiss, *Vanishing Point (Fluchtpunkt,* 1960–61), trans. E. B. Garside, Alastair Hamilton, and Christopher Levenson, in Weiss, *Exile* (New York: Delacorte, 1968) 125.
9. See Jochen Vogt, " 'Ich tötete und ich wurde getötet.' Zugehörigkeitsprobleme bei Peter Weiss," in Jost Hermand and Gert Mattenklott, eds., *Jüdische Intelligenz in Deutschland* (Berlin: Argument, 1988) 126–38.
10. See Weiss's description of this exhibition in *Leavetaking (Abschied von den Eltern,* 1960), trans. E. B. Garside, Alastair Hamilton, and Christopher Levenson, in Weiss, *Exile* 67.
11. The letter is reprinted in Matthias Richter, " 'Bis zum heutigen Tag habe ich Ihre Bücher bei mir getragen.' Über die Beziehung zwischen Peter Weiss und Hermann Hesse," in Rainer Gerlach, ed., *Peter Weiss* (Frankfurt/Main: Suhrkamp, 1984) 38–39.
12. See Richter, " 'Bis zum heutigen Tag.' " Regarding Weiss's reading of *Steppenwolf,* also see Weiss, *Leavetaking* 71ff.
13. The letter is reprinted in Raimund Hoffmann, *Peter Weiss. Malerei Zeichnungen Collagen* (Berlin: Henschelverlag, 1984) 163.
14. See Robert Cohen, "Brecht und andere 'Über-Väter,' " in Cohen, *Versuche über Weiss' "Ästhetik des Widerstands"* 181–85.
15. See "Endre Nemes über Peter Weiss," in *Der Maler Peter Weiss* 45–50.
16. See Hermann Hesse, *Kindheit des Zauberers* (1938), handwritten and illustrated by Peter Weiss with an afterword also written by Weiss (Frankfurt/Main: Insel-Verlag, 1974). See Hermann Hesse, *Der verbannte Ehemann oder Anton Schievelbeyn's ohnfreywillige Reisse nacher Ost-Indien* (1938), handwritten and illustrated by Peter Weiss (Frankfurt/Main: Insel-Verlag, 1977).
17. See Weiss, *Leavetaking* 82–83.

18. Both quotations in Weiss, *Vanishing Point* 154, 163.

19. See Helmut Müssener, *Exil in Schweden* (Munich: Hanser, 1974) 296. In the ensuing years a number of works by Peter Weiss were presented to the Swedish public. See Peter Weiss's statements in G/R 313–14.

20. The passage about Hodann's end, originally intended for the novel, was published in the *Notizbücher* (N II/898–925).

21. Karl Heinz Bohrer, ''Die Tortur. Peter Weiss' Weg ins Engagement. Die Geschichte des Individualisten,'' in Gerlach, ed., *Peter Weiss* 184–85. In contrast, see W. G. Sebald's perceptive study, ''Die Zerknirschung des Herzens. Über Erinnerung und Grausamkeit im Werk von Peter Weiss,'' *Orbis Litterarum* 41, no. 1 (1986): 265–78.

22. Gunilla Palmstierna-Weiss, ''Nachwort,'' in Peter Weiss, *Die Besiegten* (Frankfurt/Main: Suhrkamp, 1985) 156.

CHAPTER TWO

Early Texts

Peter Weiss's early life is defined by everything it lacked: familial warmth, friendship, a home country, a language, success, and a future. It was a life of exile and isolation, in London, Varnsdorf, and Alingsås, where the young painter led his attic-room existence. It was a nearly autistic life, an ivory tower existence. This early experience of barely existing, of being dead to the real world, is the theme of Weiss's earliest work published to date, where it appears turned on its head, as its title implies: "Traktat von der ausgestorbenen Welt" (Treatise about the Died-Out World). It was written in 1938–39, during the period when the twenty-two-year-old spent his second summer in the southern Swiss region of Ticino, near the revered master Hermann Hesse. It was the time when his parents fled from Czechoslovakian Sudetenland, which had just been annexed by fascist Germany, to Sweden, where Weiss was about to join them.

"Traktat von der ausgestorbenen Welt"

The world through which Peter Weiss traveled from Switzerland across Germany to Sweden was anything but "died-out": Rather, it was filled with refugees not knowing where to go, marching soldiers, and screaming victors. But "Traktat von der ausgestorbenen Welt" does not deal with this real world. In the world in which the nameless first-person narrator one day wakes up there are neither victors nor vanquished, there are no longer any people at all, no animals, absolutely no living creatures. For five days the narrator walks through this died-out world, finding traces and collecting artifacts left behind by mankind, which has vanished from the face of the earth. All the fantasy notwithstanding, this is clearly an autobiographical story; down to the fine details there is fundamental kinship between the author and the narrator who, like Peter Weiss at that time, is an aspiring poet who has "written small books and poems" and has "dreamed of one day writing a big work, a modern epic" (56).[1] In his wanderings the narrator makes his way from the countryside to the city, passing by suburbs and industrial landscapes, passing by a fair and a circus—all frequent themes in the paintings of Peter Weiss. In the entrance hall of a small, abandoned palace he finds a cembalo, so he sits down and starts to play—precisely as depicted in Weiss's 1938 oil painting "Das Gartenkonzert" (The Garden Concert). Conversely, the 1938 self-portraits—"Selbstbildnis" (Self-Portrait), "Junge im Garten" (Boy in the Garden), and "Jüngling am Stadtrand" (Young Man at the Outskirts of Town)—depict a died-out world of industrial and suburban landscapes wherein the absence of human life is underscored by the lost, lonely figure of the artist. In the last of the five short chapters of "Traktat von der ausgestorbenen Welt," the narrator finds himself alone on an island. Passing by in the distance is a colorful ship full of merry, smiling people. One of the narrator's hallucinations? The narrator's shout goes unnoticed. Then he is alone again.

Just how this cosmic catastrophe came about remains unclear. Though there are traces of a huge battle, there are neither wounded nor dead; rather, people have "completely dissolved and turned into air" (54). In the midst of very lively and colorful activity, streets, houses, fairs, and circus tents have eerily petrified. This particular end of mankind could certainly not be accounted for by war. The "Traktat" hints at causes of a different kind. Near the fair the narrator comes to a place where people literally must have vanished into the ground. An unearthly power seems to be at work here, and there is repeated mention of God. The concept of God, however, seems broadly conceived, embracing "motherliness" as well as "life, soul, faith, or death" (58). In the passages about this "high, unknown being," later also termed "dual God," a tone of religiosity unusual for Peter Weiss enters the narrative, comprehensible only perhaps if the "Traktat" is read as a "call for help from a person sick with loneliness."[2] This religious tone is not present in any of Weiss's later works, and in the epic novel, *The Aesthetics of Resistance*, the catastrophe of the Second World War is shown to have been brought about not by some unearthly power but by human beings.

The "Traktat" is the earliest literary work by Peter Weiss that has been published in its entirety. Since 1934 Weiss had been writing and illustrating short works, fictional biographies of outsiders and artists based on his own life, and abounding in *Weltschmerz* and disdain for civilization.[3] These texts were greatly influenced by Hesse's work, especially by *Steppenwolf*.[4] Asked to judge these works, Hesse in a gentle and nonhurtful way drew the young artist's attention to their immaturity and romanticization of reality. In his first letter to the twenty- year-old Peter Weiss he advised against publication: there is "much that is beautiful and promising" in these works, according to Hesse, but they "lack independence, the reader feels strongly the literary-romantic atmosphere, but also feels the literary models and impetuses."

Hesse suggested literary exercises, intense work on the text "until you get each word precisely right and can vouch for it."[5] After the "Traktat," however, these exercises had to be abruptly broken off. At the beginning of the year 1939 Peter Weiss was wrenched away from his language and all the familiar contexts of life. For a long time even painting was hardly possible. Writing? In which language?

Peter Weiss learned Swedish in an "attempt to use the Swedish language to conquer the society in which he [Weiss] was living."[6] Toward the end of the war this attempt was made somewhat easier through Weiss's contacts to a group of Swedish writers, the "Fyrtiotalisterna" (writers of the 1940s). According to Gunilla Palmstierna-Weiss, texts from this period by Stig Dagerman, Gunnar Ekelöf, Maria Wine, Erik Lindegren, and Rut Hillarp reflect the influence of surrealism and psychoanalysis and deal with man's anxiety and abandonment.[7] There was a basic kinship to this group of artists; for the painter and emerging filmmaker Weiss had just discovered surrealism for himself, and his interest in psychoanalysis had been stirred by the exiled physician and psychiatrist Max Hodann. Especially with Ekelöf and Dagerman, Weiss seems to have entertained close relationships. After the end of the war Weiss created a series of ink drawings as illustrations for poems by Gunnar Ekelöf (1907–68), and in 1947 the publishing house of Berman Fischer commissioned Weiss to do the German translation of *Den dödsdömde* (The Man Sentenced to Death), a drama by Stig Dagerman (1923–54) who committed suicide when he was barely thirty years old.

Von Insel zu Insel

Weiss's first Swedish text,[8] *Von Insel zu Insel* (From Island to Island), written in 1944, can be characterized as a surrealist rendition of mental states and obsessions. The same might have been said of the "Traktat," written seven years earlier, on which "From Island to Island" draws in a surprisingly direct manner. Just as at the end of the "Traktat" the narrator was sitting alone on an island, in the first paragraph of *Von Insel zu Insel* the first-person narrator is sitting on the shore, abandoned, still "shipwrecked," looking longingly at an island (42).[9] In later passages images and visions from the "Traktat" are drawn on repeatedly. Thus *Von Insel zu Insel* is not, as has been asserted, the first text in which Weiss depicts his traumatic early life.[10]

Von Insel zu Insel was written in Swedish and published in 1947 under its original Swedish title, *Från ö till ö*. The text consists of thirty "prose miniatures,"[11] most of them hardly one page long, in which a hypersensitive first-person narrator painfully recalls stations of the internal and external reality of his life. Even the act of birth appears as an insurmountable trauma: "It cost me my whole life to recover from birth" (9). Childhood and youth are rendered as a succession of scenes of horror and torment where the narrator is beaten by his fellow students and slapped by a stranger, and where he himself tortures animals to death, yet at the same time identifies with the tortured animals and people.

Several passages of *Von Insel zu Insel* depict the absurdity of the world: to put out the flames, a man on fire jumps into a river and drowns; in a prison courtyard inmates must carry a pile of stones from one side to the other, then return them to the original site. The text reaches a bloody paroxysm in a passage where half-naked butchers slaughter horses at an idyllic lake, a dubious aestheticization of horror that ends in a pose of noble suffering: "O . . . this hopelessness, this despair" (38). (Much more adequate is the depiction of the suffering creature in the painting "Das gestürzte Pferd" [The Fallen Horse], from that same year, 1946.)

One may be tempted to say that *Von Insel zu Insel* expresses the imagination of a disturbed mind. The fact that Weiss underwent psychoanalysis three years later seems to confirm such a conjecture. But Weiss's art was never created from pure imagination. Even the nightmarish, visionary aspects of his works were based on realistic situations. This is true to a great extent of *Von Insel zu Insel*. Thus, the first-person narrator is waiting until a factory for dyeing fabrics is built. Then, just like Peter Weiss in Alingsås, he will spend two years of his life working in this factory, writing "business letters" (23). The narrator also describes his sister's death: "We heard the horrible crash, heard the screeching brakes, saw the overturned car, saw people come running from all sides. We came closer without comprehending it. You lay there in your blood, in your blood, in my blood" (41). This is how Weiss's sister Margit died in 1934. The first-person narrator of these passages can no longer be distinguished from the real Peter Weiss. The horrors in *Von Insel zu Insel*, assumed at first glance to be imaginary, seem to draw on real events and experiences. The same holds true for a passage of a very different kind describing a "new machine for carrying out executions," built to serve the idea of "humane execution" of men, women, and children (35). This passage, as well as some of Weiss's paintings of the period can be seen as his earliest reaction to the Holocaust. The passage is also obviously influenced by Kafka. Even before the war, his Prague friend Peter Kien had drawn Weiss's attention to the author of "The Penal Colony." Only now, however, when he needed a model for the literary rendition of an event that defied description, did the Kafka lesson take effect. (Three years later, in his journalistic reports from postwar Germany, Weiss linked a description of the extermination camps openly to Kafka's "Penal Colony."[12]) Kafka was to remain a lasting influence on Weiss's literary work, to be joined later by Dante and Brecht.

In the summer of 1947 Peter Weiss was in Berlin to report about postwar Germany for the Swedish newspaper *Stockholms Tidningen*. Seven newspaper articles from Berlin were published between June and August 1947,[13] followed in 1948 by a book on the same topic.

Die Besiegten

Die Besiegten, the work Weiss wrote in conjunction with his newspaper articles from Berlin, is a complex literary object. Like *Von Insel zu Insel*, it consists of numerous prose miniatures, many hardly a page in length—impressions and recollections, visions and nightmares of a first-person narrator, and an inventory of life in a war-devastated city. In the first few of these miniatures there is a strong similarity between the first-person narrator and Peter Weiss, as when the narrator speaks of Berlin as the city of his childhood, when he seeks his parents' bombed-out house among the ruins, or when, with his "brother" (probably a reference to one of Weiss's half brothers Arwed and Hans Thierbach, who had become Nazis and stayed in Germany), he looks for his sister's grave in the cemetery (32–33).[14] After the opening passages the narrator is continually transformed: he is a German soldier, a student in a lecture hall, an officer or soldier of the occupation forces, a member of the resistance, a survivor recalling a prewar family idyll, a rapist, and a laborer working on reconstruction. In one instance the narration is even provided by a bombed-out house. But this change of roles does not give rise to a chorus of voices, as would be the case in *The Aesthetics of Resistance*. All these figures speak in the same lyrical and elegiacal tone that generalizes war and its consequences, interiorizes guilt, and deals with the causes of the war by turning them into vague anthropological metaphors—"an epidemic . . . that eventually went up in flames" (91). Weiss lifted this image almost literally from one of his newspaper articles that had already termed fascism a "dark illness" (147). But fascism is precisely not an illness or an epidemic; it is neither something inherent in nature nor a relic from former times (something "dark"). On the contrary, it is something created by human beings, created in the twentieth century under specific historical circumstances and in the name of definite interests. It is not part of nature, like an illness that must be endured, but something contrary to nature that must be combated. Peter

Weiss, whose later work contains these thoughts, did not have such insights at the time. For thirty years he had been among the weak and persecuted, and he had come to consider his weakness a virtue: "I want to preserve my weakness. I want to remain among the weak" (93).

This resigned attitude is accompanied by a complete rejection of ideology. Along with fascism, all ideology is rejected, and in the postwar climate this meant mainly the rejection of socialism—a seemingly nonideological position that was in fact the ideology of the recently ended era of the cold war. For the author of *Die Besiegten* the history of mankind is an endlessly recurring battle for survival and power (53–55). Suffering also remains eternally the same, as conjured up by Weiss in precious aesthetic images: "wounded horses, their large bloody heads raised in a mute scream" (20); in bombed-out houses "the wind's flute creates crystalline sounds" (22); and from each cross at a veterans' cemetery "a white flame glimmers forth, blurring into the sky's blue-white sea of light" (96). The real horror of these scenes tends to disappear behind flowery aesthetics.

Lacking in *Die Besiegten* are the ideological and linguistic tools for dealing with the recent history and present situation of Germany. Weiss was by no means unique in his aestheticizations and in his tendency toward vague generalizations. His lack of interest in ideology and in attempts at explaining fascism rationally—hence historically, economically, and politically—fit into the conservative and restorative tendencies of the time, tendencies that would define public discourse in the FRG into the 1960s.[15]

The two texts Weiss had written in Swedish, *Von Insel zu Insel* and *Die Besiegten,* did not lay to rest the doubts about his new language. In early 1948 he informed the publisher Peter Suhrkamp, whom he had met while on his trip to Germany, that he had started a new work and that he was again writing in German.[16] The manuscript was given the title *Der Vogelfreie* (The Outlaw). Suhrkamp rejected it as incomprehensible. (It was published by Suhrkamp in 1980 under the title *Der Fremde* [The Stranger], with authorship attributed to a certain Sinclair [an author pseudonym once used by Hermann Hesse] and without any reference to Peter Weiss.[17])

Der Fremde

Der Fremde is a hermetic text. Its narrative prose fits no literary genre—one even hesitates to call it narrative, since nothing is narrated here that can be grasped or summarized, no story, no action, no characters. No reality is described that is familiar to everyone, or to many, or even to a few. The voice that speaks or seems to speak is not a narrator who can be named or described in terms of age, origin, or appearance. Lacking identity and any clear definition, the narrator represents both the internal and external world; in his dreams, visions, and obsessions, which make up this text, reality is present only as a trace element.

There is little that can be ascertained about *Der Fremde*.[18] The text describes a twenty-four-hour period. Early in the morning a first-person narrator approaches a city, enters it, passes through it, and at the end appears to leave it. The narrator seeks contact with the city and its residents. He would like to belong with them: "I am one of you" (63). Looking for work, for any kind of meaningful activity, the narrator turns up at various places: a gymnasium where boxers are training, a glass-blowing factory, a public morgue, and an enormous construction site. To the hypersensitive "I" that narrates the text, all these stations seem places of terror from which he flees in horror. He does not fit into this world and does not even want to fit in. In a passage in the middle of the text the narrator performs an endless and liberating dance (66ff.) as an act of resistance against the constricting structures of normality. This narrator has hardly any reality, he is "a nothing. Nameless. A kind of seismograph" (82), at times losing himself to the point that he beats on himself to assure himself of his own reality (66). He experiences his existence as comparable to that of the "sole survivor after a cosmic catastrophe" (107)— an idea that recalls the "Traktat von der ausgestorbenen Welt," written ten years earlier. The narrator spends the evening in the "palace of the night" (119) where people are amusing themselves in a world of freak shows and carousels, circuses and brothels, a world made of "cardboard and glitter" (129) that the narrator longs for and nonetheless cannot be part of.

The artist here is at once expelled from and longing for the "delights of normalcy." A literary topic that conjures up Hesse, Kafka, and Thomas Mann's short novel *Tonio Kröger,* which contains this turn of phrase. But to Peter Weiss this was more than a literary topic; it was his own fate. The feeling of losing his own identity, of losing himself, derived from an existential experience. Much of this had already been present in his earlier work. In the "Traktat" there was a narrator approaching an unfamiliar city. The self-and-the-city configuration had also been the topic of many paintings, particularly of several self-portraits from the last prewar years. It had been repeated in the just completed work, *Die Besiegten.* Honky-tonk entertainment and fair and circus scenes were major themes in numerous Weiss paintings as well as in his literary work. Even the frequently evoked image of "palace of the night" in *Der Fremde* had already been found in *Von Insel zu Insel.*[19]

New, in contrast, is the vehemence with which erotic obsessions are depicted. From the opening paragraph the vocabulary and the metaphors make it clear that the image of the narrator penetrating the city, which structures the entire work, is conceived in sexual terms (the city is later also termed an "enormous womb of stone," 103). There is obsessive eroticism as well in the passages about a street of prostitutes (53) or about the guests in the "palace of the night" who become aroused by a "Negro" with a "phallus . . . like a cannon barrel." Although intended to show the emptiness and decadence of society, this passage today seems kitschy, if not vaguely racist (128ff.). The sexual fantasies were undoubtedly intended to shock, in keeping with the program of surrealism: to destroy the sexual and erotic taboos of bourgeois society. It was a program Peter Weiss had largely made his own after his encounter with surrealism, at the end of the war, and especially with Luis Buñuel's (1900–1983) films *Un Chien Andalou* and *L'age d'or*. Also evident in the erotic passages of *Der Fremde* is the influence of Henry Miller (1891–1980)—Weiss would later describe his encounter with Miller's work in *Vanishing Point*.[20] The American expatriate's novels made an overwhelming impression on Weiss. In *Tropic of Cancer* and *Tropic of Capricorn* he found a model for the literary rendition of erotic fantasies and obsessions. However, in *Der Fremde* not only the sexual taboos of society but Weiss's own sexual and emotional deformations are explored in ways which furthered the author's own liberation. A process of self-liberation that was only to be completed twelve years later with the autobiographical texts *Leavetaking* and *Vanishing Point*.

With *Der Fremde* Weiss reached an artistic impasse where there was no longer anything communicated, where no conceivable reader was being addressed. Nonetheless, this text remains part of a contradictory logic in Peter Weiss's development. The surrealist and dreamlike tone developed in texts like *Der Fremde* will impart with artistic truth even those of Weiss's works most anchored in reason and rationality, *The Investigation*, *Viet Nam Discourse*, and *The Aesthetics of Resistance*.

The Tower

Der Fremde as a depiction of a loss of self and a loss of reality, can be read as an artistic response to Weiss's own loss of identity. But how had this loss of self, this loss of identity come about? This tormenting question had caused Peter Weiss to resume psychoanalysis in 1948 (after a brief psychoanalytic experience in 1941) with very visible consequences for the next work, *The*

Tower (Der Turm), conceived as a radio play in 1948. *The Tower* is a psychoanalytic drama, more precisely a dramatized psychoanalysis. The play is constructed on the model of Freudian analysis, as Weiss makes clear in the "Prolog zum Hörspiel" (Prologue to the Radio Play). Pablo, the main character, grew up in a tower. Once in the outside world, he finds himself unable ever to really leave the tower. The tower appears as the place of a traumatic childhood, a metaphor for all that had not been dealt with and that had been repressed. Only if Pablo dared once again "to penetrate deep into the tower and deal with his past" would he be able to free himself from his childhood traumas.[21]

Pablo is a circus entertainer; more precisely (and in keeping with the goal of psychoanalysis), he is a wizard at becoming unchained, at breaking free, in essence an escape artist. At the beginning of the play Niente (Nothing), as Pablo calls himself, appears in the tower. It is home to circus performers with whom he spent his childhood and youth, and where he once performed a balancing act. He would like to perform again, though this time demonstrating his new skill as an escape artist. The tower is run by the "director" and "manageress," parent figures who once had "trained" him for his performances.[22] The two of them grant Pablo (the name once again recalls Hesse: in *Steppenwolf* Pablo is the name of the protagonist's alter ego) just one appearance, for which he is bound with rope from head to foot. With a supreme effort he succeeds in the course of the performance to free himself. While the director, manageress, and the rest of the circus performers drown, Pablo is free at last with the rope dangling from him "like an umbilical cord" (348).[23]

The play shows a "liberation process," an expression Peter Weiss was to use in 1954 to describe one of his experimental films, *Studie IV*. In *The Tower* liberation metaphors from psychology seem to have been translated too literally into a work of art. Again, as in *Der Fremde*, the main character is a "nothing" who tries to become the subject of his own existence. Once again there is the traumatic relationship to his deceased sister (328–29), once again there is the world of the circus with a lion, a dwarf, a female animal tamer, and a magician. In *The Tower*, however, not much remains of this circus world that Weiss had so often painted. The figures and their appearances are nothing more than metaphors for submission and repression, far removed from the reality of the circus as a creative, cheerful, self-contained world of fantasy. This metaphorical circus has moved into a tower, in Weiss's work a frequently recurring symbol for loneliness and being locked in. However, the circus world as metaphor clashes with the symbolism of the tower, and their real and implied meanings fail to converge. *The Tower*, nonetheless, is a less hermetic text than *Der Fremde:* the formal necessities of a play (*The Tower* was first performed on a stage in Stockholm in 1950) and the creation of actual characters and their placement in an audible and visible world led to a gain in realism. Pablo's struggle against the devastations caused in him by the parent figures of the director and the manageress makes for a credible family drama. It is a drama of revolt, as Manfred Haiduk has noted, but not of revolution.[24]

Das Duell

Weiss continued to vacillate between languages. In 1951 he returned to Swedish. In the continuing disorientation of his life, *Das Duell* (The Duel) became a text about disoriented people and their chaotic lives. Clearly influenced by Miller's novels, the text recreates the deformed existence of a deformed *bohème,* their deformed relationships and especially their deformed sexuality. As in Weiss's previous texts, there is hardly any plot, and the borders between the characters are repeatedly blurred, particularly at the transitions between passages. *Das Duell,* like the earlier work *The Tower,* is a "labor in the operating room of the mind" (126),[25] as one of the main characters says. In the course of a year, from winter to winter, Weiss recreates the mutual entanglements of four figures. Gregor is a penniless, tortured artist living in an abandoned factory. He has a relationship with Janna but loves Lea, who is pregnant by him (a presumably autobiographical constellation that recurs in *Vanishing Point*). At the beginning of the text Lea leaves her husband Robert, who works as an anonymous "warehouse manager" in the Kafkaesque wholesale operation of Lea's father, and moves in with Gregor—the name recalls Gregor Samsa in Kafka's *The Metamorphosis.* Gregor and Lea are psychologically and sexually disturbed figures, incapable of any mature relationship of mutual respect and consideration. Their life together consists of a series of tormented, sadistic, and masochistic attempts to work out their individual tales of suffering and to overcome their emotional limitations. At the end both characters are on the way to a cure— Lea leaves Gregor.

Das Duell continues the attempt begun with the radio play, *The Tower,* namely to create a more objective depiction of Weiss's biographical theme. For the first time there is no first-person narrator; the third-person narrative alternates between the perspectives of each of the four main characters. The text opens with surrealist passages of a type Weiss had already explored in *Der Fremde.* In the course of the narrative the surrealist images become fewer; toward the end language and imagery from psychology and psychoanalysis dominate. At the same time, the focus of the text narrows from the four protagonists to Lea and Gregor, and finally to Gregor, the emotionally crippled artist who, alienated from his work and life, is trying to find himself. Gregor's efforts at self-liberation are depicted by Weiss as a pandemonium of gruesome brutalities, attacks, incest, abortions, attempts at suicide, and murder; even Auschwitz is conjured up (127–28). The first part of *Das Duell* contains passages of unbearable misogyny and violence toward women:

> he tore her body, sticky from blood and spit, with his weapon he slit her womb, in her longing for destruction she whispered into his ear commanding, blind words of endearment, and he choked her while the wound of her womb, in death tremors, sucked around the penetrating weapon. (40)

Too little attention has been paid to the literal content of such passages. The issue here is not the fantasies of male dominance and male sadism—depicted openly and honestly—of a figure that, after all, is fictional. What is problematic, however, is that the misogyny of this figure is presented uncritically by the author, and that this has not been commented upon by the critics. The psychoanalytic interpreter, for instance, notes that the bloody rape in the above passage promotes "the liberation of the beloved." Although the language appears non-gender-specific in translation, the critic clearly refers to the male figure Gregor. This interpretation omits consideration of the woman Janna, bloodied and abused, who is the means by which Gregor furthers his liberation.[26] In the misogyny of his text, too, Weiss follows Henry Miller: the erotic liberation that is attempted in this kind of literature is a liberation of the man. It should be kept in mind, however, that Weiss learned much throughout his life (he remains exemplary in this respect). Years later, in a time of heightened awareness created by the women's movements, he will show insight into and understanding for the situation of women in a male-dominated society. In the figures of Lotte Bischoff, Karin Boye, and the mother of the narrator, in *The Aesthetics of Resistance,* the author of *Das Duell* provides lucid and accurate descriptions of the experiences of women in dark, violent times.

Literature as therapy. *Der Fremde, The Tower,* and *Das Duell* are texts of self-therapy through art. Such therapy is not always successful—one need only think of Lenz, Hölderlin, Kleist, and Büchner among German writers. Among Weiss's friends, the writer Stig Dagerman had killed himself at an early age. Weiss did not succumb to self-destruction. In Gregor's duel with himself and his demons the writer was able to objectify and thereby exorcise his own psychological torments and his struggle to overcome them. The cost of such efforts at objectification is evident in the text, and is itself the subject of the text. In an illuminating passage toward the end of *Das Duell*, Gregor—and along with him probably Peter Weiss—reflects about his poetic means. His literary output appears to him as the expression of an illness, as "self-help in a desperate situation" (99). The illness, the dark, destructive forces blocking his artistic work must be overcome, and the route of "consciousness" must be ventured (100).

With *Das Duell* Weiss's artistic consciousness gained strength. He decided to return to the German language and created a text entitled *The Shadow of the Coachman's Body.*

The Shadow of the Coachman's Body

This work, written in 1952 and generally referred to as a micro-novel, was published by Suhrkamp in 1960, after years of the author's efforts to have it printed. The critics were surprised and enthusiastic about this barely 100-page text by an unknown 44-year-old author, a text for which they found no comparison. The book was generally read as a kind of "word graphics," with hardly any grounding in reality; a text in which things seemed to be reduced to their "language material" and language seemed to be treated as its own topic.[27] The text, completely unlike anything on the German literary scene, was compared to the French *nouveau roman*.[28] It is not known whether Weiss at that time (or later) was aware of the works of Alain Robbe-Grillet or Raymond Queneau (the influence of absurdist French *drama,* however, from Beckett to Ionesco and Genet on Weiss's later dramatic work is undeniable). In Queneau's *Exercices de style* (1947), for example, a ridiculously insignificant event is related in more than 100 different ways: a pure exercise in language and style, albeit one of great wit and radical doubt in regard to mimesis. In contrast, the topic of *The Shadow of the Coachman's Body* is the real world. The narrative takes place in a clearly defined setting; there are individually distinguishable figures and there even is a storyline. *The Shadow of the Coachman's Body* is very different from Weiss's previous work. The paroxysmal tone and the merging of fantasy scenes and barely autonomous characters—as in *The Tower, Der Fremde,* or *Das Duell*—have been replaced by an emotionless registering. The hermetic aspect of those earlier texts is preserved mostly in the visual appearance of the printed page: blocks of text, often several pages long, that are emblematic of Weiss's prose and will recur in all of Weiss's prose works, including *The Aesthetics of Resistance.*

A first-person narrator relates three days of his stay in a remote, rural boarding house. With compulsive attention to detail he describes the landscape, the buildings, and the interiors, as well as the inhabitants of the boarding house and their doings. These inhabitants, guests and servants, are grotesque figures: the gloomy hired man, the housekeeper, the senile "captain," and the dreadful family consisting of the brutal father, the mother, an extremely disturbed son, and an infant. There is also a Mr. Schnee who collects stones, and a horrifying physician completely wrapped in bandages who is doctoring himself and wasting away in terrible pain. Soon after the beginning of the story one learns that another guest is expected, and almost imperceptibly the narrative focuses in on this guest's arrival. On the evening of the third day the expected guest arrives: it is the coachman, who remains only for the evening meal. Afterward, in the kitchen intercourse takes place between the coachman and the housekeeper, which the first-person narrator registers as a shadow-play: "the shadow of the coachman's body thrust forward again, and the shadow of the housekeeper's body came to meet him" (56).[29] Soon after, in the middle of the night, the coachman drives off.

The narrative tone of *The Shadow of the Coachman's Body* appears to be that of a visitor from Mars who has absolutely no understanding of the events he observes, makes not even the slightest effort to interpret them, and is content to describe them as precisely as possible. This narrative perspective in *The Shadow of the Coachman's Body* caused critics to perceive it as an example of "utmost objectivity in describing objects and events,"[30] and to compare the first-person narrator to a "mechanical recording device," such as a film camera or sound-recording equipment.[31] Eventually, Gunther Witting's careful reading revealed the apparently disinterested narration in *The Shadow of the Coachman's Body* as a pose.[32] This is particularly apparent in the passage in which the first-person narrator seemingly unselectively notes scraps of the guests' dialogue. From these scraps of dialogue—banalities and tired clichés—one can reconstruct a meaning. The housekeeper, for instance, describes the preparation of a dish, the captain talks about his retirement, the father fusses about the no-good son, and the doctor complains about his suffering. In a grotesquely funny passage the hired man describes how the bull mounts the cow and, as the high point of these absurdly comical linguistic acrobatics, the mother is heard complaining about the father's inadequacy in sexual intercourse. With great mastery of language (and uncharacteristically bizarre humor) Weiss creates a portrait of each character and his or her world. While the narrator appears unaware of the meaning of what he jots down, it is clearly revealed to the attentive reader. The narrator registering events without a trace of involvement turns out to be a role created by an author who is passionately involved in his narrative. In the wake of *Der*

33

Fremde, The Tower, and *Das Duell,* Weiss here once again expresses his hatred of and outrage about a (petit bourgeois) world that deforms the psyche of the individual.

How else should one interpret the now famous opening situation? The narrator, his pants lowered, is sitting in a smelly outhouse. The laconic language of the opening passage should not distract from what is actually being talked about here. Aversion and repulsion are induced by this apparent rural idyll, later recalled in *Vanishing Point* as a "place of damnation," and as "hell."[33] How else, too, should one interpret that implacable inventorying of the housekeeper's room (38–39), which does not fail to describe in minute detail every small bucolic "china statue," every "shell-covered box," every "realistically colored wooden fawn," and every "basket filled with violets"? The real-life personality, which is absent in the figure of the housekeeper as well as in the other figures of the novel, appears reified in all these objects, this accumulated tastelessness, this trashy bric-a-brac. (Twenty years later the aesthete Peter Weiss still registered his aversion to such petit bourgeois ersatz aesthetics, which he had seen in the apartments of East German communists [N II/101]). But there is another theme in *The Shadow of the Coachman's Body* that reveals the placid narrator as a role created by a passionately involved author.

There is the family: the irascible father, the oppressed and sexually frustrated mother, the eternally screaming infant, and the disturbed son who is unable to cope with life. In one passage of Weiss's malevolent satire on the bourgeois family idyll, the father chases the misguided son around the room, places him on his knee, and the mother with the infant at her breast starts sobbing. In the middle of the beating he is administering the father suffers a heart attack and, finally, with the narrator's help, has to be brought to bed (22ff.)—a passage of a liberating comical power that evokes the often mean-spirited humor of early silent film comedies. After so many previous attempts, Weiss finally succeeds in turning his own tale of suffering into a masterfully controlled literary work.

Equally successful is the integration of Kafka's influence. The former Czech national's intimate acquaintance with the world of the Prague writer can be traced in the father-son conflict as well as in the narrative tone of *The Shadow of the Coachman's Body:* this laconic registering of a small, shabby, and miserable world (not unlike the world in Kafka's *The Castle*), and even in the archaic vocabulary—"outhouse," "hired hand," "housekeeper," "coachman," and "garrison town." And, as with Kafka, Weiss's characters are waiting for redemption. This constellation calls to mind still another writer.

The influence of Samuel Beckett (1906–89) on Weiss's micro-novel was noticed early on.[34] That same year, 1952, when Weiss described characters waiting for a guest, marked the publication of *Waiting for Godot*. Obviously this was a coincidence, but then again maybe it was not. Both writers were reacting to tendencies of their time with descriptions of the "dehumanized alienation of the modern individual," as Leo Kofler states about Beckett's play. According to Kofler, the expression of this alienation is "his [the alienated person's] chattiness, as well as his muteness and lack of articulation, his emptiness, and stupidity and his absurdity bordering on the comical."[35] What Kofler notes with regard to Beckett's Vladimir and Estragon fits without reservation Weiss's captain and hired man, the father and the housekeeper.

But Peter Weiss, who occasionally characterized his micro-novel as "completely realistic" (G/R 35), stopped short of Beckett's metaphysics. In contrast to *Waiting for Godot*, with Weiss the absurd is not absolute, he does not leave his figures in complete hopelessness. Granted, the coachman who finally arrives and has intercourse with the housekeeper is not Godot nor the Messiah. But in *The Shadow of the Coachman's Body*, coitus is not reduced to the "purely copulative event," as has been asserted.[36] It is obvious that there is pleasure involved, not only for the coachman but for the housekeeper as well. That some small redemption is possible for the housekeeper, this most lowly of human beings whose miserable existence is reified in accumulated knickknacks, provides Weiss's dark, gloomy text with the trace of hope that is absent in Beckett's work.

Die Versicherung

In the work that followed *The Shadow of the Coachman's Body*, Weiss modified the redeemer figure. Instead of the anonymous coachman there is in the play *Die Versicherung* (The Insurance, written in 1952) a lewd anarchist revolutionary by the name of Leo. Unlike the coachman in Weiss's novel, he screws not only the hired help but the ruling class as well—in the literal as well as in the figurative sense. He seduces the wives of the police chief, the doctor, and other pillars of society, and ultimately places himself at the head of a revolt against this entire corrupt rabble.

Die Versicherung is less a drama—as its subtitle indicates—than a surrealist revue with music, dance, and film projections. The police chief Alfons, a pillar of society, gives a formal dinner party at which he intends to finalize numerous insurance policies covering any conceivable damages to his property. In the course of nineteen grotesque and chaotic scenes, the collapse of this society is depicted. The festive group turns up at the cabinet of one Dr. Kübel, whose delusions of grandeur match those of Dr. Caligari (of German silent film fame). While Kübel tortures his guests, Leo abducts and seduces the wife of the police chief, leaving her in a garbage can. Meanwhile, war and revolution have broken out. After losing his wife, Alfons also loses his personal papers. Drunk, he is mistaken for a bum by his own policemen, beaten, and taken to the police station. Leo has placed himself at the head of the uprising.

There is an undeniable resemblance between this surrealist work and the French theater of the absurd of the late 1940s and 1950s[37]—to the dramas of Ionesco (1929, *The Bald Soprano* [1950] and *The Chairs* [1952]), Genet (1910, *The Maids* [1947] and *The Balcony* [1955]), and Beckett. Following his first trip in 1947, Weiss had repeatedly spent time in Paris, as in 1952, 1958, and in 1960. During one of these visits he even met with Beckett.[38] Weiss himself has pointed out the importance of Ionesco (G/R 99) and Genet for his own works.[39] But all of this comes later. At the time of the writing of *Die Versicherung* no direct influence can be shown. One can only note that the postwar atmosphere of Western Europe had created in Weiss and in the French absurdist dramatists a similarity of vision and of artistic sensibility. Weiss's depiction of the "dehumanized alienation of the modern individual" once again approximates Beckett's imagery. In the fourteenth scene the chaotic Leo and the bourgeois Erna, smeared with excrement and garbage, climb out of a garbage can: humans as trash. Five years later, in 1957, Beckett will use the same image in *End Game*. It was through Beckett, however, and not through Weiss, that garbage cans became "emblems of the civilization rebuilt after Auschwitz" (Adorno).[40]

But *Die Versicherung* can no more be reduced to its absurd aspects than *The Shadow of the Coachman's Body*. It is a clearly identified world whose chaotic decline is presented here. The "CATASTROPHES REVOLUTIONS" (63)[41] that the police chief learns about from newspaper headlines, are striking at the world of power and wealth. The ridiculous compulsion of this entrenched upper bourgeoisie to insure its property against any conceivable catastrophe, even against "hurricanes, invasions, cosmic storms, explosions in space" (48), is what first sets the play in motion. But the insurance contracts come too late: the world of the police chief and his guests is "in the grips of a severe epidemic" (68) that will cause its demise. As critic Heinrich

Vormweg has noted, "There is no amount of insurance that can protect this society."[42]

Die Versicherung does not move beyond the pose of an antibourgeois revolt. Leo, with all his macho behavior, is not a revolutionary and, despite the fur he is wearing, he is also no Heracles, whose siding with the oppressed in their fight against the oppressors is repeatedly evoked in *The Aesthetics of Resistance*. *Die Versicherung* is the strongest attempt Weiss was capable of at the time of resistance against the prevailing order. Since the end of the war his literary work had been defined by his compulsion of re-creating over and over his own tale of suffering. This compulsion, which had largely blocked the study of social issues, now begins to wane.

At this point, however, Peter Weiss's literary production came to a halt: he escaped from the psychological pressure of the continuing lack of literary success. Before the end of the productive year 1952 he made his first two films, and until the end of the decade—by which time this route also turned out to be a dead end—Weiss was a filmmaker. The literary texts that followed *Von Insel zu Insel* and *Die Besiegten* had attracted no interest and were either published privately in minimal editions (*Der Fremde, Das Duell,* both in Swedish) or many years later (*The Tower* in 1963, *Die Versicherung* in 1967). Only one of Weiss's early works eventually managed to escape this fate. In 1960 *The Shadow of the Coachman's Body* was finally published in a special series by Suhrkamp, in an edition of merely 1,000 copies. It immediately created great interest. Suddenly, unexpectedly, there was success; there was a readership, people willing to pay attention to this new voice. The time of isolation had come to an end. After forty-four years the endless meandering route of the painter, filmmaker, and author Peter Weiss had revealed some kind of inner logic.

NOTES

1. The page numbers in parentheses refer to Peter Weiss, "Traktat von der ausgestorbenen Welt" (1938–39), in *Der Maler Peter Weiss* (Berlin: Frölich and Kaufmann, 1982) 56.

2. Rainer Gerlach, "Isolation und Befreiung. Zum literarischen Frühwerk von Peter Weiss," in Gerlach, ed., *Peter Weiss* (Frankfurt/Main: Suhrkamp, 1984) 153.

3. On Weiss's thus far unpublished early writings, see Heinrich Vormweg, "Der Schriftsteller als junger Künstler," in Gunilla Palmstierna-Weiss and Jürgen Schutte, eds., *Peter Weiss. Leben und Werk* (Frankfurt/Main: Suhrkamp, 1991) 24–38.

4. See chap. 1 above.

5. "Aus dem Briefwechsel mit Hermann Hesse" (1937–62), in Raimund Hoffmann, *Peter Weiss. Malerei Zeichnungen Collagen* (Berlin: Henschelverlag, 1984) 163 (Hesse's letter of 21 January 1937).

6. According to Gunilla Palmstierna-Weiss in her foreword to Peter Weiss, *Von Insel zu Insel* (1947), German trans. Heiner Gimmler (Berlin: Frölich and Kaufmann, 1984). Peter Weiss later

described in detail his battle to acquire the new language, in "Laokoon oder Über die Grenzen der Sprache" (1965), in Weiss, *Rapporte* (Frankfurt/Main: Suhrkamp, 2d ed., 1981) 170–87, esp. 176ff.

7. See Palmstierna-Weiss, "Vorwort," in *Von Insel zu Insel;* see also Gunilla Palmstierna-Weiss, "Nachwort," in Peter Weiss, *Die Besiegten* (Frankfurt/Main: Suhrkamp, 1985) 153–57.

8. Research has not determined whether this and the following texts were written entirely in Swedish. Henceforth, those texts which were first published or performed in Sweden are termed Swedish texts. On the language problems involved in the writing of *Von Insel zu Insel,* see Jochen Vogt, *Peter Weiss* (Reinbek b. Hamburg: Rowohlt-Monographie, 1987) 49–50.

9. The page numbers in parentheses refer to Peter Weiss, *Von Insel zu Insel.*

10. See Alfons Söllner, *Peter Weiss und die Deutschen* (Opladen: Westdeutscher Verlag, 1988) 45.

11. Ernst J. Walberg, "Die Ästhetik der Imagination. Peter Weiss' Frühwerk: *Von Insel zu Insel,*" *die horen* 4 (1984): 137–39.

12. See Peter Weiss, "Sechs Reportagen aus Deutschland für *Stockholms Tidningen*" (June–August 1947), in Weiss, *Die Besiegten* (Frankfurt/Main: Suhrkamp, 1985) 149.

13. In addition to the 6 articles in *Die Besiegten,* see also Peter Weiss, "Die Bibliothek in Berlin," in *Peter Weiss. In Gegensätzen denken. Ein Lesebuch,* selected by Rainer Gerlach and Matthias Richter (Frankfurt/Main: Suhrkamp, 1986) 14–18.

14. The page numbers in parentheses refer to Peter Weiss, *Die Besiegten.*

15. See Helmut Peitsch's excellent article, "Wo ist die Freiheit? Peter Weiss und das Berlin des Kalten Krieges," in Jürgen Garbers et al, eds., *Ästhetik Revolte Widerstand. Zum literarischen Werk von Peter Weiss* (Lüneburg, Jena: zu Klampen, Universitätsverlag, 1990) 34–56.

16. See Peter Weiss, "Brief an Peter Suhrkamp" (1948), in Siegfried Unseld, *Peter Suhrkamp. Zur Biographie eines Verlegers* (Frankfurt/Main: Suhrkamp, 1975) 123.

17. See Sinclair (i.e., Peter Weiss), *Der Fremde. Erzählung* (Frankfurt/Main: Suhrkamp, 1980). The page numbers in the text refer to this edition.

18. Concerning *Der Fremde,* see especially the detailed study by Rüdiger Steinlein, "Ein surrealistischer 'Bilddichter.' Visualität als Darstellungsprinzip im erzählerischen Frühwerk von Peter Weiss," in Rudolf Wolff, ed., *Peter Weiss. Werk und Wirkung* (Bonn: Bouvier, 1987) 60–87.

19. See Weiss, *Von Insel zu Insel* 46.

20. See Peter Weiss, *Vanishing Point* (*Fluchtpunkt,* 1960–61), trans. E. B. Garside, Alastair Hamilton, and Christopher Levenson, in Weiss, *Exile* (New York: Delacorte, 1968) 217–19. Missing in the English translation, however, is any reference to Miller's *Tropic of Cancer.* The translation of this entire passage is distorted, conveying the impression that at issue is a book by Amos, a character in the novel, rather than by Henry Miller. For the actual content of the passage, see Peter Weiss, *Fluchtpunkt* (1960–61) (Frankfurt/Main: Suhrkamp, 6th ed., 1973) 163ff.

21. Peter Weiss, "Prolog zum Hörspiel (Der Turm)," in Weiss, *Stücke I* (Frankfurt/Main: Suhrkamp, 1976) 453.

22. Ibid.

23. The page numbers in parentheses refer to Peter Weiss, *The Tower* (*Der Turm,* 1948), trans. Michael Benedikt and Michel Heine, in Michael Benedikt and George E. Wellwarth, eds., *Postwar German Theatre* (New York: Dutton, 1967) 315–48.

24. See Manfred Haiduk, *Der Dramatiker Peter Weiss* (East Berlin: Henschelverlag, 1977) 18.

25. The page numbers in parentheses refer to Peter Weiss, *Das Duell* (1951), German trans. J. C. Görsch in collaboration with Peter Weiss (Frankfurt/Main: Suhrkamp, 4th ed., 1982).

26. See Carl Pietzcker, "Individualistische Befreiung als Kunstprinzip. 'Das Duell' von Peter Weiss," in Johannes Cremerius, ed., *Psychoanalytische Textinterpretationen* (Hamburg: Hoffmann and Campe, 1979) 216–17.

27. Gerhard Schmidt-Henkel, "Die Wortgraphik des Peter Weiss," in Volker Canaris, ed., *Über Peter Weiss* (Frankfurt/Main: Suhrkamp, 4th ed., 1976) 15–24; Ror Wolf, "Die Poesie der kleinsten Stücke," in Canaris, ed., *Über Peter Weiss* 26; and Helmut J. Schneider, "Der verlorene Sohn und die Sprache," in Canaris, ed., *Über Peter Weiss* 46.

28. This comparison has been made since the earliest reviews. For a more recent example, see Heinrich Vormweg, *Peter Weiss* (Munich: Beck, 1981) 42ff. On this topic, see also Gunther Witting, "Bericht von der hohen Warte. Zu Peter Weiss' 'Der Schatten des Körpers des Kutschers,'" *Der Deutschunterricht* 37, no. 3 (1985): 57.

29. The page numbers in parentheses refer to Peter Weiss, *The Shadow of the Coachman's Body (Der Schatten des Körpers des Kutschers,* 1952), trans. E. B. Garside, in Weiss, *Bodies and Shadows* (New York: Delacorte, 1969) 1–57.

30. Vormweg, *Peter Weiss* 43.

31. Sepp Hiekisch-Picard, " 'In den Vorräumen eines Gesamtkunstwerks.' Anmerkungen zum Zusammenhang zwischen schriftstellerischem, filmischem und bildkünstlerischem Werk bei Peter Weiss," *Kürbiskern* 2 (April 1985): 123.

32. See Witting 57ff.

33. Weiss, *Vanishing Point* 154.

34. See Ror Wolf 27.

35. Leo Kofler, "Beckett, Warten auf Godot" (1975), in Kofler, *Avantgardismus als Entfremdung. Ästhetik und Ideologiekritik* (Frankfurt/Main: Sendler, 1987) 203.

36. Gerlach, "Isolation und Befreiung" 171.

37. Weiss mentions the French theater of the absurd for the first time in "Avantgarde Film" (1956), in Weiss, *Rapporte* 17.

38. See Peter Weiss, "Aus dem Pariser Journal," in Weiss, *Rapporte* 93–94.

39. See Peter Weiss, "Aus dem Kopenhagener Journal" (1960), in *Rapporte* 51, 67. The narrator of *Vanishing Point* also points out the great significance of Beckett and Genet for his work. See Weiss, *Vanishing Point* 140.

40. Theodor W. Adorno, "Versuch, das Endspiel zu verstehen" (1961), in Adorno, *Noten zur Literatur* (Frankfurt/Main: Suhrkamp, 1981) 311.

41. The page numbers in parentheses refer to Peter Weiss, *Die Versicherung. Ein Drama* (1952), in Weiss, *Stücke I* 35–87.

42. Vormweg, *Peter Weiss* 33.

CHAPTER THREE

Self-Liberation through Autobiographical Narration

In 1959 the inhabitants of the Congo, under the leadership of Patrice Lumumba (1925–61), rose up against Belgian colonial domination. (In 1960 Lumumba became the first prime minister of the Democratic Republic of the Congo; in 1961 he was murdered by a rival faction supported by the Belgian colonial power.)

In 1959 the physician Agostinho Neto (1922–79) returned from the Portuguese prisons of the fascist dictator Salazar to his homeland, the Portuguese colony of Angola. (In 1975 Neto would become the first president of the People's Republic of Angola.)

In 1959 the world gradually realized that a second Indochina war was underway in Southeast Asia. The conflict would soon get its definitive name: the Vietnam War.

In November 1959 in the Federal Republic of Germany, the SPD (Social Democratic Party) adopted the Godesberg Program. Giving in to the pressures from the Adenauer restoration policies and the cold war, the party adapted to the capitalist system, replacing socialist perspectives with a plan to reform the existing system.

Although Peter Weiss at the time seems not to have registered any interest in these events, his life now moved toward them.

A new worldliness in Peter Weiss's creative endeavors had been noticeable since the two texts of 1952, which marked the end of the postwar phase of Weiss's literary work, *The Shadow of the Coachman's Body* and *Die Versicherung*. Thereafter, in his film work, especially in his documentaries about topics such as the homeless, about life in prison for young criminals, about alcoholics, and about the lonely and marginalized, Weiss had turned toward the external world, toward society. The decisive event of the year 1959, however, was not of a political but of a private nature: the death of his parents. His mother died in December 1958, his father in March 1959. That same year Peter Weiss began to write again. The new work became a leavetaking from his parents.

Leavetaking

The characters and content of *Leavetaking* are familiar: the first-person narrator's father is a Jew, a textile manufacturer, the mother, a former actress; there are two half brothers, one younger brother, and two sisters, one of them named Margit. Familiar, too, is the narrator's childhood in the early 1920s in a harbor city easily recognizable as Bremen, at first in Grünenstrasse (8),[1] later in Marcusallee (15). There is the traumatic family atmosphere, the family's lack of political awareness, the half brothers' opting for fascism, and the sister's death in a car accident; there are the exile stations in London and in the Czechoslovakian Sudetenland, and the narrator's year of studying painting at the Prague Art Academy; there is the mother's destruction of her son's paintings prior to the family's flight to Sweden; there is the narrator's work in his father's factory; and, finally, in the middle of the war, there is his escape from the Swedish provinces to Stockholm and his first independent existence.

An autobiography?

To the title of this new text, *Leavetaking,* was appended the genre term "Erzählung" (story), signaling a work of fiction wherein the facts of Weiss's biography would be treated freely. This fictionalization can be shown in many instances. The narrator's entire childhood and youth are shifted to the same city (Bremen), omitting the early years of Weiss's youth in Berlin. Neither the first trip from Prague to Switzerland nor the two meetings with Hermann Hesse, key events in Weiss's life, are mentioned. The names of several real-life persons are slightly altered. Hesse is given the pseudonym Harry Haller, the name of the main character in Hesse's novel *Steppenwolf;* the Prague friend Max Barth becomes Max B. In an autobiography such changes might be explained by considerations for persons still living at the time, but why withhold from the readers the names of the narrator and his parents? On the other hand, why use the real names of Weiss's sister Margit, of his London friend Jacques Ayschmann who disappeared in Spain, or of the Prague Academy painting student Peter Kien, who was murdered in Auschwitz? In the absence of a recognizable, consistent principle, this varied use of real names appears as a delicate balancing act between factuality and literary license.

But why, then, the insistence on the genre term "Erzählung"? How much in this text is invention? What happens here that did not also happen in Peter Weiss's life? What characters appear in the text who are not also real people from the author's life? Should the shift from fact to fiction be dismissed as altogether minor? The literary genre of *Leavetaking* is not easily determined.[2]

The finding that Weiss's text straddles two genres raises more questions than it answers. Furthermore, with the publication of Weiss's next work, *Vanishing Point*, the genre debate began anew. It is also at the center of any interpretation of Weiss's plays of the Documentary Theater type, from *The Investigation* to *Viet Nam Discourse*. And in the monumental novel, *The Aesthetics of Resistance*, the genre question led to further, often loud, disputes; for, in the end, resolution of this seemingly technical question posed by Germanists is impossible without a clarification of political and ideological positions.

What needs to be clarified is the way in which Weiss treats his autobiographical and historical material. In the following pages we will explore some of the strategies by which *Leavetaking*, the authentic story of a childhood and youth, is transformed into a work of fiction.

In leafing through Weiss's book, the first impression one receives is of the hermetic appearance of the text. Already in *The Shadow of the Coachman's Body* the author had written blocks of text several pages long without paragraphs. In *Leavetaking* this characteristic visual appearance of Weiss's prose is carried to an extreme that would not be sustained either in the following *Vanishing Point* nor, years later, in *The Aesthetics of Resistance*. *Leavetaking* consists of one single paragraph which, in the German edition, is almost 170 pages long. This form is by no means imposed by the content. On the contrary, in the young narrator's development which is being related, there are such obvious caesuras as the move from Grünenstrasse to the Marcusallee, which coincides with the narrator's attending school for the first time; the sister's death; the move from Germany to England; the arrival in Czechoslovakia; and the move to Sweden. Unlike in an authentic autobiography, however, here the content is subjugated to an aesthetic concept. It was with *Leavetaking* in mind that Weiss described this aesthetic concept in 1964 as a "dense, coherent form, a single block" (G/R 37). Hermetical isolation, Weiss continued, was the basic condition of his creativity. During work he was "cut off from the whole world," he worked "from eight in the morning until late in the night, and did so for months without interruption" (G/R 33). Still later Weiss characterized his existence, this life in never-ending exile, as "hermetic." The difficulties and the pain of such an existence had induced him into making "the written [material] as dense as possible" (G/R 281), which, in turn, led to writing long, uninterrupted blocks of text.

These attempts at psychological and biographical explanations of the visual appearance of these works underscore the elusiveness of Weiss's aesthetic concept. At times the author tried to illuminate the practice of writing without paragraphs in terms of his background as a painter. In discussions and notations during work on *The Aesthetics of Resistance,* there is mention of the beauty of a page that is uniform and homogeneous in appearance (G/R 220), which Weiss compares to a painting (N II/701). After the completion of the big novel he again emphasized that this practice of writing in blocks dated from his life as a painter (G/R 280).

Literary texts organized purely on the basis of visual criteria: a rather unique occurrence in prose texts (but not in poetry, where visual appearance can be a determining aspect of a work). Weiss was aware of this, as well as of the inadequacies of his attempts at explanation. There remains a part that cannot be explained and that may be termed artistic peculiarity. It is one of the elements through which Weiss's texts become fiction.

In undertaking to write the *authentic* story of their youth, writers may look for sources that confirm, correct, and supplement their own recollections. They may, for instance, study notes and diaries of family members, visit the early settings of their life, and inquire about the later life of childhood friends and foes. All this the narrator of *Leavetaking* undertakes, and these searches and sources are related in the text. Right at the beginning, as the siblings dissolve the deceased parents' household, the reader learns that the narrator keeps for himself his father's notations and his mother's diary (7). Later, the first-person narrator reports that while writing down his life, he is pouring over his parents' notes and letters (23). There are literal quotations from his father's testament and from one of his letters to his mother (23), as well as from the mother's diary (51). A visit by the narrator to the places of childhood is also mentioned (14–15). Granted, a fictional narrator, too, can mention his parents' writings or revisit the places of his or her childhood. However, the diary of Weiss's mother actually existed, and Peter Weiss quoted from it in his Copenhagen journal.[3] There is also little reason to doubt the authenticity of the father's notations used by the narrator; everything related about his father's situation on the Eastern front during the First World War and his war injury applies to Eugen Weiss. As far as can be determined, even the secondary figures of Weiss's "story" coincide, in name as well as in biography, with real persons: the childhood torturer Friederle Nebeltau who, it is learned, later became an officer of the *Wehrmacht* (15), as well as the narrator's later friend, Peter Kien, whose end in Auschwitz has already been mentioned.

With all these facts being authentic, is *Leavetaking* an autobiography after all?

Leavetaking begins, "I have often tried to come to an understanding of the images of my father and my mother." What is meant here, of course, is the common desire to gain clarity about one's origins. But the implications of this sentence are also very specific. In Peter Weiss's life there had been concrete attempts to come to an understanding of the images of his parents—in his work as a painter, and especially in the texts written since 1946. The first sentence of *Leavetaking* refers to these works, even though German readers were unfamiliar with them at the time; unjustly so, as Weiss undoubtedly felt after numerous efforts in vain to have them published. Evidently there was much in these works that he continued to consider valid and that he did not wish to be lost. Hence, various topics, figures, and constellations were taken from these works and, sometimes literally, integrated into *Leavetaking*. The description of the sister's death, for instance, was taken from *Von Insel zu Insel* (46);[4] the farcical passage, in which the weakly father places the son over his knee, whereupon the son screams solely for the purpose of appeasing the father (53), was first created in *The Tower* and recurred in *The Shadow of the Coachman's Body;*[5] the passage where the young narrator seeks out a whore, but is then so repulsed that he leaves before sexual intercourse takes place (76) first appeared in *Von Insel zu Insel;*[6] the narrator's fleeting recollection that as a child he had once seen his mother's genitals (77–78) had already been described in *Der Fremde,* as had the metaphor of the city as a "womb of stone" (81).[7] *Leavetaking* is laced with images and quotations from Weiss's earlier fiction which, as was shown, often adhered precisely to Weiss's real biography.

The closer one reads *Leavetaking,* the more confusing its particular mixture of fact and fiction, autobiography and novel becomes. The realism of many of its passages is undermined as the narration turns into surreal poetry, removing any secure ground from under the reader: as when the narrator recalls that as a child he found himself on the chimney of his parents' house, "I sprang with a leap into the sky" (8); the evocative description of the narrator's feeling of abandonment at night in his parents' house ends with the casual observation, "From the ditch I caught the half-extinguished cries of a drowning child" (26); and the hated London warehouse, in which he works as a volunteer, becomes a phantasmagoria, its wares lying in "stalactite caverns," while "in the subdued light of the jungle, orange-yellow salesgirls fluttered around like butterflies," the whole building becomes a "primeval tropical world" (60). Not only the images but the words themselves at times become autonomous, as in the description of a mechanical puppet show at a fair where, after a brief pause, "everything moved along again, shook again, bobbed again, dragged along again, hacked again, cracked again'' (13); or when the narrator decorates the display window of the London warehouse ''with matches and hatchets, sandpapers and capers, guns and buns, ash trays and hair sprays.'' (62). Here, Weiss's language achieves a freedom and play-fulness that far exceeds the ''word graphics'' of *The Shadow of the Coach-man's Body.*

Thus far, I have made little mention of the depressing, shocking *content* of *Leavetaking,* the obsessive passages about sexuality, masturbation, and in-cest, about fantasies of torture, and about the psychological and physical hell of this childhood and youth. Much of this has been discussed in the previous chapters dealing with Peter Weiss's life and early literary work. *Leavetaking* (and its continuation, *Vanishing Point*) represents the sum of this life and work at the end of the 1950s (just as *The Aesthetics of Resistance* can be re-garded as the sum of Weiss's entire life and work). This sum includes not only the past but the present as well, the author's consciousness at the time of writing. In the year 1959 this consciousness was far removed from the con-sciousness of the young man of the story, an aspect easily overlooked in the interpretation of *Leavetaking.*[8] Peter Weiss had come a long way since his last literary work, the chaotically antibourgeois play of 1952, *The Tower.* The per-son who is recalling his nearly autistic childhood in *Leavetaking* is in the throes of a process of turning toward the world, toward society and its prob-lems. The narrator of 1959 is able to view his own tale of suffering no longer merely in terms of individual psychology but in its social and historical con-texts as well: as when he terms the child's stay in the arbor as an ''exile'' (9); and later when the attic will be called ''exile'' (21). Here Peter Weiss's early existence receives a new, a political interpretation.

Also new in Weiss's work and thinking is this insight: ''I comprehended nothing of the living conditions of the workers, their struggle, their prob-lems'' (84). The narrator of 1959, while showing empathy and understanding for the psychological deformations of his former ego, is helpless when it comes to explaining his former disinterest in the real world and in the his-torical process, his lack of solidarity with the lower classes. This is the tone of several passages in *Leavetaking,* such as the brief description of the funeral procession of Tomáş Masaryk (1850–1937) through the city of Prague. Alien and uninvolved, the young man walks among the masses of people mourning the first president of Czechoslovakia (74). He is unaware and uninterested in who it is who is being carried to the grave (even though Masaryk had been generous in granting exile status to German and Austrian refugees). The book concludes with a painfully frank settling of accounts with the narrator's former self: "The war did not open my eyes" (86), and "emigrating had taught me nothing" (86). Only the narrator of 1959 recognizes that the battle then being waged ought to have concerned him, and he is filled with regrets about his former lack of awareness, "I had never come to any conclusions about the revolutionary conflicts in the world" (86). The concluding passage leaves no doubt, however, that the author of *Leavetaking* had since learned that, in the battles of one's time, it is necessary to keep one's eyes open, to draw lessons from one's own fate and the fate of one's fellow human beings, and to take a stand.

"In contemporary German literature there is no more radical description of a failed youth." This assessment by Karl Heinz Götze[9] touches upon what ultimately makes the beauty of this work: its high degree of truthfulness. This truthfulness is the result of an unlivable youth, long years of isolation, an artist's existence developed under extremely adverse conditions, of more than twenty years of painting with hardly any recognition, of repeated false starts and dead ends as a filmmaker and writer, and, finally, of an emerging awareness of the state of the world. Which leads one to the paradoxical conclusion that the beauty of *Leavetaking* is the result of an existence that up to that point Peter Weiss had been able to see only as deformed, misguided, and wasted.

Peter Weiss's life, thinking, and art in the early 1960s convey a sense of intense, rapid, and profound change that manifests itself as a restlessness, a confusing succession of travels to Paris, Morocco, Southern France, the Italian part of Switzerland, Denmark, and again Paris. This restlessness is also reflected in his artistic output during these years: *Leavetaking* was concluded; Weiss's last film, *Hinter den Fassaden* (Behind the Facades) was shot, and notes about the making of this film ("Aus dem Kopenhagener Journal" [From the Copenhagen Journal]) and about the author's stays in Paris ("Aus dem Pariser Journal" [From the Paris Journal]) were readied for publication; while at the same time he began to work on *Vanishing Point*. Weiss also wrote essays about a naive French mailman's lifelong work on an enormous sculpture ("Der grosse Traum des Briefträgers Cheval" [The Postman Cheval's Big Dream]) and about Strindberg ("Gegen die Gesetze der Normalität" [Against the Laws of Normality]).

Weiss's essays and notations indicate a change of paradigm in his conception of art. In the opening passage of the Paris journal Weiss describes his impressions from having attended three exhibitions about surrealism. He acknowledges the demise of a movement that had been a strong influence on his work since the 1940s. The works of de Chirico, Max Ernst, Duchamp, Man Ray, Magritte, Tanguy, and Dali were now in museums and galleries—defined by Weiss as "the treasure chests of their enemies"—to be viewed comfortably from "velvet easy chairs." This type of art had ostensibly lost its subversive power. Works once felt to be "high-explosive bombs" had been tamed by society, their impact reduced to one of "meditations" and "dream material." The artistic means of these artists, Weiss continues, were not up to the task of depicting the horrors that had engulfed much of the world in the recent past. On one occasion, when he found himself in the presence of the long revered surrealist French poet André Breton (1896–1966), Weiss noted that his former fascination with Breton's work now seemed like a figment of his imagination.[10] (Still, years later Weiss would name his daughter with Gunilla Palmstierna-Weiss after Breton's surrealist text of 1928, *Nadja.*)

In quest of new means of expression for a literary rendition of the real world and its social issues, Weiss became interested in the artistic methods of two Swiss artists working in Paris, Jean Tinguely, a sculptor working with iron, and the conceptual artist Daniel Spoerri. Tinguely, whose works have since acquired international fame, created bizarre, playful sculptures with movable parts out of scrap iron, which make a lot of noise when set in motion. Weiss describes an occasion when Tinguely paraded several of these sculptures through Paris, an anarchical happening that ended abruptly when the police arrested Tinguely (N I/9–10). What especially fascinated Weiss about this happening was that, however briefly, art seemed to have succeeded in intervening in real life, that the separation of art and life was overcome—a demand that had been at the core of the historic avant-garde movements, dadaism and surrealism, as described by Peter Bürger in his *Theory of the Avant-Garde.*[11] Eventually, though, Weiss had to register defeat: artistic happenings like Tinguely's were incapable of achieving lasting changes in people's lives. In his essay "Aus dem Pariser Journal," Weiss assigns to the artist the role of revolutionary in a society whose class differences Weiss judged to have been largely eliminated. It was an idealistic demand, but one that documented how intensely he was now interested in a link between art and the real world. Weiss's notebooks include a description of another Paris happening comparable to Tinguely's action. In summing up this second event, Weiss notes that there were several "charged moments" and "orgiastic beginnings," but here too the "separation between art and life" could not be overcome (N I/19–23).

Like Tinguely, the conceptual artist Daniel Spoerri was concerned with preserving for posterity lowly artifacts of civilization, the daily trash people leave behind. Spoerri was interested in what people left behind after a meal: dirty dishes and silverware, food remains, dirty glasses, half-filled ashtrays, and wrinkled napkins on a bespotted tablecloth; all of which he glued down and exhibited as a tableau, a seemingly uninvolved, exact inventory of common, useless objects. "Maybe he wants to show something of the stupefaction and senselessness of a terminal situation," Weiss noted. It was what he himself had done in *The Shadow of the Coachman's Body*. The micro-novel, too, showed a kind of terminal situation, and Weiss had used the same method of creating a seemingly uninvolved, exact inventory of common objects and pointless happenings. But in the Paris journal Spoerri's work also prompts Weiss to point out the problems inherent in such an artistic method. Mere inventorying, which avoids any valuation and judgment, in which everything seems equally important or unimportant, and which aims to let things speak for themselves, might express an uncritically affirmative attitude toward society. Spoerri's work might ultimately serve the system and contribute to the "preservation of order."[12]

Vanishing Point

Peter Weiss gave literary expression to his evolving thinking about art in *Vanishing Point*, the second installment of his fictionalized autobiography. It was begun in the fall of 1960 immediately after completion of *Leavetaking* and finished in the summer of 1962 (N I/71). *Vanishing Point* describes the life and creative problems of representatives of a European *bohème* exiled in Stockholm[13] during the period from November 1940 until the spring of 1947. The characters in the novel are based on real people, even when the real names are not used: for example, Max Bernsdorf (Max Barth), Anatol (Endre Nemes), and Hoderer (Max Hodann). The events coincide in great detail with the biographical facts of Weiss's life. This again raises the question of literary genre, of autobiography versus novel, of authenticity and fiction. The various aspects of this issue, as debated above in conjunction with *Leavetaking*, equally apply here. In keeping with the classification of the book as a novel (in the German original the title is followed by the subtitle "Roman" [novel]) and Weiss's own intentions, *Vanishing Point* will here be read as a novel.

Characters and themes of *Vanishing Point* are familiar from Weiss's earlier literary work (particularly *Das Duell* [The Duel]) and documentary films: artistic *bohème*, outsiders, marginal existences—the latter being the narrator's characterization of himself (132)[14]—and their struggle for artistic existence, their desperate attempts to find themselves, their difficult friendships, and the destructive and self-destructive round of their sexual relations. Especially the first-person narrator, a twenty-four-year-old painter driven out of Ger-

many by the Nazis, who arrives in Stockholm at the beginning of the novel
(91), closely resembles the nihilist Gregor from *Das Duell*. He emphasizes
his lack of belonging, his complete independence from any ties of family,
race, or nation (93, 111), as though it were a great accomplishment. He turns
this lack of belonging on its head, making it appear as a virtue of which he
can boast, "I did not want to belong to any race, ideal, city or language, and
I wanted to see strength solely in my detachment" (115). The narrator's art
is just as removed from the real world as his existence. The political and ideological demand of the hour—namely the battle against fascism—seems to
him unimportant in comparison to his artistic work (98). At times he appears
indifferent, even toward his own works: these paintings that "lay under thick
bell jars" (114), that express no intentionality whatsoever, and that depict
nothing more than "a sort of inventory" (139)—the key term Weiss had used
in criticizing Daniel Spoerri's artistic concept. Indifference also character-
izes the young painter's attitude toward his lovers. Changing sexual partners,
pregnancies, abortion, fatherhood, marriage, and divorce: the emotional
chaos of these relations makes it clear that it is not only the young painter's
work that is under a bell jar but he himself.

Unlike in the earlier *Das Duell*, however, here the main character's most
important acquaintances and friends are conceived as his opposites. The
writer Max Bernsdorf, the painter Anatol, and the sculptor Karel Kurz attempt unceasingly, through intellectual and artistic activities, to influence the
course of history, to resist and change it. Like the socialist physician Hoderer,
they are committed antifascists. They find in their solidarity with the persecuted a sense of community, even in exile. Beyond the individual tragedies of
their fates—the endless flight of Bernsdorf and the suicides of Hoderer and
Kurz—they represent the future (143). The narrator becomes aware of this
through Anatol's paintings, which deal with all the issues that his own paintings conceal and ignore.

Yet he continues to cling to the concept of "freedom of expression" of all
art (141), which to him means that art needs to serve no practical purpose.
He has just discovered the art of the 1920s, that "historical avant-garde" (Peter Bürger) of dadaism and surrealism that had so strongly influenced Peter
Weiss in the 1940s. At the time he wrote *Vanishing Point*, however, Weiss had
already progressed to a critique of the historical avant-garde and its ability to
reflect historical developments. He was now more interested in the gathering
and exhibiting of artifacts, an aesthetic concept he had found in the works of
Tinguely and Spoerri, and which he had experimented with in *The Shadow of
the Coachman's Body:* a style of writing that gave the impression of being

objective and dispassionate (and that had led some critics to compare the narrator of the micro-novel to a film camera or a sound recorder). In late 1960, at a time when Weiss had already begun writing *Vanishing Point,* there is a programmatic notation in the notebooks about this emerging new concept: "To describe things precisely the way they are. Common, insignificant, worn out objects. To ascribe no other meaning to them than their own. No exaggerations, nothing out of the ordinary or surprising" (N I/42).

This concept, which seems a complete reversal from the style of *Der Fremde* or *Das Duell,* is further developed in *Vanishing Point.* In a conversation with the writer Fanny (220–21) and in contrast to her defense of the traditional concept of fiction, her "playing with imaginary figures," Weiss has the narrator sketch out a new, reality-based conception of literature. Against traditional forms of narration that seem to him unsatisfactory and constricting, he posits a type of writing based on forms such as "diary, notes, sketches, the various stages of a picture." At the end of the novel the narrator, who only a short time earlier had been painting pictures that were separated from reality as if underneath a "bell jar," insists on the unity of art and life and no longer wants to admit them as separate spheres: a demand already made by the historical avant-garde movements, but which Peter Weiss had discovered for himself only after his experiences with the happenings in Paris.

What emerges from all these concepts is the quest for a more realistic art that is closer to life. *Vanishing Point* describes this quest and is at the same time its result. The excesses of a text like *Das Duell* have almost completely disappeared. Gone too is the nearly hermetic aspect of Weiss's earlier texts. Consequently, there is a strong gain in realism. Yet there is also a certain impoverishment. In *Vanishing Point* Weiss dispenses to a large extent with those magical visions and dream images that were at the core of the artistic quality of *Leavetaking.* From now on the aesthetics of Weiss's literary work will be driven by the dialectics of obsessive fidelity to reality and free flights of creative fantasy. In *Marat/Sade* the flights of fantasy and imagination will dominate. At times, as in *Viet Nam Discourse,* the obsession with facts will lead to a striking reduction of artistic means and to a kind of *minimal art.* In *The Aesthetics of Resistance* the contradiction between factuality and free invention will be brought to a new synthesis.

The aesthetic doubts about his own works, triggered in the young painter by Anatol's paintings, are expanded into the political realm by Hoderer. The physician and Marxist intellectual argues that the apparent radicalism in the narrator's paintings is merely a pose of the kind that does not endanger those in power. In sentences that Weiss lifted almost literally from his Paris journal,

Hoderer predicts that works of art like those of the young narrator would some day be treated by the ruling class as harmless luxury objects with a potential for making money. In contrast, Hoderer posits the concept of an art with "utilitarian value" (140), an art capable of intervening in life. He challenges his young friend to show solidarity by participating in the struggles of his time.

Discouraged by the course of the war and by his deteriorating health, the fictional Hoderer commits suicide in 1943 (the real Max Hodann committed suicide in 1946), but the thinking of this "vigilant selfless person" (134) will not be without consequences in the narrator's life. Gradually he begins to understand that he cannot remain neutral. Still immersed in his own private tale of suffering, he now hopes that some day it will be possible for him to describe his private experiences in such a way that they would also reflect historical events.

The bell-jar existence develops cracks. Real life increasingly intrudes into the narrator's life, forcing him out of his own narrow sphere. Two episodes illustrate the young artist's breaking out of his ivory tower. One is the interval spent as a helper on a farm, the other the months he works as a lumberjack in the forests of northern Sweden, both autobiographical experiences of Peter Weiss. Weiss had already used his experiences on a remote farm as the basis for the narrative, *The Shadow of the Coachman's Body*. In the retelling of the same episode in *Vanishing Point*, however, there is no longer a figure comparable to the coachman, no redeemer appears among the exploited farmhands. Observing their exploitation and misery, the narrator of *Vanishing Point* begins to understand that only the exploited themselves can bring about their redemption. But his attempts at political agitation among this rural underclass are deflected by a rigid, ossified reality. This experience is repeated among the lumberjacks in northern Sweden. Here too the young idealist tries to agitate for changes, and here too he abrades himself against a wall of stolid agreement with the prevailing conditions. His comments and, to an even greater extent, his presence awaken mistrust among his fellow workers, who perceive him as a privileged son of the bourgeoisie who has lived a sheltered life; an educated person whose interest in art and literature is as alien to them as his insistence on physical hygiene. Nonetheless, the narrator is free of arrogance toward the lumberjacks' proletarian existence. This willingness to learn from them, rather than his political agitation, shows his readiness to shed bourgeois attitudes.

The narrator experiences the spring of 1945 as the end of an epoch. Upon seeing film images of Auschwitz, he leaves the movie house in tears. His existence is inextricably connected with Auschwitz in a twofold way: through his half Jewish background and through the fate of his Prague acquaintances, Peter Kien and Lucie Weisberger. The narrator experiences his Jewishness mainly as an absence: he had been reared in Germany as a Christian; he had been baptized and confirmed; he had participated in tormenting his Jewish fellow students; and he had been on the side of "the persecutor and hangman" (96). His father's response to the increasing anti-Semitism had been a radical denial of his own Jewishness, a denial which finally erupts into self-hatred when he screams at his younger son, "you bloody Jewish lout" (125). Only a short time before leaving Germany is the narrator told of his Jewish ancestry. Years later he will comprehend that his Jewishness was his salvation: it had protected him from being on the side of the perpetrators.

Thus, he belonged among the victims. The fascists had already sealed his fate; that he escaped creates an insurmountable psychological trauma. Burdened by the feelings of guilt of one who survived, the narrator repeatedly, as if under a compulsion, recalls the fate of Peter Kien and Lucie Weisberger. When last heard from both were in the Theresienstadt concentration camp. In the middle of the war the narrator makes a desperate, senseless attempt to rescue Lucie Weisberger. He does so mainly to allay his own guilt feelings.

Under the impression of the film images of Auschwitz, in the spring of 1945 the narrator once again gives in to unrestrained feelings of guilt, wallowing in them. His pain threatens to fizzle out in self-pity. But he is able to overcome this self-pity by remembering how Hoderer had urged him to use reason and to make a commitment. Torn between self-pity, thoughts of suicide, and the growing realization that he is no longer able to remain above the struggles going on around him, he finally asks the central question of the epoch, "Whose side should I take?" (196). The whole novel culminates in this question. That the narrator does not yet have an answer adequately reflects his level of consciousness. Without being able to choose any political party, he now realizes that he must take sides.

Thus, this novel depicting a young man's growing political awareness in the early 1940s reveals Peter Weiss's political consciousness at the beginning of the 1960s. Here the narrative structure of *Vanishing Point* must be kept in mind. The novel is not related by the young painter—the narrated first person who at the beginning of the story in the fall of 1940 becomes twenty-four years old—but by a narrator who is twenty years older and who, in Stockholm in the year 1960, is looking back at a time long past. It is this older narrator whose consciousness determines the story, the characters, and the central character. It is from his perspective that the lack of reality in the young artist's paintings and his enduring lack of involvement in the struggles of his time are criticized, and it is this older narrator's consciousness that the young painter gradually begins to approximate.

A few years after writing *Vanishing Point* Weiss, who since *The Shadow of the Coachman's Body* had been regarded as a kind of "pure," nonpolitical artist, publicly professed his radical political commitment[15]—a political coming out that was still considered a "spectacular political decision" twenty years later.[16] Yet, as has been attempted to show here, the radicalization of Peter Weiss is clearly apparent in *Vanishing Point*. It is also evident from his other writings during the early 1960s. In his vocabulary one can now find expressions, such as "struggle against exploiters,"[17] "revolutionary act" (N I/9), "revolutionary thinking," "class,"[18] and "capital."[19] But Weiss's notations also attest to his difficulties in making these concepts applicable in practice. For instance, were class differences in the capitalist countries to be regarded as minor, as is assumed in the Copenhagen journal,[20] or did such a belief serve only to lull social criticism, as Weiss noted in the Paris Journal?[21] The notations contain no answers. But the delay with which Weiss registered political events grew shorter.

In the summer of 1960 a photograph of Patrice Lumumba, the leader of the Congolese fight for independence, was placed in the notebooks, with the comment: "The face of the third world that is suddenly staring at us from a newspaper" (N I/17, 19). Peter Weiss had caught up with historical events.

NOTES

1. The parenthetical page numbers refer to Peter Weiss, *Leavetaking* (*Abschied von den Eltern*, 1959, 1960), trans. E. B. Garside, Alastair Hamilton, and Christopher Levenson, in Weiss, *Exile* (New York: Delacorte, 1968).
2. This is the point of departure for Reinhold Grimm's study of *Fluchtpunkt*, whose insights apply equally to *Abschied von den Eltern*. See Reinhold Grimm, "Blanckenburgs 'Fluchtpunkt' oder Peter Weiss und der deutsche Bildungsroman," in *Basis* 2 (1971): 234.
3. See Peter Weiss, "Aus dem Kopenhagener Journal" (1960), in Weiss, *Rapporte* (Frankfurt/Main: Suhrkamp, 2d ed., 1981) 52ff.
4. See Peter Weiss, *Von Insel zu Insel* (1946), trans. (from Swedish) Heiner Gimmler (Berlin: Fröhlich and Kaufmann, 1984) 41–42.
5. See Peter Weiss, *The Tower* (*Der Turm*, 1948), trans. Michael Benedikt and Michel Heine, in Michael Benedikt and George E. Wellwarth, eds., *Postwar German Theatre* (New York: Dutton, 1967) 327. See also Peter Weiss, *The Shadow of the Coachman's Body* (*Der Schatten des Körpers des Kutschers*, 1952), trans. E. B. Garside, in Weiss, *Bodies and Shadows* (New York: Delacorte, 1969) 24.
6. See Weiss, *Von Insel zu Insel* 21.
7. See Sinclair (i.e., Peter Weiss), *Der Fremde* (Frankfurt/Main: Suhrkamp, 1980) 133, 103. See also the passage about *Der Fremde* in chap. 2 above.

8. As with Karl Heinz Bohrer, "Die Tortur. Peter Weiss' Weg ins Engagement. Die Geschichte des Individualisten," in Rainer Gerlach, ed., *Peter Weiss* (Frankfurt/Main: Suhrkamp, 1984) 182–207, esp. 193ff.

9. Karl Heinz Götze, "Der Ort der frühen Bilder. Peter Weiss und Bremen. Eine Spurensuche," in Hans Höller, ed., *Hinter jedem Wort die Gefahr des Verstummens. Sprachproblematik und literarische Tradition in der "Ästhetik des Widerstands" von Peter Weiss* (Stuttgart: Akademischer Verlag, 1988) 188.

10. All quotations from Peter Weiss, "Aus dem Pariser Journal," in Weiss, *Rapporte* 83–85.

11. Peter Bürger, *Theory of the Avant-Garde* (*Theorie der Avantgarde*, 1974), trans. Michael Shaw (Minneapolis: University of Minnesota Press, 1984).

12. Both quotations from Weiss, "Aus dem Pariser Journal" 91–93.

13. See Grimm 237.

14. The page numbers in parentheses refer to Peter Weiss, *Vanishing Point* (*Fluchtpunkt*, 1960–61), trans. E. B. Garside, Alastair Hamilton, and Christopher Levenson, in Weiss, *Exile*.

15. Weiss's speech was originally given in English at Princeton University. See Peter Weiss, "I Come Out of My Hiding Place" (written by Peter Weiss in English), *The Nation* 30 May 1966: 652, 655.

16. See Marcel Reich-Ranicki, "Peter Weiss. Poet und Ermittler, 1916–1982," in Rainer Gerlach, ed., *Peter Weiss* (Frankfurt/Main: Suhrkamp, 1984) 9.

17. Weiss, "Aus dem Kopenhagener Journal" 54.

18. Peter Weiss, "Gegen die Gesetze der Normalität" (1962), in Weiss, *Rapporte* 72.

19. Weiss, "Aus dem Pariser Journal" 90.

20. See Weiss, "Aus dem Kopenhagener Journal" 54.

21. See Weiss, "Aus dem Pariser Journal" 90.

CHAPTER FOUR

Success on Theater Stages
All Over the World

For someone with Weiss's biography, the success, the recognition, and the attention he now began to receive required some getting used to. When in late 1962 he was awarded the Charles Veillon Prize for *Vanishing Point,* the author, now forty-six years old, reacted with an irony that hardly concealed his bitterness (N I/77, 78). Furthermore, his "official" entrance on the West German literary scene—his first participation at a meeting of Gruppe 47 (Group 47), the prestigious postwar group of West German writers, in the fall of 1962—turned out to be traumatic. He was now one of those either very promising or already recognized German-language authors who once or twice a year were invited by novelist Hans Werner Richter to give readings at a place of Richter's choice. The meeting in the fall of 1962 took place at Wannsee near Berlin, the place where 150 years earlier Heinrich von Kleist, having concluded that there was no help for him on earth, had put a bullet through his head. Years later, Weiss recalled Kleist's suicide in his embittered notes from his first Group 47 meeting. He had found himself at a gathering that was teeming with rancor, envy, rivalries, power struggles, and cultural politics (N II/730). Successful writers such as Grass, Enzensberger, and Walser each had a group of followers. According to Weiss, who had expected an "exchange of ideas about the difficulties of our craft" (N II/728), there was only "animosity," and the focus of the meeting was not on shared interests but on "market values." Weiss's "great expectations" in going to Wannsee (N II/730) had obviously been unrealistic. The differences between writers such as Grass, Enzensberger, Andersch, or Johannes Bobrowski did not suddenly disappear. Nor were the meetings of Group 47 exempt from market forces. These were especially in evidence at the concluding event, the awarding of the prize for the best reading, which was determined by an open vote. In his notes Weiss parodied the award as a sports event, a race in which he and GDR lyricist Bobrowski were the "favorites," with Bobrowski the ultimate winner "by a nose" (N II/731). Weiss concluded that he should have avoided joining the pack of hounds in quest of a prize.

It must be emphasized that these notes were committed to paper fifteen years after the event, in the summer of 1978, when Weiss, exhausted from having completed volume two of *The Aesthetics of Resistance,* was hospitalized for an infection. In a state of depression he recalled being dominated mainly by feelings of not belonging and of never-ending exile. The belated recognition of his literary work, which his first reading at the Group 47 meeting clearly signaled, was given short shrift.

The text that Peter Weiss read in Wannsee was *Das Gespräch der drei Gehenden* (*Conversation of the Three Wayfarers*), written during the preceding weeks. It was by no means the kind of text one might have expected from the author of *Vanishing Point.* There is hardly a trace of that new worldliness, of that turning toward society and its problems, which was very much in evidence in the just-completed novel. The new text seems like a return to old positions and concepts.

What may have contributed to this turnaround may have been Weiss's discontent with *Vanishing Point.* The publisher had initially rejected the book. Weiss, made insecure from years of lack of success, thought his text a "total failure" (N I/57). The manuscript was set aside; then came trips to Switzerland and Paris. Weiss next turned to the work of August Strindberg (1849–1912). In commemoration of the fiftieth anniversary of the Swedish dramatist's death, he wrote a speech in which Strindberg is praised as a writer who "opposed the laws of normality."[1] In the early summer Weiss translated Strindberg's drama, *A Dream Play,* into German. Then in late August 1962 work on the manuscript of *Vanishing Point* was taken up again and the revised version sent off to the publisher. But the author apparently remained dissatisfied, formulating his merciless criticism of this work in his notebooks (N I/96–97) as well as in "Aus dem Pariser Journal" (From the Paris Journal),[2] and repeating it in an interview more than a year later in 1964 (G/R 39). For reasons of formal unity, according to Weiss's notes and statements, *Vanishing Point* contained inadmissible simplifications and his early development was made to look too smooth. Weiss felt that he had made this development appear as the logical result of his endurance and strength, when in reality there had only been false starts and dead ends, "delusional ideas," and "lack of a standpoint." While writing this book he had lacked the courage to again confront himself with his perilous existence, his book was a "falsification." These statements, in their pitiless baring of psychic wounds, focus on psychological rather than on literary analysis. This is underscored further by the fact that Weiss made no attempt to distinguish between himself and the narrator of his novel.

If *Vanishing Point* is somewhat less successful than *Leavetaking,* Weiss's reluctance to open psychological wounds, to deal truthfully with his own shortcomings is not the main reason, as has been shown in chapter 3. Nonetheless, Weiss's psychologizing self-criticism helps to understand why, after the newly found realism of *Vanishing Point,* he proceeded to write a text like *Conversation of the Three Wayfarers,* which was much closer to his earlier work.

Conversation of the Three Wayfarers

Self-analysis had once again become necessary. This time nothing would be spared as the numerous entries in the notebooks concerning Weiss's childhood and sexual obsessions indicate, entries which continue into 1963 (N I/ 67ff.). Toward the end of 1962 terms such as "altered states," "deliriums," "mirages," "borderline states," "hallucinations," and "mental illness" occur with increasing frequency in the notebooks. Once again, Weiss seems obsessed with his innermost experiences; and once again he seems to be talking only to himself. Appropriately enough the new text Weiss was working on was to be titled "Das Gespräch eines Gehenden mit sich Selbst" (A Wayfarer's Conversation with Himself, N I/73, 102). This "conversation" is once again a hermetic text; one must go back all the way to 1948, to *Der Fremde* (The Stranger), to find anything comparable in Weiss's oeuvre. As in that early work, nothing tangible is narrated; there is no story that can be summarized. Once again there is no plot, there are no individually developed characters. Like *Der Fremde,* this conversation of a wayfarer with himself consists of grotesque and bizarre visions and fantasies. As in the earlier book, it is impossible to say anything definite about the structure of the new text. The opening passage introduces three men named Abel, Babel, and Cabel, who are so much alike that they can be taken for brothers (61).[3] Having encountered each other by coincidence, they take turns telling stories while walking next to one another. After this brief introduction there is no further mention of the three figures. What follows are thirty brief first-person tales of bizarre, farcical, surreal, and unbelievable incidents. It is impossible to tell which of the three figures is speaking. Considering their similarity, it is altogether possible that they are one and the same, as the title implies. But Weiss eventually changed this title, and the published text is now called *Conversation of the Three Wayfarers.* The title change, however, was not intended to remove any ambiguity—in an interview, Peter Weiss dismissed the question of whether there were one or three figures narrating the text as having little relevance (G/R 40).

The incidents related in *Wayfarers,* as one of Weiss's interviewers accurately noted, resemble *tall tales* (G/R 40). They seem exaggerated, as if the three figures were trying to top each other with their improbable stories. Their bizarre, grotesque humor, however, only underscores the horror and obscenity of these tales. In one passage one of the narrators throws a dart at his father, hitting him in the middle of the forehead; a mother dying in a hospital bed urinates on her son; there are visions of concentration camps (81–83, 113–14); and a man-size fly sits at a breakfast table, repulsively devouring an insect. Elsewhere, there is a description of "small heads of cabbage thickly planted together" like "burst skulls, set in rows in a field" (113)—a vision of horror that recalls Weiss's chilling drawing "Adam, Eva und Kain" (Adam, Eve, and Cain, 1946), in which a plow pulled by Adam and Eve and guided by Cain tills a field of corpses. The landscapes of Weiss's childhood, the subjects of many of his paintings, are also evoked in the various descriptions of harbor facilities, docks, shipbuilding yards, tugboats, industrial plants with smokestacks, freight depots, and street fairs.

Especially unbelievable is a tale one of the three narrators repeatedly resumes about a ferryman and his family, his six grotesque sons Jam, Jem, Jim, Jom, Jum, and Jym. In Switzerland during the 1950s there was a radio series of uncanny and fantastic stories, "Verzell du das em Färimaa" (You Tell That to the Ferryman). Although it is unlikely that Weiss was familiar with that series, it may be that in Swedish as well as in German-Swiss culture the association of tall tales with ferryman stories derives from comparable folk mythology.

The surreal "fragment" (as Weiss called his text in the original German version) can nonetheless not be characterized as "pure," nontendentious art. Rather, its tendency can be described as a bitter parody of bourgeois institutions, such as marriage, school, official ceremonies, military recruitment, the office routines at some fancy capitalist enterprise, and, repeatedly, of bourgeois family life (especially in the ferryman stories). In all these tales, however, stronger than any critique is a feeling of helplessness, of being delivered to an impenetrable, horrible world—to the world of Kafka and of Beckett, whose influence on *Conversation of the Three Wayfarers* is strongly in evidence. Like the odes written by Jom, one of the sons of the ferryman, Weiss's text reflects a sense "that he knows nothing, that he understands nothing, that he cannot grasp just why he is where he is now or why he is at some other place" (96).

Conversation of the Three Wayfarers remains a fragment. However, Weiss continued with his attempts at a surreal type of writing. Another fragment from that period, about a man who "could hear the stones talk," which was eventually published in the notebooks, gives the impression that it had become impossible for Weiss to say anything definite (N I/92ff.). In late January 1963 Weiss began work on still another project: "Bericht über Einrichtungen und Gebräuche in den Siedlungen der Grauhäute" (Report about Institutions and Customs among the Grayskin Settlements).[4] A first-person narrator from a distant part of the Third World describes his impressions upon entering a modern big city. "Grauhäute" is a satire on alienated life in a large capitalist metropolis. It is also, as has been noted, a parody of a modern-day white explorer of an alien Third World culture.[5] Thus, "Grauhäute" becomes Weiss's first attempt at dealing with the issues of imperialism and colonialism. However, the ideological basis of this satire remains vague. Weiss does not yet seem to have overcome the difficulty he had noted a year earlier: "I have no idea of a position" (N I/56), which may help to explain why this text, too, was to remain a fragment. With this venture into social satire, however, it appears that Weiss had found a way out of this phase of protracted alienation.

Night with Guests

During this difficult yet fertile period, while Weiss was still working on "Grayskin Settlements," there was yet another attempt at social satire. Within a few days in late January 1963, he wrote the play *Nacht mit Gästen* (*Night with Guests*). With this piece Weiss resumes his dramatic work, which had been interrupted for ten years since *Die Versicherung* (The Insurance). There is an obvious thematic similarity, as the anarchist drama *Die Versicherung* was already a kind of "night with guests." Employing stiff doggerel, the new work relates a tale of terror of the kind once presented by street singers at fairs: the evil Jasper Ruddigore intrudes into the house of a family, intending to rob and stab its members; the father promises him a chest filled with gold; while the father fetches the chest, Jasper sleeps with the man's wife; meanwhile, a "warner" appears, intending to alert the family to a dangerous robber who is in the neighborhood; at this moment the father returns with the chest; in the ensuing chaos Jasper Ruddigore stabs the wife, the warner stabs the father, then the warner and Jasper stab each other; and the poor orphans discover that the chest contains not gold but dried turnips.

Night with Guests is a bloody dance around the golden chest. The play's social satire springs from the same consciousness that created the satire on consumerism in "Grauhäute." And, along with the children frightened by Jasper Ruddigore, it seems to be Peter Weiss himself who is asking:

> Where is Peter Wright?
> His red shirt blazing bright
> He's kind in word and deed
> He helps all those in need.[6]

But no Peter Wright appears on the scene. The hope for a red (shirted) messiah is not fulfilled. By now, however, Weiss's political radicalization could no longer be overlooked. The classification of the author as a "pure" artist, which had emerged with *The Shadow of the Coachman's Body,* was no longer tenable. The irritated response of conservative critics to *Night with Guests* was to dub it "a Punch and Judy show as agitprop," referring to the crudely didactical political theater developed in the Soviet Union in the wake of the revolution. Perceiving nothing but artistic decline, they called the work "uncouth and primitive, even silly."[7]

The inadequacies of *Night with Guests,* however, lie elsewhere. With his dramatization of a street ballad, a form that presupposes reduction and simplification, Weiss had achieved a degree of stylization that he himself on occasion compared to the Japanese Kabuki theater.[8] Such a degree of stylization obviates the possibility of making a concrete statement about the contemporary world, as has been rightly noted.[9] Weiss's street ballad is not about any historic epoch or specific society or class. In this regard, his satire does not go beyond the vague and unspecific social and political critique of his anarchist drama *Die Versicherung* of 1952.

At the same time, with the resort to the formal elements of a Punch and Judy show, to street ballad and prank, the freak show, folk theater, and rhyme, *Night with Guests* represents a gain in theatrical means. There is also, in Weiss's effort toward stylization and toward an antilyrical, antipsychological drama, a turning toward the epic theater and the techniques of alienation and toward the theater of Brecht (Brecht's name is mentioned in the *Notizbücher* for the first time, shortly before the writing of *Night with Guests*). Thus, in Weiss's presumed decline there was also progress, as his next play was to make clear.

Marat/Sade

In November 1962, before he started work on *Night with Guests,* Peter Weiss's interest was directed by his young stepson toward a tale of terror from the French Revolution (N I/143; see also G/R 44). In the middle of the upheaval one of the revolution's bloodiest leaders had been stabbed to death in his bathtub by a beautiful young woman. Evidently, there was material

here for another street ballad and, when work on *Night with Guests* was finished, Weiss began research on the revolutionary Jean-Paul Marat (1743–93)
and his murderess Charlotte Corday (1768–93). But the legend of the beautiful virgin who stabbed the bloodthirsty revolutionary and thereby saved the
nation's honor, according to the distorted picture of the event perpetuated by
a victorious bourgeoisie,[10] resisted easy dramatization. Corday was not an
adequate antagonist for Marat; a new counterpart had to be found. Two writers were given consideration: both contemporaries of Marat, both authors of
erotic novels, and both friends of the revolution—the Marquis Donatien Al-
phonse François de Sade (1740–1814) and the less well-known Nicolas Rétif
de la Bretonne (1734–1806). In Weiss's notebooks Rétif de la Bretonne is
mentioned as a descendant of François Villon, an anarchist vagabond and ero-
tomaniac ("already started to fuck at age ten" [N I/45]) who associated with
the lowest classes and spent much time in dance halls and bordellos. In his
writings he gave expression to the suffering and revolutionary mood of the
people.[11] But the concept of a confrontation "MARAT vs. R de la BRE-
TONNE" (N I/148) was not further explored. What took shape eventually
was a confrontation between Marat and Sade.

Two historic facts in the life of the marquis made him the ideal counterpart
to Marat. After the murder of Marat, Sade had delivered a eulogy to the revolutionary leader; his involvement with Marat could thus be based on actual
fact. Sade had also performed dramas (written by himself) with the inmates
at the insane asylum of Charenton, in the vicinity of Paris, where he was interned from 1803 until his death. Reality itself provided a dramatic concept
that no imagination could surpass. Thus, Sade became Marat's antagonist,
with enormous consequences for the content and tendency of the play.

Initially, Marat had been the sole main character of the work, conceived as
a radio play (N I/143) and written by Weiss between 1 March and 20 April
1963. Suhrkamp distributed the as yet unpublished manuscript to various theaters. Weiss turned immediately to a new project with the working title
"Mockinpott," completed only in 1968 (this will be discussed in chapter 7).
In July 1963 he met for the first time with the director Konrad Swinarski (N
I/156), who was to stage the premiere of *Marat/Sade* at the Schiller Theater
in West Berlin, in April 1964. In the fall Weiss gave a number of readings
from his works in the Federal Republic. He was also busy preparing for the
premiere of *Night with Guests,* which opened on 6 November 1963 in the
workshop of the Schiller Theater in West Berlin. Throughout this busy period, work on *Marat/Sade* continued. In late October Weiss again read at a
meeting of Group 47; this time from the new play about Marat. The author,

who had spent much of his life in isolation and loneliness, was now besieged with so many demands that he had to cancel readings in order to finally return to writing.

But the distractions continued. In early 1964 Weiss was asked to head the newly founded film academy of West Berlin. He seriously considered the appealing offer, but it evidently came ten years too late, and Weiss declined.

During these months there were a growing number of visits to East Berlin, the capital of the German Democratic Republic. It was a difficult time. With the building of the wall in August 1961 the inhuman ideology of the cold war had assumed material reality for the inhabitants of that divided city. There was a split in the world from which the Swedish visitor could not be immune. In the GDR he was interested more in the situation of the arts than in the socialist organization of production. He noted that there were shortcomings—"intimidation" of artists and "narrow-mindedness of cultural bureaucrats"—which he contrasted with the free development of the arts in the Soviet Union after the October Revolution (N I/165–66). Weiss was to publish his criticism of communist cultural bureaucrats in 1965 in his essay "10 Arbeitspunkte eines Künstlers in der geteilten Welt" (An Artist's Ten Working Points in a Divided World). In the notebooks one can also find a critique of East German political elites and hierarchies that, Weiss observed, were unpopular with the people (N I/220). He was to continue his criticism of the situation of the arts in the GDR and of the Stalinist deformations of socialism right up to his death. But, as a result of his friendship with theater people, writer colleagues, and literary scholars, Weiss also gained greater understanding of the development of the GDR and the historical causes of Stalinist deformations. In his unwavering solidarity with liberation movements of the Third World and his support for a socialist change of the first, Weiss would always consider the GDR and other noncapitalist countries his most important allies.

Among the visitors attending the *Marat/Sade* rehearsals in the Schiller Theater was Peter Brook, the British director who wished to stage the work in London. This interest was to have major consequences for *Marat/Sade,* especially for the reception of the play in English-speaking countries, as will be shown later. Weiss noted that Brook was "delighted" with the costume designs created by Gunilla Palmstierna-Weiss, Weiss's collaborator, long-time companion, and, since January 1964, his wife. Palmstierna-Weiss at that time was intensely involved with designing the costumes for *Marat/Sade* and had even gone to Paris for research. Her work was to contribute significantly to the international success of the play, and, after the premiere in Berlin, she also collaborated on the stage and costume design for Peter Brook's London production and its filming.

In March 1964, in the middle of rehearsals for the new play, Weiss traveled to Frankfurt to attend the so-called Auschwitz trial. Auschwitz would become the topic of his next play. But before he could start work on this new project the premiere of the Marat play took place in West Berlin in April 1964. Its title alone was to assure its becoming a theater sensation: *Die Verfolgung und Ermordung Jean Paul Marats dargestellt durch die Schauspielgruppe des Hospizes zu Charenton unter Anleitung des Herrn de Sade (The Persecution and Assassination of Jean-Paul Marat as Performed by the Inmates of the Asylum of Charenton under the Direction of the Marquis de Sade)*.

The title sums up the content of the work, even though somewhat imprecisely, for the play deals only marginally and discursively with Marat's persecution. What is portrayed is the murder of Marat. The outcome of the work is thus prefigured in its title, as was the case with Büchner's great drama about the French Revolution, *Danton's Death*. The unusually long title also provides initial information about the performers (inmates of an asylum), director (Marquis de Sade), time (during Sade's stay in Charenton), and place of performance (the asylum of Charenton); but this abundance of information turns out to be confusing. For the play is, of course, not performed by the inmates of an insane asylum but by actors in a contemporary theater under the guidance of a director hired for the job. The author is not the Marquis de Sade but Peter Weiss. The playful title of the work reveals a glimpse of its structure, a complex weaving of time, place, and plot, of actors, stage, and historical figures, and of reality and fiction.

The historical facts: Jean-Paul Marat was a physician and naturalist. During the early stages of the French Revolution he became a member of the National Assembly and a radical publicist who, in his newspaper *L'Ami du Peuple (Friend of the People)*, championed radicalization of the revolution. He was murdered in his bathtub on 13 July 1793. (During the revolutionary turmoil he at times had had to hide in the sewers of Paris, which led to a skin disease whose itching he relieved by spending hours in a bathtub.) With the execution of Louis XVI several months earlier, on 21 January 1793, the revolution had entered its most radical stage. The war of revolutionary France against the monarchist powers that surrounded it was going poorly. To keep the army battle ready the Convention (the National Assembly) increased the number of military conscripts. This led to peasant uprisings in several parts of France, followed by rising prices and a bread shortage in the cities, especially Paris.

The *enragés* (the angry or the possessed), the most politically aware among the impoverished masses (the *sansculottes*)—one of whose leaders was the priest Jacques Roux (1752–94)—caused riots in late February. The republic was threatened from within and without. The Convention became radicalized. The liberal upper-bourgeoisie represented by the Girondistes, who until then had dominated the National Assembly, was crowded out by the Montagnards, the revolutionary wing of the bourgeoisie and petit bourgeoisie. Girondiste ministers were replaced by Montagnards. Three representatives of the Montagnards moved to the center of power: Robespierre, Danton, and the most radical, Jean-Paul Marat. Unlike Robespierre and Danton, however, Marat remained on the side of the lower classes, even when the uprisings broke out anew in May 1793. The uprisings ended with the defeat and arrest of the Girondistes, and the seizure of power by the Montagnards.

This ushered in "the third and most advanced phase of the bourgeois-democratic revolution."[12] Robespierre was now intent on reconciliation with the bourgeoisie. In contrast, Marat urged radicalization of the revolution. At this historic moment, when the future of the revolution hung in the balance, he was assassinated. Among the persons eulogizing him was the Marquis de Sade.[13] One may well ask how the nobleman from Provence, notorious for his sexual obsessions, ended up on the side of the most radical representative of the bourgeois revolution.

On 14 July 1789 the people of Paris had stormed the Bastille, a garrison-like prison, thereby starting revolutionary upheavals in all of France. Among the Bastille prisoners released that day was Sade, who at that point had already been incarcerated for more than ten years. However, the reason for his imprisonment was not his opposition to a despotic monarchy but rather his imagined as well as real sexual debaucheries. Later, it would again be his "monstrous writings" (Weiss) that would lead to his renewed incarceration.[14]

Nonetheless, it cannot be doubted that Sade opposed the monarchy and the nobility whose brutalization and sexual depravity he had recounted in horrifying detail in his *120 Days of Sodom* (1785), a sick chronicle of a sick society. He supported the liberation of the individual and the elimination of a ruling caste that for so long had kept him in prison. Thus, he found himself at times on the side of the revolution to which he was now indebted for his release. He seems, however, not to have shared the Montagnards' radical demands, such as the redistribution of feudal lands, being himself the owner of feudal property; but it could do no harm to display his fidelity to the republic by eulogizing Marat.[15] Little did it help him. Sade was soon back in prison, suspected of counterrevolutionary activity. After the execution of Robespierre (1794) he was set free one more time, only to be interned once and for all, a few years after Napoléon seized power, at the Charenton Asylum. While there he did a lot of writing, including plays that he also staged, using fellow inmates as performers. Never, however, did Sade either write or put on a play about Marat's assassination.

Drawing on and generally adhering to these historic facts, Weiss in 1963 thought up a play that takes place in the Charenton Hospice on 13 July 1808. More accurately, Charenton in 1808 forms the framework for a play that takes place fifteen years earlier. In the plot of the framework the inmates and the hospice director Coulmier, along with his family, gather in the hospice's bath house to watch some of the inmates perform a play about the murder of Jean-Paul Marat. During the performance Coulmier and his family from time to time intervene to critique opinions expressed by the characters or to restore order among the inmates who are getting restless. While reenacting the murder of Marat the inmates/actors at Charenton become so excited that they cause a tumult that, at Coulmier's command, the attendants try to suppress. As this tumult reaches a feverish pitch the curtain is lowered.

Within the framework of the events at Charenton, the drama of Marat's murder forms a play within a play. The events surrounding Marat's murder are performed by patients—interned because of mental illness or "for political reasons"—who in turn are played by actors.[16] On a temporal level Sade's play about the 1793 murder is written and performed in 1808; this (fictional) play was actually written in 1963 by Weiss, and is performed (or read) at the present time. *Marat/Sade* has a complex, multilayered structure, in which one may loose oneself to the point where it seems nearly impossible to make any definite statement about the play. Nevertheless, *Marat/Sade* is not a precursor of postmodern arbitrariness. It has an objective tendency that can be brought out through rational discourse. Still, it is useful to keep in mind the multilayered structure of the play: statements about *Marat/Sade* should always contain a measure of doubt.

In Weiss's dramatic fiction the play within a play is written and staged by one of the hospice inmates, the Marquis de Sade. It shows Marat sitting in the bathtub in his living room on 13 July 1793, completing notes for a speech he is to deliver to the National Assembly the following day, the fourth anniversary of the storming of the Bastille. Marat reflects on the course of the revolution, discussing it with Jacques Roux, the leader of the *enragés,* and the Marquis de Sade (thus, Sade is a character in his own play). In a parallel plot development Charlotte Corday arrives in Paris from the provinces, buys a knife, and has a discussion with the Girondiste deputy Dupperet whose political position she shares. On 13 July she twice calls on Marat in vain, but on her third visit she is admitted and stabs him.

The focus of the play within a play that makes up the main part of *Marat/Sade* is on Jean-Paul Marat, who is not only a naturalist and physician but also a writer (a fact that is emphasized particularly in scene 28) who wants to go beyond his journalistic efforts by intervening directly in the historic events. The parallel to the writer, Weiss, who was himself in a process of radicalization and moving toward political activism, is apparent. In the National Assembly Marat represents the left wing of the bourgeoisie and supports the rights of the Fourth Estate, the *sansculottes*. His demands for pushing the revolution still further, and his insistence, along with the *sansculottes*, on the redistribution of wealth clearly go beyond the historic possibilities of the late eighteenth century: they are directed at Weiss's own time. This is brought out in the programmatic speech in scene 23. Marat begins with a warning against the "lies . . . about the ideal state" that are spread by the Girondistes (54). Never had the rich been prepared to "give away their property / of their own free will" (54). If at times the condition of the workers improved, it was only as a means of having the profits of the entrepreneurs increase even more. Here Marat's argumentation is no longer directed merely at late eighteenth-century France. Subsequently, the anachronisms in his speech become more pronounced: for instance, when he mentions the owners "in their marble homes and granite [in the original German: steel] banks" (56), or when he later speaks of "agents, stockbrokers, and speculators" (76). Marat's accusation that those in power "rob the people of the world / under the pretense of bringing them culture" (56) seems directed more at twentieth-century imperialism than at eighteenth-century colonialism. And Marat's warning to the revolutionary masses not to let themselves be deceived by a slight improvement in their living standard seems aimed more at the era of Weiss than that of the French Revolution:

> Don't be taken in
> when they pat you paternally on the shoulder and say
> that there's no inequality worth speaking of (55–56).

That class differences were no longer worth speaking of had been a claim Weiss himself had supported in his essay "Aus dem Kopenhagener Journal" of 1960. Two years later, however, in "Aus dem Pariser Journal," Weiss signaled his doubts by asking whether such a claim might not serve to "lull" social criticism. The change in Weiss's thinking can be further traced in the notebooks, where, in the fall of 1963, Marat's warning to the Fourth Estate was first formulated: "There will come times when people will say that class conflicts no longer exist" (N I/93). In the play, ultimately, Marat dismisses out of hand the notion that class differences had disappeared.

Marat's critique of the concept of private property championed by the Girondiste upper bourgeoisie represents the most advanced position of the French Revolution. At the time, however, Marat's concepts did not prevail; given the political and economical realities of his time, they probably *could not* prevail. To this extent, Marat is, in fact, "a premature hero," as Manfred Haiduk has noted.[17] Haiduk's phrase refers to Friedrich Engels's work, *Der Deutsche Bauernkrieg* (The German Peasants War), where it is stated about Thomas Münzer, the radical leader of the peasants' revolt: "The worst thing that can happen to the leader of an extremist party is to be forced to take over the government in an epoch when the movement is not yet ripe for domination by the class he represents and for implementation of the measures which this class domination requires."[18] In the context of the French Revolution the revolutionary movement was not yet ripe for domination by the *sansculottes,* the masses of the Fourth Estate, or for a socialist form of society. The time was ripe for the bourgeoisie, represented by the Gironde and its ideology which, as Marat ironically notes, "writes into the declaration of the rights of man / the holy right of property" (35). (The enduring consequences of this right can be seen two centuries later: in order to obtain recognition and economic support from capitalist countries, the formerly socialist European countries are required to introduce those human rights favored by the West, especially the right to a free market—which is just another word for what Marat, in Weiss's play, terms "the holy right of property"). By demanding the elimination of this "right," by combating the economic goals of the bourgeoisie, Marat was a precursor of Karl Marx, as Peter Weiss noted.[19] But there are also important differences. Marx's thinking was shaped by his ongoing analysis of the possibilities *and limits* of his epoch—by his historical materialism. Marat's demands, in contrast, are characterized by their idealism and voluntarism:

> Against Nature's silence *I use* action
> In the vast indifference *I invent* a meaning
> . . .
> The important thing
> is *to pull yourself up by your own hair*
> (26–27, emphasis added).

In these lines it is the wish and will of the individual that appears to control material reality, exactly in the sense of the classical idealism of Schiller, who had his character Wallenstein say, "It is the mind that creates the body."[20] Nothing in *Marat/Sade* or in Weiss's comments about the play indicates that Marat's idealism ought to be questioned. Rather, it appears to reflect Weiss's own idealism. In this regard, too, the dramatist resembled his creation.

In the play Marat is said to be "a hundred years ahead" of his time.[21] This evaluation makes a connection between his actions and the rise of the industrial working class in the late nineteenth century and, ultimately, with the October Revolution. Today, the negative outcome of this historic event can be ascertained. The question of whether Marat was ahead of his time by a century or even longer, or, as Sade mockingly suggests, whether even in July 1793 his thinking was lagging behind historical developments (33), seems to have been answered—against Marat and in favor of Sade. But history has a way of bringing back issues that the victors had long assumed had been laid to rest.

In the play within a play, Marat's position is not the most radical; that role is assigned to Jacques Roux and the four singers who represent the *sansculottes,* or the Fourth Estate. Cucurucu, Polpoch, Kokol, and Rossignol repeatedly remind Marat of everything that still needs to be accomplished and try to push the revolution along:

> Marat we're poor and the poor stay poor
> Marat don't make us wait any more
> We want our rights and we don't care how
> We want our revolution NOW (11, see also 35, 70–71).

Roux demands that the food warehouses be opened and the churches closed, and that ownership of the means of production be handed over to the people (44). Even more than Marat, Roux tries to drive the revolution beyond the material limits set by the epoch. He anticipates the goals of the proletarian revolution with his prophetic words at the end of *Marat/Sade:* "When will you learn to see / When will you learn to take sides" (101). Even more than Marat, Roux embodies "the premature hero." Soon after Marat's death he was to be arrested by the revolutionary government and was to commit suicide, but the play ends before he meets his fate. In *Marat/Sade* Roux's extreme position provides a kind of utopian vanishing point against which Marat's goals as well as the accomplishments of the bourgeois revolution up to our present must be measured.

In Weiss's drama of the revolution the Marquis de Sade is the great counterpart of Marat. But it should be kept in mind that the marquis too had contributed to bringing about the revolution (46). Sade also shares with Marat a hatred of the aristocrats, these "monstrous representatives of a dying class" who could be spared endless boredom only by the guillotine (23), as well as a disdain for the members of the bourgeoisie outdoing each other in trying to demonstrate their patriotism. In the year 1808 at Charenton, Sade still holds positions supportive of the revolution. Coulmier, the director of the asylum, repeatedly feels compelled to object to the rebellious talk in Sade's play and to praise the progressiveness of Napoléonic society. In so doing he "unintentionally calls attention to what he would like to conceal,"[22] and what is revealed with heavy irony in Sade's play (especially in the herald's monologues)—namely, the bad social conditions in Napoléonic France. Coulmier, this embodiment of the restoration who in his own mind sees himself as a representative of the revolution, is the counterpart of Sade in the Charenton scenes. A comparison with Coulmier's speeches reveals to what degree the thinking of the Marquis de Sade remains indebted to the revolution and the goals of Marat.

Sade's dispute with Marat breaks out at the point where Marat challenges the people to the use of force, where he proclaims approval of the coming horrors of the revolution:

> And what's a bath full of blood
> compared to the bloodbaths still to come
> Once we thought a hundred corpses would be enough,
> then we saw thousands were still too few (15).

The revolutionary terror predicted here by Marat (it would start only after Marat's death in October 1793) is depicted in a pantomime in scene 11. Entitled "Deaths Triumph," the scene is a tribute to the painting of the same name by Brueghel, the first great inspiration for Peter Weiss's painting. While the pantomime of beheadings ordered by the revolution takes place, Marat reminds those who lament this bloodbath of how long they had exploited and robbed the people before there finally occurred this resort to revenge (21). Sade himself is among these belatedly righteous people. He, too, had wanted revenge, he maintains (48), but when his revenge fantasies became horrible reality, he shied away. He tells of his tailor, "a gentle cultured man" who murdered a Swiss (one of the king's Swiss guards) in a horrifyingly brutal manner (32). When forced to witness a heinous mop-up action against a Carmelite convent (48), Sade becomes sick. When he became a member of the revolutionary tribunal, he realized that "I couldn't bring myself / to deliver the prisoners to the hangman" (48). He counters Marat's vision of mass executions to come with the description of the horror of the execution of a single human being: the dismemberment of Damiens in 1757 after his assassination attempt on Louis XV.

By no means does the marquis, by his unbearably detailed descriptions of scenes of horror, wish to appeal to pity, for, as he contemptuously states, "Compassion is the property of the privileged classes" (26). Sade's topic is the reality of the human body. Just as there are idealistic positions held by Marat, Sade's stance here is materialistic. All his sexual excesses, the tortures meted out and suffered, and the long years of suffering in prison have taught him "that this is a world of bodies" (92). He is obsessed with this thought. He repeatedly, insistently talks of the reality of the body, its ecstasy and its pain, as when he speaks of

> the orifices of the body
> put there
> so one may hook and twine oneself in them (93)

or when he tells Marat, "You lie in your bath / as if you were in the pink water of the womb" (33), when he conjures up the horrors of the revolution in a scene he witnessed of

> women running by
> holding in their dripping hands
> the severed genitals of men (49)

or when he calls Marat's attention to the body of his future murderess, Corday,

> Marat
> forget the rest
> there's nothing else
> beyond the body (91).

Sade's materialism is a materialism of the body.

The same can be said of Peter Weiss. His work, with its recurring obsessive passages about sexuality and torture, is suffused with the realization that this is a world of bodies. As a consequence of Weiss's turning toward Marxism, this obsession became increasingly grounded in material reality. Specifically, it came to include the way in which these "bodies" produce their lives and organize themselves by forming classes and different kinds of societies. Thus, the liberation loudly demanded by the oppressed at the end of *Marat/ Sade* has two sides to it, "Revolution revolution / copulation copulation" (101). Pain and ecstasy of the body; a continuing obsession which in *Marat/ Sade* makes Weiss once again conjure up that gruesome vision from his painting "Adam, Eve, and Cain" of 1946 in which corpses are being ploughed into a field. This image, already recreated in *Conversation of the Three Way-farers,* is evoked here by one of the mentally disturbed inmates:

> The earth is spread
> The earth is spread thick
> with squashed human guts (32).

This obsession with the suffering of the body is also reflected in Corday's anticipatory description of her own execution, "Now I know what it is like / when the head is cut off the body" (86). Fifteen years later, in *The Aesthetics of Resistance,* the guillotine execution of women, antifascist resistance fighters, again had to be described. Peter Weiss had long thought that this scene would defy description; and perhaps only he, having prepared for it through all of his oeuvre, was capable of putting it into words. The chapter on these executions in *The Aesthetics of Resistance* must be considered one of the great passages of the literature of our time.

In his awareness of this "world of bodies" Sade seems superior to Marat. Superior, too, is Sade's insight about the blurred distinction between perpetrators and victims, "I do not know if I am hangman or victim" (31), and "In a criminal society / I dug the criminal out of myself" (47). Such insights, it should be recalled, tormented Peter Weiss from his early years when he realized that only through a twist of fate was he spared from becoming a Nazi perpetrator, just as only through a series of coincidences he was later spared from becoming a Nazi victim. His artist's creative imagination had made him aware of the frailty of his identity and of his whole existence.

In *Marat/Sade* it is the marquis who formulates this insight. Here again he appears superior to the rationalist Marat, who perceives only perpetrators and victims. The marquis objects to such simplification. He is completely overwhelmed by the physical reality of the execution of a single human being, Damiens. Anyone capable of imagining in such unbearable detail the horror of a single death has to be appalled at the thought of exterminating thousands.

Marat, of course, believes that these deaths are "necessary" or unavoidable if the revolution is to succeed. The Marquis de Sade a pacifist and humanist, and Marat a bloodthirsty monster, as portrayed by bourgeois historians? Not quite.

Sade, who wants to have nothing to do with revolutionary terror, also wants to have nothing to do with impeding it: "I . . . watch what happens / without joining in" (50). In exact contrast to Marat, he is a writer who does *not* want to intervene in the course of historical events. He represents no program, no morality, and certainly not the future. His attitude is indifference, apathy, satiety, and repulsion. He cares nothing about France, about any country (40–41). He cares nothing about the masses (40–41), about idealists, or about "any of the sacrifices / that have been made for any cause" (41). He considers the new rulers the same kind of crooks as their predecessors. He finds ridiculous the revolutionary ideas about the equality of human beings (57). In a solipsistic movement he announces his resignation from the revolutionary committees (50), he turns away from reality—"for me the only reality is imagination" (34)—and retreats into his own individual existence, "I believe only in myself" (41).

To adequately appreciate Sade's postrevolutionary hangover it is necessary to keep in mind the structure of *Marat/Sade*. In the play within a play it is not Sade himself who is speaking. Rather, an image of him is conveyed that the marquis—in Weiss's fiction—created fifteen years later in Charenton. Since the murder of Marat, Sade has seen the Thermidor (the fall of the revolutionary government and the execution of Danton and Robespierre); he has experienced the end of the people's movement and the return of the conservative bourgeoisie, the rise of Bonaparte and the 18th Brumaire when Bonaparte seized dictatorial power; and finally, by the time he is interned in Charenton, Sade has lived through the completion of the restoration which had culminated in the crowning of Napoléon as emperor.

Sade in Charenton can regard the revolution only from the perspective of defeat; he cannot declare Marat right. "In the year 1808 Sade is incapable of writing and staging a Marat drama in which the people's tribune [Marat] could be given historical justice."[23] This must be kept in mind in any discussion as to whether, in *Marat/Sade,* the marquis or Marat prevails. The issue of who is right, which still dominates the debate over Weiss's drama, has at times been conducted in a purely formalist manner. Thus it was argued that Sade wrote the play (within the play), that Sade created Marat, and that Sade's superiority could be asserted merely by looking at the formal structure of *Marat/Sade.*[24] This line of argument omits consideration of the reality of the stage as well as the contradictory elements, the ambiguity and plurality of meanings of Weiss's dramatic creation. This purely formal argument can save the interpreter the trouble of seriously examining Marat's arguments. There might be better justification for an argument based purely on content, which holds that the demands of the French Revolution have long since been implemented; hence Marat is ultimately right.

Weiss himself became involved in this dispute over the tendency of his play. His various statements show that he was initially leaning toward Sade who, vacillating between his hatred of the ruling class and his aversion to the bloodbath of the revolution, adheres to a "third approach."[25] After having insisted until only a short time before the writing of *Marat/Sade* that he had no idea of his own standpoint (G/R 57), Weiss now claimed Sade's "third approach" for himself and critics accepted this claim. Under the influence of the GDR staging of *Marat/Sade* in Rostock, however, Weiss began to move closer to Marat's position and eventually came to insist "A staging of my play in which Marat does not ultimately appear as the moral victor would be inappropriate."[26] West German critics turned Weiss's change of allegiance against him, even though it would not appear all that unusual for an author to interpret his or her own work and on occasion to change that interpretation.

The dispute was not without effect on the five versions of *Marat/Sade* that Weiss created between 1963 and 1965. Although the spoken words were not significantly changed, Weiss introduced his evolving interpretations into the play by revising the stage instructions, which were modified through the various versions.[27]

Marat's radical Jacobinism was greeted with little understanding by West German audiences in the year 1964, as was noted soon after the premiere of *Marat/Sade*.[28] In stagings in the capitalist West, Sade's superiority was generally emphasized, an interpretation that cannot be explained merely by pointing out that the cold war was at its peak. The theatricality of Weiss's undertaking, this ebullient amalgam of song, dance, and pantomime, of comical, tragic, melodramatic, lyrical, scenes, and of strong eroticism and unbearable brutality, portrayed by mental patients in an insane asylum, easily seduces directors into stagings that affirm the marquis's position.

That was clearly the case with Peter Brook's London staging at the Aldwych Theatre in the fall of 1964. The filmed version of Brook's staging, also directed by Brook, was to determine for years to come the thinking about *Marat/Sade* in the English-speaking countries. Audiences got to see severely disturbed mental patients, who, incessantly and fascinatingly preoccupied with their morbid ticks and behavior, delivered indifferently a text that was incomprehensible to them. Dwelling with dramatic artistry on the madness of the figures, Brook showed far less interest in the ideological disputes in the play. The English director coercively merged Brechtian alienation with Antonin Artaud's *Theater of Cruelty*.[29] What may have been gained for the stage in terms of theatricality, however, was lost in the filming. Brook had far less experience with filmmaking than with theater. During the filming he further heightened the onstage excesses by using such avant-garde techniques of the time as handheld cameras, wide-angle lenses, and hectic montage. In a formal sense the result is somewhat amateurish; the events get out of control, madness prevails. This concept corresponds only vaguely to the objective tendency of Weiss's play. The rational core of the dialogue between Sade and Marat—and most particularly Marat's revolutionary struggle for the rights of the *sansculottes* and the Fourth Estate—were largely lost.

And so it is not surprising that some interpreters of *Marat/Sade* to this day maintain that Weiss was not intent on rational insight.[30] This is refuted by the play's dialectical structure, wherein ideological positions are constantly juxtaposed and which, beyond al all the theatrical excesses, stimulates reflection. The theses and antitheses of Marat, Sade, Roux, and Coulmier are altogether suited for fostering rational analysis among audiences and readers alike.

NOTES

1. Peter Weiss, "Gegen die Gesetze der Normalität" (1962), in Weiss, *Rapporte* (Frankfurt/Main: Suhrkamp, 2d ed., 1981) 73.

2. See Peter Weiss, "Aus dem Pariser Journal" (1962), in Weiss, *Rapporte* 86–87.

3. The page numbers in parentheses refer to Peter Weiss, *Conversation of the Three Wayfarers* (*Das Gespräch der drei Gehenden*, 1962), trans. Rosemarie Waldrop, in Weiss, *Bodies and Shadows* (New York: Delacorte, 1969).

4. See Peter Weiss, "Bericht über Einrichtungen und Gebräuche in den Siedlungen der Grauhäute" (1963), in *Peter Weiss. In Gegensätzen denken. Ein Lesebuch*, selected by Rainer Gerlach and Matthias Richter (Frankfurt/Main: Suhrkamp, 1986) 119–35.

5. Sepp Hiekisch-Picard, "Zwischen surrealistischem Protest und kritischem Engagement. Zu Peter Weiss' früher Prosa," in Heinz Ludwig Arnold, ed., *Text + Kritik* 37 (Peter Weiss), completely revised 2d ed. (1982) 31.

6. Peter Weiss, *Night with Guests* (*Nacht mit Gästen*, 1963), trans. Laurence Dobie; Stanley Richards, ed., *The Best Short Plays, 1968* (Philadelphia: Chilton, 1968) 141.

7. Otto F. Best, *Peter Weiss* (Bern: Francke, 1971) 71.

8. See Peter Weiss, *Stücke I* (Frankfurt/Main: Suhrkamp, 1976) 456.

9. See Manfred Haiduk, *Der Dramatiker Peter Weiss* (East Berlin: Henschelverlag, 1977) 38.

10. See the comments about Marat and Corday in Karlheinz Braun ed., *Materialien zu Peter Weiss' "Marat/Sade"* (Frankfurt/Main: Suhrkamp, 1967).

11. See Walter Markov and Albert Soboul, *1789. Die Grosse Revolution der Franzosen* (Cologne: Pahl-Rugenstein, 2d ed., 1980) 63, 88.

12. Markov and Soboul 283. My summary of the historical events generally follows Markov and Soboul.

13. See Sade's speech in Braun, ed., *Materialien* 14–15.

14. See Braun, ed., *Materialien* 8.

15. See Haiduk 51.

16. The reference to patients interned "for political reasons," contained in the description of the characters that opens the German text, is missing in the English translation. The play is quoted here from its English edition: Peter Weiss, *The Persecution and Assassination of Jean-Paul Marat as Performed by the Inmates of the Asylum of Charenton under the Direction of the Marquis de Sade* (*Die Verfolgung und Ermordung Jean Paul Marats dargestellt durch die Schauspielgruppe des Hospizes zu Charenton unter Anleitung des Herrn de Sade*), trans. Geoffrey Skelton (New York: Atheneum, 1981). Page numbers in the text refer to this edition.

17. Haiduk 49.

18. Friedrich Engels, *Der Deutsche Bauernkrieg* (1850) (East Berlin: Dietz, 1974) 122.

19. See Weiss, *Stücke I* 463.

20. Friedrich Schiller, *Wallensteins Tod,* act III, scene 13.

21. The quotation is contained in the German version of the passage "Poor Marat, you lie prostrate''; it has been omitted from the English version (85).

22. Haiduk 90.

23. Karlheinz Braun, "Schaubude—Irrenhaus—Auschwitz. Überlegungen zum Theater des Peter Weiss," in Braun, ed., *Materialien* 140.

24. See Peter Schneider, "Über das Marat-Stück von Peter Weiss" (1964), in Braun, ed., *Materialien* 132. See also Rainer Nägele's refutation of this line of argument in his "Zum Gleichgewicht der Positionen. Reflexionen zu *Marat/Sade* von Peter Weiss," in Reinhold Grimm and Jost Hermand, eds., *Basis. Jahrbuch für deutsche Gegenwartsliteratur* 5 (Frankfurt/Main: Suhrkamp, 1975): 151–53.

25. See Peter Weiss, "Author's Note on the Historical Background to the Play," in Weiss, *Marat/Sade* 106.

26. Peter Weiss in a conversation in Spring 1965; see Braun, ed., *Materialien* 101.

27. For the various versions of *Marat/Sade,* see Braun, ed., *Materialien* 29–65.

28. See Henning Rischbieter, "Swinarskis Inszenierung in Berlin," in Braun, ed., *Materialien* 79.

29. See Peter Brook, "Introduction," in Weiss, *Marat/Sade,* English version, v–vii. Influenced by Brook's approach, some interpretations of *Marat/Sade* tend to overemphasize the connection with Artaud's concept of the theater. See also Susan Sontag's review of Brook's theatrical staging which had a lasting influence on the reception of the play in the United States. Susan Sontag, "Marat/Sade/Artaud," *Partisan Review* 32, no. 2 (Spring 1965): 210–19.

30. See Christian Bommert, " 'Offene Fragen im phantastischen Tumult'. Die Revolutions-interpretation in Peter Weiss' 'Marat'—Drama," in Harro Zimmermann, ed., *Schreckensmythen—Hoffnungsbilder. Die Französische Revolution in der deutschen Literatur* (Frankfurt/Main: Atheneum, 1989) 342.

CHAPTER FIVE

Dante, Marx, and Auschwitz

" "His entire oeuvre is designed as a visit among the dead," a perceptive critic commented about Peter Weiss.[1] Confirmation of this can be found in Weiss's essay of 1965, "Gespräch über Dante" (Discussion about Dante): "After all we live with our dead. Each of us has memories of persons no longer present. As long as we exist they also endure. We often get into conversations with them. Our very existence is a consequence of theirs."[2] A year later, on the occasion of his fiftieth birthday, Weiss noted, "I live with many dead" (N I/500). At times he felt closer to the dead who had once touched his life than to the living (N I/810–14). These dead included his sister Margit, Uli Rothe, Peter Kien, Jacques Ayschmann, Lucie Weisberger, Max Hodann, and now also his parents. The death of all of them had either directly inspired or played key roles in numerous Weiss paintings, films, and texts. Peter Kien and Lucie Weisberger, whom the young painter had got to know during his year at the Prague Academy, had perished in concentration camps. In the middle of the war Weiss had attempted, from Stockholm, to rescue Lucie Weisberger from Theresienstadt: an effort that was doomed to failure and that left him with indelible feelings of horror and guilt.

It seemed almost inevitable that Peter Weiss would some day create a work that dealt with the extermination camps. It was the only way he could come to terms with the never-ending horror of the realization that he, too, might have become one of the perpetrators. Equally as strong were the never-ending feelings of guilt since, as a half Jew, he had escaped certain death: that "drastic guilt of having been spared" (Adorno) shared by so many survivors, from Adorno to Günther Anders.[3] Just how Peter Weiss reached the point where he was able to deal with the topic of Auschwitz, until then not considered a subject that might adequately be portrayed through literature, requires explanation.

In 1949 Adorno, writing about the incommensurability of the extermination camps, had stated that to write a poem after Auschwitz was a barbaric act.[4] Up to today, thinking about Auschwitz and its representation in art and literature has not recovered from this verdict. In 1990 Günter Grass still made Adorno's statement the focus of his Frankfurt lecture on poetics.[5] In the early 1960s, however, the problem was less with finding a literary expression for Auschwitz than with the continued silence about it. Mass extermination in

Nazi concentration camps was not a major topic during the Adenauer years. Worse yet, many Nazis had been restored to office and honor by Konrad Adenauer, chancellor of the Federal Republic from 1949–63. Heading the list was lawyer Hans Globke who, in 1935, had formulated the practical application of the race laws in the Nazi state and who, in 1953, was appointed to one of the highest posts in the Adenauer administration. The replacement of Adenauer by Ludwig Erhard in October 1963 changed nothing in this state of affairs. The title of FRG philosopher Wolfgang Fritz Haug's 1967 study, *Der hilflose Antifaschismus* (Helpless Antifascism), expresses the essence of the period, as does Alexander and Margarete Mitscherlich's research on "the basis of collective behavior," also published in 1967, which has since become famous under its title *Die Unfähigkeit zu trauern* (The Inability to Mourn).

In such a time, Peter Weiss noted during the early stages of his work on *The Investigation,* he considered it "an enormous task" (N I/252) to bring to public consciousness the mass extermination that had occurred under fascism. At the beginning of this task Weiss had to find a solution to the seemingly unsurmountable problem of creating a literary form for what had occurred in Auschwitz, Bergen-Belsen, Mauthausen, Buchenwald, Maidanek, and Sobibor. In March 1962 Adorno had reiterated his statement about Auschwitz and poetry.[6] In early 1964 Weiss himself, reflecting about what the Nazis had called the "final solution of the Jewish problem," wrote in his notebooks, "We have to say something about it, but we are still unable to" (N I/211). Just a few weeks later, however, after attending the Auschwitz trial for the first time, Weiss notes: "At first I thought it couldn't be described, but those were acts committed by human beings against human beings on earth" (N I/226). The statement cautiously reflects doubt about Auschwitz constituting a radical break with everything that had preceded it. As incomparable as the events in the extermination camps may have seemed to him, Weiss began to comprehend them as deeds committed by human beings and, thus, part of a historical continuum. Weiss goes on to note that, up to then, art had indeed been capable of dealing with the most dreadful atrocities committed by human beings against other human beings: an insight befitting the author of the just completed *Marat/Sade* and an admirer of Brueghel and of Picasso's famous painting "Guernica." The difficulties of the new project, however, turned out to be enormous. Overcoming them required intensive study, as well as an expansion of thought, which is how Weiss repeatedly circumscribed the intellectual process. He eventually overcame these difficulties by turning to the work of Dante and the tenets of Marxism.

Weiss's interest in Auschwitz appears to have been awakened as early as the fall of 1962. An entry in the notebooks lists the titles of two works about the "final solution of the Jewish question" (N I/67). The topic then seems to have been dropped for almost a year. Then, from the late summer of 1963 until the summer of 1965 the notebooks are filled with entries on Auschwitz as well as on Dante and on Marxism.

In December 1963 the "criminal case against Mulka et al.," as the Auschwitz trial was officially termed, got under way in Frankfurt am Main. A short time later, in January 1964, Weiss made the notation quoted above, that it was not yet possible to find an adequate artistic expression for Auschwitz. Soon thereafter, Dante's name is mentioned for the first time (N I/211). While studying the work of the Renaissance painter Giotto, Weiss came across the fact that Giotto had several times met with Dante. This constellation stimulated his fantasy, as is revealed from the text, "Vorübung zum dreiteiligen Drama divina commedia" (Preliminary Study for a Three-Part Drama: The Divine Comedy), in which Weiss described the genesis of *The Investigation*. At first he considered making the meeting of these two "innovators in the arts of writing and painting" into the subject of a drama; for example, by having Dante accompanied on his wanderings not by Virgil but by Giotto.[7] In the first weeks of the year 1964 the notations about Dante and Giotto increase noticeably, as Weiss tries various ways in which to link the world of the two Renaissance figures with the present. In the process a first, tentative concept for the Auschwitz topic is found: "Dante and Giotto stroll through the concentration camps" (N I/215). It once again prompts the question of whether this topic could be portrayed at all (N I/215).

On 13 March 1964, in the middle of the rehearsals for *Marat/Sade*, Weiss attended the Frankfurt trial. From this point on there are numerous entries concerning this trial and Auschwitz, interspersed with bibliographical listings on the "final solution." In the summer of 1964 Weiss wrote the fragment, "Frankfurter Auszüge" (Frankfurt Excerpts), his first attempt at finding a form for the Auschwitz trial.[8] The decision in favor of a play about Auschwitz had been made.

From the notebooks it is apparent that the new work about the destruction of human beings under fascism was merely part of a project that grew increasingly monumental in scope. In the tradition of Dante, Weiss was undertaking to re-create in literature the totality of the human condition of his time. The denunciation of fascism in the new play about Auschwitz was part of a larger struggle against *all* forms of colonialist and imperialist exploitation and repression in Europe, as well as in Africa, Latin America, and Asia. In the racial hatred of his own epoch Weiss perceived a growing parallel to the anti-Semitism of the "final solution." Of the racists of the 1960s, he noted, "They would at any moment be willing to have the blacks gassed" (N I/249). The burgeoning of this divine comedy project led to endless attempts to find a workable concept. Efforts to define for his own time Dante's concepts of hell, purgatory, and paradise proved to be especially difficult. New key words about history, society, psychology, characters, ideological positions, and experiences are continuously assigned to the three Dante sites.

From Weiss's notations and essays there emerge the outlines of a concept that can be approximately summed up as follows: *Inferno* (hell) is the place of the powerful, the rulers, the exploiters, the repressors, and the torturers; *Paradiso* is the place of the victims, the "blessed . . . who are still waiting for their liberation"; *Purgatorio*, finally, is the place of contemporary battles, hence, also the place of doubts and contradictions. In Weiss's notations purgatory increasingly becomes the main focus of the project as well as the most difficult concept to define.[9]

Under the influence of the staging of *Marat/Sade* in Rostock (GDR), Weiss had changed his allegiance from the positions championed by Sade to those of Marat. He was also moving closer to Marxist and communist positions, and the newly gained insights led to a more precise and more militant redefinition of Dante's three realms. Attacks on socialism or remarks asserting that there was no longer any class conflict, a belief to which Weiss himself had adhered for a time, were now associated with the *Inferno*. *Purgatorio* was conceived more clearly as a place where the struggles for a new social order took place, its essence caught in a rallying cry (expanded by Weiss) from the Communist Manifesto: "Proletarians of all countries and oppressed peoples, unite." *Paradiso* now culminated in a "commitment to communism."[10]

Weiss's changing ideas on his divina commedia project never came together in a unified work. Even such a fundamental question as whether *The Investigation* should be assigned to the realm of the *Inferno*, the place of the perpetrators, or to *Paradiso*, the place of the victims, proved to be unsolvable. In Weiss's conception Auschwitz would have had to be assigned to paradise (N I/308, 599),[11] which must seem absurd to anyone not familiar with Weiss's approach to reading Dante against the grain.

In addition to the long-pursued concept of retaining Dante's threefold division, there existed also a conception for dividing his own version of the *Divina Commedia* into several one-act plays dealing with events in Angola, the Congo, South Africa, Latin America, Cuba, and with Germany's past (N I/537, G/R 115). Although this idea was not carried out, it nonetheless serves to illuminate the process by which first the topic of Auschwitz, then the struggle over Angola, and then the increasingly important events in Vietnam were split off from the divine comedy project and developed into independent works—*The Investigation, Gesang vom lusitanischen Popanz (Song of the Lusitanian Bogey)*, and *Viet Nam Diskurs (Viet Nam Discourse)*. Peter Weiss never wrote a divine comedy drama, but the years of work on this project left their mark on all his works after *The Investigation*.

In the year 1965, in addition to the "Vorübung zum dreiteiligen Drama divina commedia," Peter Weiss published a second essay on his Dante project, the "Gespräch über Dante." Trying to gain clarity about his appropriation of Dante's work, he reflects on what elements from *The Divine Comedy* he might still use and what is most remote to him. The fundamental question, Weiss states in the "Gespräch," was whether the complexity of events in his own epoch could at all be reproduced in their "totality."[12] He had to go as far back as the Renaissance to find comparable attempts to recreate in a work of art or literature the essence of an era in its totality. Weiss's project, which recalls Hungarian Marxist philosopher Georg Lukács's concept of totality, may appear dated in view of the belief of major representatives of modernity—from Joyce to Kafka to Beckett—that only fragments from the totality of events are accessible to the individual, and that extensive totality can no longer be rendered in a work of art. Weiss, however, was always out of step with his time, as he himself had been aware of since his early years as a painter; he was "always actually opposed to the trends and motifs that dominated in the era" (G/R 301). The roots of Weiss's concept of totality can be traced to his beginnings as a painter, to his preoccupation with Bosch and Brueghel, which had led to such paintings as "Die Maschinen greifen die Menschheit an" (The Machines Attack Mankind, 1935) and "Das grosse Welttheater" (The Great Theater of the World, 1937), paintings which attempt to render just such a totality. There is a continuity in Weiss's work, despite all the ruptures and meandering detours of his personal and artistic development. The study of Marxism, as a universal attempt to formulate the laws that govern nature, society, and thought, only served to encourage Weiss in his search for an artistic expression of the totality of the human condition. The divine comedy project eventually grew beyond all proportions. To Weiss's critics it appeared as a somewhat foolish undertaking, but they were also impressed by its sheer magnitude.[13] Any definitive evaluation of Weiss's Dante project should keep in mind, however, that, with *The Aesthetics of Resistance*, the stubborn author, Weiss, ultimately came very close to achieving that totality which major representatives of modernity had no longer thought possible.

As his focus shifted from the totality of his project to the topic of Auschwitz, Weiss's reading of *The Divine Comedy* concentrated more and more on details. The entire work had always caused him great difficulties and had always seemed very remote. The "unity" and "conviction" of Dante's epic poem appeared unattainable, and its "idealized perspective" could not be recreated. *The Divine Comedy* was an "exalted vision" and, at times, it seemed to Weiss that he lacked "even the remotest ideas" for its concepts of hell, purgatory, and paradise.[14] Against Dante's promises of paradise, Weiss stresses his own completely secular position: the human condition should be changed in the here and now. Clearly with Auschwitz in mind, he writes in the "Vorübung" that no more did the torturers belong in hell than the victims in paradise. Rather,

> they belonged only to us . . . ,
> and what they had done, what had happened to them,
> belonged to us.[15]

Again, addressed in the two Dante essays is the question of whether Auschwitz could be portrayed at all. For the author of *The Divine Comedy* it had still been possible to find words for the horrors he had to describe. For Weiss, in contrast, there remained only facts: "documents, files, record books, / charts, numbers, and books, libraries."[16] Weiss found this obsession with facts, which would characterize *The Investigation* and which anticipates the program of the West German Documentary Theater of the 1960s and 1970s, altogether prefigured in Dante. For in *The Divine Comedy* each figure and each place is called by its authentic name. One of these authentic names is Beatrice, the beloved of Dante's youth, who had died of illness at an early age. It was here that Peter Weiss found a common ground. Among *his* dead there had also been a Beatrice, a mysterious youthful acquaintance he could not forget. About her death, however, there could only be conjectures, "Maybe she was beaten to death. Maybe gassed. She had long become ashes when I was still describing her beauty to myself." Lucie Weisberger as Beatrice, Weiss as Dante who, in quest of a "youthful beloved"[17] from days long past, finds himself in hell. This is how Peter Weiss came to Auschwitz.

On 13 December 1964 he and other observers of the Frankfurt Auschwitz trial traveled to the former concentration camp in southwest Poland (N I/

321). Weiss spent one day in that place for which, in his own words, he had been destined but which he had escaped. He made a precise inventory of that inferno:

> Washroom, tiled floor. Black pipes. Large shovels. A stretcher made of linen. Troughs on the walls, as though for livestock. Wheelbarrows. Ominous looking poles.
>
> . . . .
> Four standing cells. Size: 19 ½ x 9 ½ inches. Air hole, 2 ½ inches. Concrete floor. At the bottom of the heavy iron door there is a hinged opening to crawl through. Iron bars on the door and peephole.
>
> . . . .
> The courtyard: finely ground sand. Stone edges at the sides with drainage trenches. (N I/324, 325, 326)

One would like to be spared the knowledge of what purpose had been served by the drainage trenches, the four standing cells, the troughs on the walls. But the author of the unbearably detailed description of Damiens's death (in *Marat/Sade*) has nothing of the sort in mind. One is forced to take note of what happened in Auschwitz. Immediately following his return from the visit to the concentration camp, Weiss wrote an essay which was published in Sweden and, in slightly revised form, in the Federal Republic in 1965 under the title "Meine Ortschaft" ("My Place").[18] What is described in this text, as well as Weiss's own biographical links to the fascist extermination camps, would become the basis for *The Investigation*. With this essay, Weiss also found the tone that would characterize the Auschwitz play.

Weiss repeatedly attended the Auschwitz trial at the beginning of 1965. By that time, work on *The Investigation* was already far advanced, the division of the events into Danteesque songs had been decided: "Song of phenol / of cyclon B / of the swing" (N I/308–09). (A comment is needed on the use of the word "song." Weiss uses the German word *Gesang,* which means song. But *Gesang* is also used as the translation of *Canto,* in the German translation of *The Divine Comedy,* whereas in the English translations of *The Divine Comedy* the Italian word *Canto* is retained. The English translators of Weiss's works, who may not have been aware of the close link of some of these works to Dante, always use the word song, as in "song of phenol," or in the title of the play *Song of the Lusitanian Bogey,* which might more aptly have been titled *"Canto* of the Lusitanian Bogey." In keeping with these translations the word "song" will be used here.) On 19 April 1965 the new work was completed under the title "Anus Mundi" (N I/367). A short time later the definitive division into eleven "Songs" and the definitive title, "Die Ermittlung," were noted (N I/367). On 19 October 1965 in a spectacular theater event, *The Investigation* simultaneously premiered on sixteen stages throughout the Federal Republic, West Berlin, and the German Democratic Republic.

The Investigation

"We must drop the lofty view / that the camp world is incomprehensible to us" (108).[19] Not an inappropriate demand of the present and future generations that the Third Witness makes in Peter Weiss's "Oratorio"—thus, the subtitle of *The Investigation*. What, if not the hope of gaining some measure of understanding, would be the incentive for confronting the issue of mass extermination under fascism? *The Investigation* proceeds to systematically destroy any such hope. From one scene to the next, the play seems intent on revealing the complete and utter incomprehensibility of the events. In the face of a relentless succession of atrocities, attempts at rational analysis grow faint. But this dulling effect is balanced by a counterprinciple that is at work in *The Investigation* and which Peter Weiss would formulate several years later in *Trotsky in Exile*: "When things are beyond rational comprehension . . . , that's the very time we must apply our reason. It's our only weapon."[20] Spectators and readers of *The Investigation* are caught up in the dialectics of the play, which numbs their faculties to reason while at the same time urging them toward rational analysis.

Weiss's first assumption had been that the events of Auschwitz defied portrayal on stage. That must have become even more evident when Rolf Hochhuth's drama *Der Stellvertreter* (*The Deputy*) premiered in 1963. The last act of this play, in which the pope's complicity in the extermination of the Jews is shown, takes place in Auschwitz. Hochhuth's attempt to depict mass extermination onstage naturalistically, crying children and barking dogs and all, had proved inadequate.[21] That Hochhuth's play was a popular success did not preclude its negative evaluation as drama by Weiss and others. In the 1980s the American television series "The Holocaust" again depicted Auschwitz naturalistically, and it, too, was commercially successful. Yet how could this attempt at a re-creation of the camps, which necessitated selecting extras on the basis of their emaciated appearances, be anything but a mockery? For an adequate rendition of Auschwitz by the means of art one might turn to the thirty-minute short film of 1955 by Alain Renais, *Nuit et Brouillard* (Night and Fog).

The year 1963, however, also marked the publication of one of the most profound studies of mass extermination under fascism. Hannah Arendt's report on the Eichmann trial, *Eichmann in Jerusalem,* with its famous subtitle, "A Report on the Banality of Evil," has had a lasting influence on the debate on this topic up to today. Arendt is mentioned in the notebooks in 1964. While Weiss was working on his address for the Lessing Prize, he noted the title of Arendt's essay about Lessing, "Von der Menschlichkeit in finsteren Zeiten" (On Humanity in Dark Times) (N I/320). Weiss's library also contained Arendt's study on Eichmann. The subtitle of Arendt's book signals her approach to the topic: not Eichmann in Nazi Germany, but Eichmann in Jerusalem; not the event itself but the present-day confrontation with it; and not the deeds but the later attempt at finding out the truth about them. All this also applies to Peter Weiss's play. *The Investigation* is not a historical drama of mass extermination (like *The Deputy*), but a legal drama from Weiss's present in 1964. It deals with the Frankfurt Auschwitz trial, the third largest trial of German war criminals (and the first in the Federal Republic) after the Nuremberg trials, held by the Allies (1947), and the Eichmann trial (1961).

In addition to his own notes of the trial, Weiss used numerous sources that were listed in the first edition of *The Investigation,* especially Bernd Naumann's reports of the trial, published at the time in the *Frankfurter Allgemeine Zeitung* and, later, as a book (in the United States it appeared with a foreword by Hannah Arendt). In the notebooks Weiss strongly emphasized the importance of Naumann's reports for his play (N I/390–91). As Manfred Haiduk and others have pointed out, Weiss adhered to his sources with great accuracy, often retaining whole passages literally,[22] down to the speech mannerisms of the trial participants and the "distorted officialese" (N I/231) of the accused and even of the victims.

Since the actual events that were to be related onstage exceeded any superlative forms available in language, Weiss dispensed with their use, as he dispensed with any attempts at artful linguistic re-creation, with images and metaphors. The account of the events tolerated not even the minimal dramatization through punctuation. Weiss permitted himself nothing more than a slight rhythmization of the language. Still, the degree by which Weiss intervened creatively in his work is by no means slight.

The apparent formal minimalism of *The Investigation* is the result of years of endlessly renewed attempts to depict and describe horrible experiences and visions that seemed beyond the means of artistic expression. A less creative writer than Weiss would have done more, as the example of Hochhuth shows. Even so, the material from the legal proceedings needed to be refashioned in a fundamental and decisive way in order to reduce it to a performable length (were it ever staged in its entirety, *The Investigation* would still require three theater evenings). The almost 400 witnesses were reduced to 9, the number of judges, prosecuting attorneys, and counsels for the defense was reduced to 1 each. Weiss's treatment of the documentary material went far beyond the "reduction of the author to an arranger,"[23] as further analysis of the play's aesthetics shows.

In a formal sense the play preserves the classical unity of time, place, and action. The events in the concentration camp that took place twenty years earlier and that are being investigated by the court are the subject of reports by witnesses and the accused. They form a subplot within the framework of the action in the courtroom. To this extent the structure recalls *Marat/Sade*, where the murder of Marat constitutes a play within a play. But unlike in *Marat/Sade*, there is no attempt here to transform the events at Auschwitz into events onstage. What happened in the camp, the actual subject of *The Investigation*, is merely related, and the continuity of the three unities is never interrupted. In terms of content the perspective on the past is determined by the present, wherein the trial takes place. In terms of form, in place of the unbound theatricality of *Marat/Sade*, there is a renunciation of any physical representation.

Weiss provides this basic concept with a formal structure gleaned from *The Divine Comedy*. In Dante's work the three realms of hell, purgatory, and paradise are each divided into thirty-three cantos (with the exception of the *Inferno*, which includes an additional song, bringing the entire text to 100 songs). *The Investigation* consists of eleven songs, each divided into three parts, so the structure of *The Divine Comedy* is substantially retained. The eleven songs of *The Investigation* correspond to eleven stations of a route of horror leading from the ramp, where the trains arrive, to the crematorium ovens: a progression analogous to Dante's route through the nine circles of hell down to that place of eternal ice in which Lucifer is forever frozen. If there is eternal ice in the innermost circle of Dante's hell, at the end of the descent into the concentration camp there is fire. As with Dante's poem, there is also a female figure at the center of Weiss's text (in the fifth song, almost precisely in the middle of the play). In Weiss's complex identification strategy this figure, Lili Tofler, is identified with Dante's Beatrice, and Beatrice in turn is identified with Lucie Weisberger (N I/305–6). But while Dante's quest for the beloved dead eventually leads into the fields of paradise, Weiss's quest leads to Auschwitz.

The few comparisons show similarities but also differences in Weiss's adaption of Dante's epic poem. The criticism occasionally heard—that the Dante-inspired form of *The Investigation* remains external to its content[24]—

overlooks Weiss's creative use of the structure of Dante's work. According to the necessities of the content, Dante's structure was in some instances duplicated, in others loosely applied, and, where necessary, completely abandoned. On the whole, as Weiss's preliminary studies show, much more than merely certain formal aspects of *The Divine Comedy* were integrated into the Auschwitz play. In its similarities and dissimilarities with Dante's work, *The Investigation* turns out to be the work of a creative mind that, as Weiss himself programmatically stated, had read Dante "against the grain."[25]

There were pitfalls in linking *The Divine Comedy* with Auschwitz that were brought out in a polemic by Martin Walser, who in 1965 criticized popular clichés linking Auschwitz to Dante's inferno and the practice of qualifying events that occurred in the camps as "Danteesque." Such metaphors indeed reflect an inability to come to terms with Auschwitz. The incommensurable appears as something long familiar, ultimately "eternal and human," and the concentration camp is turned into a grandiose and horrific work of art. Walser summed up his protest (it was not aimed at Peter Weiss) simply and convincingly: "After all, Auschwitz was not hell but a German concentration camp."[26] Peter Weiss would undoubtedly have agreed with this warning against attempts to turn Auschwitz into a metaphor.

Weiss was indeed far from considering the extermination camps as a "Danteesque hell," as was revealed in his conception of the *Divina Commedia*, which placed Auschwitz in the *paradiso*. Weiss had no other alternative, since there remains an insurmountable difference between Dante's inferno and Auschwitz; those suffering in the inferno were guilty and were being punished for their crimes. But what were the victims of fascism being punished for? What crimes had the millions of men, women, and children committed that brought them to this end? And even assuming that some of them might have been guilty of some crime, Hannah Arendt's irrefutable statement would still apply: "No humanly possible crime could have been commensurable with this punishment, no conceivable sin could have been commensurable with this hell."[27] The victims of fascist extermination constitute a category that was not prefigured in Dante's text.

The majority of these victims were Jews, as is known. But the word Jew is not mentioned in *The Investigation*. Strangely enough, in the discussion of Weiss's play this omission has hardly prompted any comment. The Germans also are not mentioned, no more than are Poles, gypsies, or gays; even the name Auschwitz is never mentioned. This is altogether surprising in a documentary work which frequently adheres literally to its sources. Peter Weiss systematically eliminated from his text any specific references to nationality or race contained in reports of the trial. This decision was the result of a thought process, at the inception of which Weiss still found it possible to use the Nazi term, "final solution" (N I/211). The notes for the Auschwitz trial occasionally mention Jews and "Polacks" (N I/223), Russians, Jews, and gypsies (N I/231). In these notes Weiss also reflects on his own Jewishness (N I/228). His enduring realization that he could have been not only on the side of the victims but also on the side of the perpetrators ultimately affected the concept of the new play. In an interview given in October 1965, at the time of the premiere of *The Investigation* Weiss emphasized that Auschwitz could occur not only in Germany, thus shedding light on why Auschwitz is only referred to as "the camp." Weiss also insisted that, in *The Investigation*, it was not Jews who were being exterminated but human beings. He added that had there been a "different twist of the historical kaleidoscope," many of the victims might have been on the side of the Nazis, and that what determined people's fate was the "social structure" (G/R 101). This conviction, which Weiss forcefully reiterated one year later,[28] is also expressed in the play. The Third Witness, the most lucid and politically aware of all the figures in *The Investigation*, states:

> Many of those who were destined
> to play the part of prisoners
> had grown up with the same ideas
> the same way of looking at things
> as those
> who found themselves acting as guards
> They were all equally dedicated
> to the same nation
> to its prosperity
> and its rewards
> And if they had not been designated prisoners
> they could equally well have been guards (108).

If, as this passage makes clear, it is inappropriate to speak of an unbridgeable gap between witnesses and accused,[29] the interpretation of the director Peter Palitzsch who had staged the play in Stuttgart also seems untenable. Palitzsch, apparently taking the above lines of the Third Witness literally, had the roles of the accused and of the witnesses performed by the same actors and actresses. As a consequence, perpetrators and victims appeared as randomly interchangeable.[30] Such a concept leaves no room for individual decision. Weiss's play, in contrast, is designed to show that even under the most extreme of circumstances there is still room for choice, for decisions in favor of humanity. We will return to this topic later on.

Weiss did not rigidly adhere to his concept of not mentioning nationalities and ethnic groups. The few exceptions are worth noting: at one time a "Polish woman" is mentioned (136); and in another instance the sadistic high school student, Stark, screams at a woman he is about to execute, calling her "Sarah" (147), the official first name given by Nazi Germany to all female Jews (the official first name for male Jews was Israel). Also, "Soviet prisoners" are mentioned several times (149, 152 [twice], 225, 267). Had *The Investigation* been a historical play, hardly anyone could have taken offense at this insistence on the sufferings of people from the Soviet Union. After all, the systematic decimation of the Soviet population under German fascism was beyond dispute. However, since the focus of events in *The Investigation* was on the epoch of the trial, that is, the 1960s, the repeated reference to "Soviet prisoners" became a political issue, as Weiss had intended. From an open letter he wrote in 1965 to Hans Werner Richter, spiritual head of the Group 47, it becomes apparent why there had to be this insistence on the nationality of the *Soviet* victims. The West German population, Weiss wrote, had learned nothing from the war, and he added bitterly, "At one time they [the West Germans] had allowed themselves to be chosen as a bulwark against Judaism, now they are the bulwark against communism."[31] During the cold war, which followed the "hot" war that had ended in 1945, the object of hatred had been switched but the hatred had remained. In 1956 the Communist Party of the Federal Republic (KPD) was banned and, with the construction of the Berlin wall by the GDR in 1961, anticommunism had reached a new peak. Peter Weiss, further elaborating his "bulwark" statement, pointed out that the Nazis' plans from the very beginning had included not only what eventually became known as the "final solution of the Jewish question" but also the destruction of the communists. Weiss perceived the anticommunism of the 1960s as a continuation, under changed historical circumstances, of a paramount tenet of fascist ideology.[32] The frequent reference to Soviet prisoners of war was intended to call the audience's attention to this fact.

It was this continuity from the Nazi state to the Federal Republic of the 1960s—a continuity not only of anticommunism but also of the economic structures that had lead to fascism—which Weiss sought to unmask in *The Investigation*. For this purpose an understanding of the correlation between capitalism and fascism was necessary. The notebooks show that Peter Weiss was increasingly preoccupied with this problem. An early notation, made soon after Weiss first attended the Frankfurt Auschwitz trial, concerned the "involvement of the arms industry" (N I/232), and toward the end of that same year, 1964, there is this thought: "Capitalist society driven to the most extreme perversion—exploitation even of blood, bones, ashes" (N I/316).

These notations point to the dual form of exploitation through which industry profited from Auschwitz. On the one hand factories were set up in the vicinity of the camp in which prisoners were forced to labor until their death (usually only a few weeks). Right at the beginning of *The Investigation* several of these industries are mentioned by name: "They were branch plants / of I-G Farben / Krupp and Siemens" (6). Precise details are given about the organization of this industrial exploitation until death, about the route to work, the number of hours spent working, and the wages. The yearly revenue of the firms, as revealed by the prosecutor, amounted to several billion marks (131). On the other hand, industry profited from what had in 1941 become the main purpose of Auschwitz: the mass extermination of human beings. Specifically mentioned in the play is Degesch, the company that supplied the gas (229), and Topf und Söhne, the firm that built the crematoriums.[33]

In addition to these "traditional" forms of exploitation, there was a third form of capitalist exploitation that entered the history of mankind only through fascism. The prisoners themselves were processed as raw material by industry. While they were still alive, this was done, for instance, by "various / pharmaceutical concerns" (124) in whose name one Dr. Clauberg burned young women's ovaries or used a syringe to insert a "cement-like mass" into their uteruses (115–16). There is no mention of what conceivable purpose these "experiments" might have had. After death, the corpses were further processed: jewelry was removed; the hair shorn, bundled, and put into bags; and gold teeth were removed. At times there was so much to be done that the personnel (all prisoners) were forced to work in two shifts (258). Finally, some of the flesh was cut out of the corpses (182) for use in bacteriological experiments (200).

In thorough detail *The Investigation* deals with what was inflicted on the human body. For Auschwitz, too, was "a world of bodies," in the turn of phrase used by the Marquis de Sade in *Marat/Sade*.[34] Now, however, Weiss's obsession with the reality of the body is grounded more strongly in material reality. For the minute descriptions of the destruction of bodies are intended to make visible the organized "industrial processing system," to use a term by Martin Walser.[35] Surrounded by other factories, Auschwitz was itself a factory and, like the others, it too supplied products necessary for the war.

Weiss's use of the records of the trial reveals the economic and "rational" aspect of the extermination of human beings by fascism, which until then had generally been hidden behind ideological veils (anti-Semitism and racism).

In the course of the Auschwitz trial Weiss's interest was increasingly directed toward the continuity of the economic powers and the profits they had derived from the extermination of human beings. He noted that the goods stolen from the victims were "worth billions," which were still in German hands (N I/235). Later he noted, "The same industries that profited from the concentration camps are the ones that today are again on top" (N I/361). As an example of individual profiteering there is one Dr. Capesius who, having been a "representative of the Bayer company prior to the war" (15), was responsible for the camp pharmacy in Auschwitz (16). His duties included management of the Cyclon B gas used in the gas chambers, as well as of the phenol, which was injected into the hearts of victims selected for this kind of death (202). In addition to these products of the chemical industry, Capesius had custody of the luggage containing jewelry and gold teeth. These he used after the war to furnish a pharmacy and—fantasy pales before reality—a beauty parlor: "Be beautiful / with beauty treatments by Capesius" (234).

There is also a former chairman of the board of one of the industries working in Auschwitz. At the time of the trial he was drawing a DM 300,000 annual pension from his former company, and he was living in a palace where he collected precious objects (129). Such examples recur frequently enough in *The Investigation* to gradually reveal a supra-individual pattern of continuity extending to a number of the most important industries of the Federal Republic. This pattern is summed up by the prosecuting attorney:

> Let us once more bring to mind
> that the successors to those same concerns
> have ended up today in magnificent condition
> and that they are now in the midst of
> as they say
> a new phase of expansion (131).

Here the investigation of the past becomes an investigation of the present of the year 1965. This present was in the grip of the cold war, and any political attack on the Federal Republic was subjected to this bitter ideological struggle. In *The Investigation* this led to certain one-sided positions. Thus, most other aspects of Auschwitz receded somewhat behind Weiss's emphatic critique of the role of capitalism played in the creation of the camps, a critique that was equally emphatically extended to the capitalist system of the Federal Republic. Several of these other aspects will be discussed below. First, however, it is necessary to deal briefly with the debate that developed around Weiss's critique of capitalism and that turned *The Investigation* into a key work of the cold war.

At the time Weiss wrote *Marat/Sade* he claimed for himself a "third approach" in the dispute between the two power blocs. Now, however, only a few weeks prior to the premiere of *The Investigation*, he published in Sweden and in the GDR an essay entitled "10 Arbeitspunkte eines Autors in der geteilten Welt" (An Author's Ten Working-Points in the Divided World). It contains a brief analysis of the two power blocs and tries to clarify the artist's tasks in this historic situation. Weiss takes stock of his thinking that, especially since *Marat/Sade,* had been evolving as a consequence of his analysis of the French Revolution, his experiences with the GDR, his attempts to come to terms with Auschwitz—both as the site of fascist mass extermination and as the low point of the capitalist system—and his intensifying efforts to depict world-historical events in a gigantic work modeled on *The Divine Comedy.* He renounces the bourgeois class of his origins and the aesthetic existence and lack of commitment of his years as a painter. The last section of "10 Arbeitspunkte" begins with what in the Federal Republic amounted to public heresy: "For me, the guidelines of socialism contain an abiding truth."[36] With this rather general and somewhat vague statement, Weiss delivered himself to his opponents. They never asked which socialism Weiss was referring to, that of Marx and Engels, or that of Luxemburg, Lenin, Trotsky, Gramsci, Stalin, Ulbricht, and Castro—and, at the time, Weiss probably would not have been able to answer.

Only in the summer of 1965 had he begun to read Marx's *Das Kapital* (N I/380). Weiss apparently never systematically worked through the writings of the Marxist classics. He was far more interested the *history* of socialism and the labor movement than in its *theory.* The critical Marxist of the 1970s, the author of *The Aesthetics of Resistance,* probably would not have felt comfortable with the turn of phrase "abiding truth." Already in the "10 Arbeitspunkte" the dogmatism and restrictions on artists and writers in the GDR are repeatedly and emphatically criticized (even in the concluding sentence), and the notebooks, too, contain many critical entries after visits to the GDR. But Weiss's nuanced attitude toward the socialist German state was ignored by an antagonistic press.

Weiss's public avowal of socialism distorted judgments. The author was accused of having, in *The Investigation,* "put Auschwitz in the service of the

Cold War," of having placed "Auschwitz in the service of the Ulbricht Reich" (Walter Ulbricht was the head of state of the GDR from 1960–73). In these polemical pronouncements—they were made by Ludwig Marcuse—the play itself appears only as an afterthought, easily dismissed as a "well documented record" of Auschwitz.[37] With such attacks Marcuse and others were distracting from the long overdue discussion of the facts presented in *The Investigation,* a distraction that appeared to many as a "scandalous waste of an important topic."[38]

In the GDR, too, as was inevitable in that historic period, the intentions of the play were at times distorted. The critique of West German capitalism contained in *The Investigation* was emphasized to an extent that distracted from the GDR's own shortcomings in coming to terms with Auschwitz, Judaism, and anti-Semitism. On the day of the premiere of *The Investigation,* however, the GDR held a public reading at the Academy of Arts in which leading writers, actresses, and politicians, such as Stephan Hermlin, Helene Weigel, and Alexander Abusch, participated. An act by the state appropriate to the importance of *The Investigation,* it equally honored the sponsor and the play.

Perhaps the most unbearable aspect of the killing and dying in Auschwitz was its "normality." From the arrival of the trains to the smoke in the chimneys, the sequence of events became a daily routine in a world that had become the negation of any normal daily routine. In *The Investigation* the Fifth Witness describes this Auschwitz "normalcy" which all prisoners had to learn, this Auschwitz in which it was normal to be stolen from and to steal, to fight with one's fellow prisoners for food and a place to sleep, and to lose all feelings and become indifferent in the midst of suffering; a place where

> It was normal
> that all around us people were dying
> and it was normal
> to live in the face of one's own death (41).

And, somewhat later,

> The question
> of right and wrong
> didn't exist any longer (57).

This system, designed to destroy any humanity in the *inmates,* also destroyed the humanity of the *camp personnel.* In the upside-down world of fascism, this loss of humanity was declared the expression of a new humanity of the "master race." The words of the Reichsführer SS Heinrich Himmler to his troops remain etched in one's memory: "Most of you will know what it means if 100 corpses are lying about, if 500 are lying about or if 1000 are lying about. To have endured this and, apart from exceptions of human weaknesses, to have remained decent, is what made us tough. This is a never-written and never-to-be-written glorious chapter of our history."[39]

Guard duties in the extermination camps were carried out by average people. In *The Investigation* there are no references to the personnel as sadists. In their use of language, in their arguments, and in their entire bearing the torturers appear as average people, mostly members of the lower middle class. As far as is known, not one of them was accused after the war of any sadistic or deviant behavior. They lived in the Federal Republic typically as teachers or train conductors. One of the most bestial worked as a nurse, trustingly called "Papa Kaduk" by his patients (55). On the occasion of the staging of his play in Sweden, Weiss emphasized the averageness of the accused, who, in most instances, had had an average family life, "with all the banal and touching details familiar to us."[40]

Weiss's statement recalls Arendt's tenet of the "banality of evil." At the time of the Frankfurt trial she continued to maintain that the cruelties in the camps "[were] not committed by bandits, monsters, or raging sadists, but by some of the most respected members of an honorable society."[41] Against Arendt's and Weiss's insistence on the banality of evil, one might point out that by no means must sadists always rage, that it is altogether possible that monstrous people can be members of an honorable society and lead an "average family life." And that, unlike Eichmann, the accused in Frankfurt did indeed commit the horrible deeds themselves.

Why Weiss, nonetheless, insists on their banality becomes obvious from the example of Corporal Stark, a high school student who was just as easily inculcated with love of Goethe as with bestial behavior. His development, described in detail in Song 6 of the play, draws attention to the system that produced these perpetrators and behind which they now seek to hide from responsibility, "It was not my job / to question this purpose" (100), "I made no decisions / I had no such authority" (52), "But I only did what I had to do" (53). With such evocations of their "unquestioning execution of their duty" (196), the accused try to present themselves as indifferent toward, even as in disagreement with, the unlawful Nazi state. In contrast, Arendt has shown that this kind of absolute "obedience" conceals a basic agreement with the laws and institutions of the state. In questions of morality, Arendt emphasizes, there can be no appeal to the duty of obedience; it is one's duty to resist against an unlawful state or, at least, to withhold support.[42]

The court's insistence that they should have resisted or at least refused to carry out certain commands is rejected by the accused in *The Investigation* with their last and strongest argument: "Anyone who spoke of it [torture] / risked the death penalty" (100), anyone refusing to kill "would have been put up against the wall" (190). If that had been true, all arguments would fail. Like their other excuses, however, these assertions of the accused are refuted. In Song 2, a female witness states,

> that each one of the men in charge
> could take a stand
> against conditions in the camp
> and change them (58).

A witness for the prosecution confirms that his refusal to participate in the selections on the ramp did not result in punishment. In Song 8 the prosecuting attorney points out that there is no known instance of anyone having been punished for refusal to participate in the killings. The tireless efforts of an ambulance man by the name of Flacke or of a Dr. Flage to preserve some degree of humanity in the camp provides incontrovertible evidence that genocide could not have been carried out, at least could not have proceeded so smoothly, if there had been more such people.

Even though the contrary is constantly asserted by the accused, the Nazi organization of the extermination of human beings was a system with loopholes. In the most extreme situations there was still room for individual action and responsibility. In *The Investigation* this is shown to be true not only for the perpetrators but also for the victims; for the victims resisted their role no more than did the perpetrators. By the hundreds of thousands, by the millions, they obediently went to their death. Several persuasive reasons for this are given in *The Investigation,* from the belief that any resistance would have been pointless, to the very understandable and, at the same time, utterly incomprehensible conviction of the victims who, even within sight of the gas chambers, regarded the fate immediately confronting them as inconceivable. In addition, and in contrast to the perpetrators, they knew with absolute certainty that the slightest attempt at resistance would result in their death. Nonetheless, it is necessary to keep in mind the assertion of the perceptive Third Witness that these people were not heroes. It is necessary, too, to keep in mind his reflection, which extends the issue of individual responsibility and resistance against a world out of joint right into the present:

> We
> who still live with these pictures
> know that millions could stand again
> waiting to be destroyed
> and that the new destruction
> will be far more efficient
> than the old one was (110).

This is a survivor's warning to the living—in view of future possible (nuclear and environmental) catastrophes—to abandon our attitude of an indifferent or hopeless waiting for the end, to make use of the opportunities for individual action that are available to us, and not to render "unconditional obedience" to any law or state. As Hannah Arendt teaches, in questions of morality there can be no such thing "unconditional obedience."

These, then, are some of the efforts undertaken in *The Investigation* in order to remove the aura of incomprehensibility and uniqueness that surround the mass exterminations under German fascism. To come to an understanding of Weiss's play, the reader or spectator also has to abandon the belief that the world of concentration camps remains incomprehensible. What happened in Auschwitz needs to be placed in a historic continuum whose roots can be traced in history and which, in a different form, might conceivably happen again.

In keeping with Weiss's intentions, the focus of this analysis was on the economic interests that brought about the concentration camps. It should be pointed out, however, that the expansionist necessity of capitalism by no means provides a complete explanation for the Nazi mass exterminations. In history there are indeed parallels for Auschwitz, and yet the industrial mass-production of corpses by the Nazis remains without precedent. It is a complete "rupture in civilization."[43] One must recognize that any attempt at rational explanation runs up against that limit where "the word fails and the thought process breaks down" (Arendt).[44] Still, one cannot abandon attempts to comprehend these events rationally.

NOTES

1. W. G. Sebald, "Die Zerknirschung des Herzens. Über Erinnerung und Grausamkeit im Werk von Peter Weiss," *Orbis Litterarum* 41, no. 1 (1986): 266.

2. Peter Weiss, "Gespräch über Dante," in Weiss, *Rapporte* (Frankfurt/Main: Suhrkamp, 2d ed., 1981) 152.

3. Theodor W. Adorno, *Negative Dialektik* (Frankfurt/Main: Suhrkamp, 1970) 356. See also Günther Anders, "Auschwitz 1966," in Anders, *Besuch im Hades* (Munich: Beck, 2d ed., 1985) 30.

4. Theodor W. Adorno, "Kulturkritik und Gesellschaft" (1949), in Adorno, *Prismen* (Frankfurt/Main: Suhrkamp, 3d ed., 1987) 26. Concerning the historical-philosophical basis of this famous statement by Adorno, see Detlev Claussen, "Nach Auschwitz. Ein Essay über die Aktualität Adornos," in Dan Diner, ed., *Zivilisationsbruch. Denken nach Auschwitz* (Frankfurt/Main: Fischer, 1988) 54–68.

5. See Günter Grass, *Schreiben nach Auschwitz. Frankfurter Poetik-Vorlesung* (Frankfurt/Main: Luchterhand, 1991) 14ff.

6. See Theodor W. Adorno, "Engagement" (1962), in Adorno, *Noten zur Literatur* (Frankfurt/Main: Suhrkamp, 1981) 422–24.

7. See Peter Weiss, "Vorübung zum dreiteiligen Drama divina commedia" (1965), in Weiss, *Rapporte* 128, 130.

8. See Peter Weiss, "Frankfurter Auszüge," *Kursbuch* 1 (June 1965): 152–88.

9. For Weiss's attempts to characterize the three realms, see Weiss, "Vorübung" 137–38; see also Weiss, "Gespräch über Dante" 168 (here also the quotation).

10. From an unpublished text by Peter Weiss quoted by Manfred Haiduk, in Haiduk, *Der Dramatiker Peter Weiss* (East Berlin: Henschelverlag, 1977) 119–20. See also the notation concerning purgatory in N 1/365.

11. See Rolf D. Krause, *Faschismus als Theorie und Erfahrung: "Die Ermittlung" und ihr Autor Peter Weiss* (Frankfurt/Main: Peter Lang, 1982) 31, 464–65 n. 11. See also Burkhardt Lindner, *Im Inferno. "Die Ermittlung" von Peter Weiss* (Badenweiler: Oase, 1988) 72.

12. See Weiss, "Gespräch über Dante" 163.

13. See Heinrich Vormweg, *Peter Weiss* (Munich: Beck, 1981) 92–93.

14. All quotations from Weiss, "Gespräch über Dante" 143–44.

15. Weiss, "Vorübung" 134–35.

16. Weiss, "Vorübung" 136.

17. Both quotes from Weiss, "Gespräch über Dante" 154.

18. See Peter Weiss, "My Place" ("Meine Ortschaft" 1964), trans. Christopher Middleton, in Middleton, ed., *German Writing Today* (Harmondsworth, England: Penguin, 1967).

19. The page numbers in parentheses refer to Peter Weiss, *The Investigation* (*Die Ermittlung*, 1964), trans. Jon Swan and Ulu Grosbard (New York: Atheneum, 1966).

20. Peter Weiss, *Trotsky in Exile* (*Trotzki im Exil*), trans. Geoffrey Skelton (New York: Atheneum, 1972) 117. I am using my own translation, which is more literal than Skelton's and brings out the emphasis of the sentence.

21. See Klaus Harro Hilzinger, *Die Dramaturgie des dokumentarischen Theaters* (Tübingen: Niemeyer, 1976) 33ff. and n. 3.

22. Haiduk 134.

23. Vormweg 97.

24. See Ludwig Fischer, "Dokument und Bekenntnis oder Von der Schwierigkeit, durchs Schreiben ein Sozialist zu werden. Erwägungen zum schriftstellerischen Weg des Peter Weiss," *Text und Kontext* 5, no. 1 (1977): 98ff.

25. Weiss, "Gespräch über Dante" 148.

26. Quotes from Martin Walser, "Unser Auschwitz," *Kursbuch* 1 (June 1965): 190ff., 192.

27. Hannah Arendt, "Das Bild der Hölle" ("The Image of Hell" 1946). Eike Geisel, in Arendt, *Nach Auschwitz. Essays und Kommentare 1* (Berlin: Tiamat, 1989) 51.

28. See Weiss's interview with Oliver Clausen in Clausen, "Weiss/Propagandist and Weiss/Playwright," *The New York Times Magazine* 2 October 1966: 132.

29. As does Jürgen E. Schlunk. See Schlunk, "Auschwitz and Its Function in Peter Weiss's Search for Identity," in *German Studies Review* 10, no. 1 (February 1987): 21.

30. Regarding Palitzsch's staging, see Haiduk 153–54.

31. Peter Weiss, "Unter dem Hirseberg" (1956), in Weiss, *Rapporte 2* (Frankfurt/Main: Suhrkamp, 1971) 10. Repeated almost verbatim in G/R 78.

32. See Peter Weiss, "Antwort auf eine Kritik zur Stockholmer Aufführung der 'Ermittlung,' " in Weiss, *Rapporte 2* 46–47.

33. This company is not mentioned in the English version.

34. See chap. 5 above.

35. Walser 193.

36. Peter Weiss, "10 Arbeitspunkte eines Autors in der geteilten Welt," in Weiss, *Rapporte 2* 14–23.

37. Ludwig Marcuse, "Was ermittelte Peter Weiss?" *Kürbiskern* 2 (1966): 86–87.

38. Thomas von Vegesack, "Dokumentation zur 'Ermittlung,' " *Kürbiskern* 2 (1966): 83. Vegesack also provides an overview of the critical response to *The Investigation*.

39. Walther Hofer, ed., *Der Nationalsozialismus. Dokumente, 1933–1945* (Frankfurt/Main: Fischer, 1957) 114.

40. Weiss, "Antwort auf eine Kritik" 45.

41. Hannah Arendt, "Was heisst persönliche Verantwortung unter einer Diktatur?" ("Personal Responsibility under Dictatorship," 1964), trans. Eike Geisel, in Arendt, *Nach Auschwitz* 91, see also 130.

42. Arendt, "Was heisst persönliche" 95–97.

43. "Zivilisationsbruch"; the term comes from Dan Diner, see n. 4 above.

44. Hannah Arendt, *Eichmann in Jerusalem. Ein Bericht von der Banalität des Bösen* (*Eichmann in Jerusalem: A Report on the Banality of Evil*, 1963), trans. Brigitte Granzow (Munich: Piper, 6th ed., 1987) 300.

CHAPTER SIX

Solidarity with Liberation Movements
of the Third World

" "I do not identify myself any more with the Jews than I do with the people of Vietnam or the blacks in South Africa. I simply identify myself with the oppressed of the world."[1] With these words in the fall of 1966 Peter Weiss summed up a development in his thinking that had begun during work on *The Investigation.* Already in the spring of 1964 one of his notations indicated that, in addition to the personnel of the concentration camps, the colonialists of South Africa, Spain, and Portugal were to be assigned to (Dante's) hell (N I/227). Anti-Semitism was increasingly thought of as a "parallel" to racism (N I/270). Weiss's turn toward the liberation struggles of the Third World was the logical outflow of his thinking about fascism and Auschwitz. After *The Investigation* was completed in early summer of 1965, he resumed work on his divine comedy of the twentieth century. Within the framework of this never-completed project there is an increase in notations about parts of the world that Weiss had become aware of only recently: Southeast Asia and Latin America and, to an growing extent, the Portuguese colonies in Africa, Mozambique and Angola. Entries in the notebooks focus on a Dante-inspired "song about colonialism" (N I/395). During this period Weiss was involved in two much publicized disputes.

The second issue of *Kursbuch* (August 1965), an important West German cultural journal of the 1960s and 1970s, was devoted to the Third World. It contained contributions by Frantz Fanon, Carlos Fuentes, and Fidel Castro, and closed with a contribution by publisher Hans Magnus Enzensberger.[2] In his article Enzensberger sided with the view that the division of the world should no longer be understood in terms of capitalist versus socialist societies, but in terms of "rich" versus "poor" countries, a concept that had the merit of directing attention away from the cold war among white people and toward the problems of the nonwhites in the Third World. Enzensberger stressed the distance between "them" and "us," and emphatically denied that solidarity was possible with the inhabitants of the colonized countries; no power of imagination would suffice to put oneself in the place of these people. He ended with the laconic assertion that he had no solutions to offer. Weiss agreed neither with Enzensberger's analysis nor with his conclusion.

He immediately wrote a response, stating that he, contrary to Enzensberger, remained committed to the view of a division between the capitalist and the socialist world.[3] Weiss maintained that from these two opposite social systems no unified, wealthy front directed against the Third World could be construed. Moreover, Weiss emphatically guarded against the use of the term "Third World," since it was based on "class thinking" and stressed a Eurocentric standpoint. For the same reasons he rejected the term "underdeveloped countries," without, however, proposing a better term (G/R 132; and see N I/549). Weiss also insisted that the capitalist countries could not simply be called "rich." There were large class differences in the wealthy countries that might lead to struggles altogether comparable to those in the Third World. For the exploited here and there, only socialism would bring liberation.

Weiss expressly guarded against the line of demarcation Enzensberger drew between "us" and "them." Using a complex strategy of identification with the victims, Weiss had been able in *The Investigation* to convey the reality of fascist concentration camps. He now understandably insisted that it was also possible to imagine the everyday horrors in the colonized countries. In contrast to the publisher of the *Kursbuch,* Weiss declared his solidarity with the oppressed whose struggle he wanted to support through his work.

From then on Peter Weiss would not let himself be deterred from publicly using his now world-famous name in support of his convictions, and not the least where socialist countries and specifically the GDR were concerned. The staging of *Marat/Sade* in Rostock had yielded contacts within the GDR that were virtually indispensable for Weiss's intellectual development and for his work. Nonetheless, he became involved in a dispute with his new comrades when he expressed his opposition, in late 1965, to the restriction of the artistic activities of the GDR poet and songwriter Wolf Biermann. A discussion about Biermann with high GDR cultural bureaucrats (including Kurt Hager and Alexander Abusch) brought no change (N I/396). Weiss decided to take a public stand by writing a letter, dated 28 December 1965, to Wilhelm Girnus, publisher of the GDR literary journal *Sinn und Form.* The letter was eventually published in the FRG but not in the GDR. Weiss used the occasion of the repressive measures against the obstreperous East German songwriter as a pretext to elaborate on criticism he had already formulated in his essay "10 Arbeitspunkte" about restrictions on artistic work in the GDR. He warned that socialism, more than any other form of society, had an obligation to guarantee freedom of the word. As he had in the "Ten Working Points," he referred to the fruitful development of Soviet arts in the years following the Soviet October Revolution. (Lenin himself, who had no great appreciation for artistic experiments, had demanded generosity and tolerance toward art.) In the realm of art, Weiss continued, a socialist society should be able to tolerate "the deviant, the vehement, the wild, the offensive, and even the frightening." The letter ended with the challenge, "Let Biermann sing, be irritated about it, and make things better!"[4] The comrades did not accept Weiss's suggestion. Ten years later Biermann was expelled from the GDR. In the wake of this expulsion, writers such as Thomas Brasch, Sarah Kirsch, Reiner Kunze, and others either left or were forced to leave the GDR; a loss that could never be undone, and that undoubtedly accelerated the decline of the socialist German state.

A decision in favor of an Angola play had still not been taken in November 1965. In the notebooks there are numerous entries about the colonization of Central America and the Caribbean: in Nicaragua, Costa Rica, Jamaica, and other "banana republics" (N I/404) such as the Dominican Republic, Colombia, Panama, Guatemala, Honduras, and Cuba. A play about the plundering of Central America by the U.S. conglomerate United Fruit Company began to take shape (N I/411ff.). In early December there are notations about Vietnam and Algeria (the latter had just wrested its independence from France). Eventually, a concept was found from which the next work would emerge, "The real Salazar suddenly confronts the *Bogey* Salazar" (N I/429, emphasis added; Antonio Salazar [1889–1970] dictatorially ruled fascist Portugal and its colonies until his death). From then on there is an increasing number of entries concerning a play about the liberation struggle of the Portuguese colonies. Many of these notations would be included almost verbatim in the new work.

Song of the Lusitanian Bogey

The play about the Portuguese colonies Angola, Mozambique, and Guinea was written in late 1965 (N I/474), and its premiere, in Swedish translation, took place in Stockholm in January 1967. Its curious title is *Song of the Lusitanian Bogey (Gesang vom lusitanischen Popanz)*. The word "song" in any work of Weiss since *The Investigation* is a reference to the cantos of Dante's *Divine Comedy*. Just as *The Investigation* is divided into eleven Danteesque songs, the two-act *Song of the Lusitanian Bogey* is subdivided into eleven sections or scenes. But unlike in the Auschwitz play, here the individual scenes are not further subdivided; the formal proximity to Dante's epic poem is looser. In the title (and in the play itself) Portugal is called by its ancient Latin name Lusitania. The designation, no longer in use, creates distance. More importantly, it is a reminder that in the great days of the Roman Empire, Portugal had itself been a colony. The Roman Empire had crumbled, its colonies were lost, and Lusitania had eventually become the independent country of Portugal: dialectics of history which, in Weiss's depiction of the independence struggle of the Portuguese colonies, should be kept in mind.[5] This historical dialectic underlies the play and provides the thread of hope that runs through this dramatization of the Angolan struggle for independence. A bogey, finally, is a scarecrow, a scapegoat. The disintegrating colonial power of Portugal is offered up to ridicule: a now-hollow colossus that is toppled at the slightest push.

In *Song of the Lusitanian Bogey* the history of the original colonization of Angola, the present social conditions in Portugal and in its African colonies, and the first phase of the liberation struggle are shown onstage. That these events are actually put onstage is an absolute precondition for this work. Unlike *The Investigation*, *Lusitanian Bogey* is not a play whose meaning is largely disclosed through reading. It is more like a libretto, the word "song" in the title should be taken quite literally. Much of the text is sung, either by a solo voice or alternating with a chorus, as a canon or a ballad; in its first staging the entire play was accompanied by music.[6] There is also dance and pantomime; and there are heroic tableaus, shadow plays, cabaret and circus-like intermezzos. As in *Marat/Sade*—but in extreme contrast to *The Investigation*—there is an abundance of theatrical elements. The simple and pregnant forms of farce, freak show, fair, and folk theater, and of rhyme and doggerel, take up the theatricality of the drama about Marat and Sade as well as of the early play *Night with Guests*. The rough-hewn manner of that play, the dispensing with individually drawn characters and psychologizing, and most of all the simplicity and directness of its social satire had earned *Night with Guests* the disqualifier "agitprop." Now, however, on the occasion of an interview about *Song of the Lusitanian Bogey*, Weiss himself drew a parallel between the new play and those crude but effective agitational forms that had emerged in Russia after the revolutionary upheavals of October 1917. In *Song of the Lusitanian Bogey*, Weiss explains, the events are presented onstage in the drastic, simple manner of agitprop theater (G/R 138). *Lusitanian Bogey* is a polemical, partisan play; it is a "pamphlet," as has been correctly noted.[7]

The pamphlet aspect is made clear immediately in the first scene, in the dramatically effective completion of the bogey and in the introduction of that "trinity of military, clergy, and industry,"[8] which has held power in Portugal

101

for more than thirty years. The action onstage is accompanied by empty phrases about "god, patriotism, and family" (8)[9] and about the defense of the "sacred rights of property" (9; already in *Marat/Sade* there had been mention of the "holy right of enrichment"); and there are tirades against the "spreading of poisonous / internationalism," with more than a hint of anti-Semitism as well as of anticommunism. Ruling by a strong leader is deemed necessary since, in the words of the powers that be, "man is not capable / of guiding himself / He needs the direction of an authority" (6). After the oratorio about *German* fascism, *Lusitanian Bogey* constitutes a satirical attack on *Iberian* fascism (in Spain Generalissimo Franco had been in power ever since the end of the civil war in 1939), which was still able to hold sway twenty years after the end of World War II. This Iberian fascism, however, is now nothing more than a bogey: a stage figure "larger than life, and menacing" (8), yet at closer scrutiny "scrap iron" (8), wobbly, with shabby trappings of power such as a cylinder, an honorary ribbon, and a crucifix, its aggressive chatter repeatedly turning into a yawn. The former empire of Portugal is in the last stages of decline: this is the historical moment at which Weiss's dramatization of the history and of the liberation struggle of the colonized sets in.

The second scene of *Lusitanian Bogey* shows the conquest of Angola by Diego Cão in the year 1482.[10] Powerful Brechtian language is used to describe events that are generally known. For the pattern was repeated over and over, regardless of whether the name of the white conqueror was Cão, Cortés, or Pizarro, or whether the victims were Africans, Aztecs, or Incas. White Europeans were searching for a sea route to India and the people of the Third World had to pay the costs—and up to the present they have not stopped paying. About these costs Weiss provides the audience with a precise accounting that includes data on the yearly and monthly wages and bills due and on the price of a kilo of corn meal, beans, or dried fish. The bottom line of this accounting reveals that a cotton-picker cannot afford to buy a cotton skirt.

Also among the costs are numbers about the forced labor of diamond diggers and miners, and of women and children forced to work on plantations. In addition, there is the destruction of the indigenous culture, which coincided with the deliberate exclusion of the colonized from any education, "So many as possible should neither read nor write" (7), for which again numbers are provided. At the slightest hint of resistance against the rules and regulations of the colonial power, the costs increase enormously. The methods of torture extend from the "billy" that tears holes in the hands (24) to that "standing statue'' (58), which must have seemed horribly familiar to Peter Weiss since he had already described this form of torture in *The Investigation.* [11] An extreme form in which the colonized had to bear the costs of colonialism is shown in the example of those men from the Cabinda enclave, who had petitioned the colonial government for permission to set up a separate school for their children. The men are arrested. Then, as one of the wives describes it:

> An airplane flew with what was
> left of our husbands in sacks
> far out over the sea
> After days the tide then washed
> back what was left onto the beach
> Arms legs the torsos (38–39).

Here once again is Weiss's tormented obsession with the pain that can be inflicted on the human body; there is once again, as in *Marat/Sade,* this obsession with the reality of the body; and once again, the human body is shown as that primal matter from which all thinking about the human condition must start. The horrors inflicted by the colonized on the bodies of the *colonizers* are also noted:

> They have taken the owner of a sawmill
> and his family
> and tied them to the boards
> and run them lengthwise
> through the buzz saw (46).

The horrors perpetrated on the colonists are to be understood as a reciprocal action by the colonized who are relentlessly victimized by the white rulers. The colonists, of course, take note only of the violence against themselves and thus conclude, ''We do not fight against men / we fight against / untamed beasts'' (46). Hence, the colonized ultimately are denied their humanity; that, too, is part of the costs they have to pay. They are truly, as Frantz Fanon (1924–61), the physician and theoretician of Third World liberation movements from the Caribbean island of Martinique, noted, ''the damned of the earth.'' [12] Peter Weiss had read Fanon, [13] and was undoubtedly aware that the title of Fanon's book is taken from the ''International,'' the song of the international labor movement. The European industrial proletariat had for a long time been the damned of the earth. The improvement of their lot, particularly since World War II, made it possible for Fanon, Weiss, and others to redirect the Eurocentric focus toward those who were still the damned of the earth: the colonized, the people of the Third World.

The cost accounting that Peter Weiss presents in *Song of the Lusitanian Bogey* also has its plus side—for the white colonialists. Capital investments in Angola yield 30 percent dividends (39). The companies that chalk up such profits are mentioned by name, just as the companies that had made profits in Auschwitz had been mentioned in *The Investigation*. Those few names in *The Investigation* had caused a scandal that revealed to Weiss the agitational value of naming names. In *Lusitanian Bogey* the uncommented-upon enumeration of industrial corporations that participated in the plundering of the Portuguese colonies is turned into a formal element:

> For the Anglo-American Diamond Company
> For the Oppenheimer Group
> For Morgan
> For De Beers
> For Guggenheim
> For Ryan and the Forminiere
> For the Union Miniere du Haut-Katanga
> For the Guaranty Trust Bank (39).

(Such uncommented-upon lists of names will constitute a main narrative element in *The Aesthetics of Resistance*.) With these lists Weiss made good on one of the demands in his letter to Enzensberger, where he had encouraged West German authors to examine the extent to which their own country was involved in the exploitation of the Third World. In the letter Weiss had listed West German companies conducting business in South Africa.[14] As a further example of the *German* responsibility for plundering colonized countries, Weiss in his letter had mentioned a trip to Angola and Mozambique by cabinet minister Jaeger, at the time minister of justice and vice president of the Bundestag (Parliament) of the FRG. After his return Jaeger had promoted the idea that the term "foreign domination" was no longer appropriate for the Portuguese colonies and that Mozambique was an "island of peace" and the "race question was solved."[15] For Weiss, this passage in his letter to Enzensberger was not to be the end of this paradigmatic incident. In the ninth scene of *Lusitanian Bogey* Jaeger's trip is depicted in sentences lifted almost verbatim from the letter to Enzensberger.

The Angola play contains yet another concept Weiss had laid out in opposition to Enzensberger. Enzensberger had denied that solidarity with the colonized was possible, since no power of imagination could suffice to transpose oneself into the reality of these people. The play shows that Weiss had precisely this kind of imagination. In order to enable the spectators to experience the reality of the colonized, however, he had to ignore his own aesthetic concept according to which the figures onstage would not be individually drawn characters but would merely represent "ideas . . . , forces opposing one another" (G/R 123). In Scene 5 these "ideas" and historical "forces" are vividly brought to life through the fate of the Angolan maid, Ana: her life in a tin shack at the outskirts of the town of Nova Lisboa, her job with the white ruling class, her arrest after she dares contradict her employers, the beatings that cause her to abort in the sixth month of pregnancy, and her incarceration in an anonymous dungeon without hope of ever seeing her family again. This exemplary life brings home to white European and American theatergoers the daily realities of the life of the colonized.

Within the carefully balanced structure of *Song of the Lusitanian Bogey,* the figure Ana is the Angolan counterpart, even in name, of the Portuguese domestic, Juana, whose comparable existence is described in the first scene. The language of these two women is Brechtian in tone. Juana begins her tale with the words, "my job of work goes this way" (14); a linguistic *gestus* close to Brecht's "I have such a life" with which Puntila's three proletarian "brides" begin their life stories in *Herr Puntila and his Man Matti.*[16] The notion Enzensberger had rejected—solidarity with people that belong to a different class, a different culture—was indeed possible for Brecht as well as for Weiss. And it was also possible to transpose oneself into the reality of the other without being patronizing or overbearing, without any false closeness. Doing so, however, was not merely a question of empathy. It required an understanding of the human being as an "ensemble of social relations," as the young Karl Marx had formulated in the sixth thesis on Feuerbach.[17] Since *Marat/Sade* Weiss had been studying Marx's concept of "social relations." In Weiss's interest for Marx, too, there was now a closeness to Brecht.

In *Song of the Lusitanian Bogey* the only two individually drawn figures are again women. In *The Investigation* it had been a woman, Lili Tofler, whose individual fate had served as a focus for the horrors of Auschwitz. In Weiss's early writings up to *Vanishing Point* women had appeared primarily in obsessively erotic scenes or, as in *Das Duell,* in misogynist rape fantasies. *The Investigation,* however, revealed a new and different kind of heightened interest in women that is primarily concerned with their social situation.

In *Lusitanian Bogey* this interest is clearly signaled by the fact that the cast consists of more women than men (four women and three men). This was by no means self-evident, as only the names of *men* such as Agostinho Neto and Mario de Andrade and their counterparts Holden Roberto or Jonas Savimbi had become known from the war in Angola. The contribution of women to the liberation struggle had not drawn much attention from those who report or write history. Weiss counterbalanced the world of the men in various ways with the world of the women, most obviously in the scenes about Ana and Juana. He also created an archaic (and, seen from today, feminist) antiphony where the pains of childbirth are wished on men:

> *Chorus* The earth it rips open it tears open it heaves open
> 2 Let the men feel the pains of the women in labor
> *Chorus* The earth it rips open it tears open it heaves open
> 2 Let the men feel the pains of giving birth
> *Chorus* The earth it rips open it tears open it heaves open
> 2 Let the men feel the bloody giving of birth
> *Chorus* The earth it rips open it tears open it heaves open
> 2 Let [the men] be in labor and the fruit burst forth (16).

These lines convey still another aspect of Weiss's exploration of the other. Beyond the alien world (for male theatergoers) of the women this passage also conveys a sense of an alien culture. Such reminders of the "cultural other" are used sparingly in *Lusitanian Bogey,* as when the images of the "antelope man," "rabbit man," or "fieldmouse man" are evoked (28), or when the fantasies, born of the despair of the resistance fighters, suspend the laws of reality:

> I will laugh the bark off the trees
> I will swim straight up the waterfall
> I will dance the rocks to pieces
> I will sing the lion dead
> I will blow out the moon (46).

Such alien and poetic speech conjures up images of black African culture. A cautious attempt to suggest the "other," yet avoid the superficially exotic. In these passages the war of the African people against the colonial power Portugal is shown to be inseparably linked with their struggle to preserve their own culture.

Viet Nam Discourse

The Vietnam War began with the defeat of France, the colonial power, in the northwest Vietnamese settlement of Dien Bien Phu on 7 May 1954, and ended with the evacuation of the last members of the U.S. forces from the roof of the American embassy in Saigon on 30 April 1975.

In December 1960, at the end of Dwight Eisenhower's presidency, there were approximately 750 American "military advisers" in South Vietnam. At the time of John Kennedy's assassination on 22 November 1963 their numbers had increased to more than 16,000; at the peak of the American aggression, at the end of Lyndon B. Johnson's presidency in December 1968, there were 536,000 U.S. soldiers in Vietnam. The war ended during the term of President Gerald Ford, the successor to Richard Nixon (Nixon had been forced to resign in August 1974 due to the Watergate scandal). At the conclusion of the war, as is generally known, approximately 60,000 Americans had been killed and, as is generally less well known, approximately 2 million Vietnamese men, women, and children had also been killed.[18]

The Vietnam War was not only a trauma for those directly involved, the Vietnamese and the Americans, it affected and touched people all over the world. Its effect on many Europeans is comparable to the effect of the Spanish Civil War on an earlier generation. In the Federal Republic the Vietnam War, to use a turn of phrase of the early Karl Marx, forced the petrified conditions to dance. Conditions which, under federal chancellors Adenauer, Erhard, and, since November 1966, the former Nazi Kurt Georg Kiesinger, had successfully diverted West Germans from reflecting about the Second World War—from remembering and from mourning. People had been busy with the reconstruction of their lives and their country, with the economic miracle, and with anticommunism—all under the umbrella of an unquestioning and uncritical allegiance to the United States.

This state of affairs heavily influenced the attitude of the Federal Republic toward Vietnam, as Weiss bitterly noted, observing West Germany from his exile in Sweden. He pointed out that American claims about Vietnam, which no longer had any credibility even in the United States, were still believed in the Federal Republic in 1968 (G/R 143), where people were "pro-American and reactionary" and basically more American than the Americans (G/R 149). This careful observer of the political scene in the FRG also did not fail to notice that resistance was beginning to develop among the younger generation, students and pupils (G/R 147) who would trigger the 1968 movement within the following weeks and months. On the whole, however, the Federal Republic appeared to Weiss as a "morass" (G/R 147).

Weiss's polemical assessment of the political situation in West Germany provides the basis for an understanding of the form and content of *Viet Nam Discourse*. The dramatist was himself heavily involved in the debate over Vietnam. In April 1966 he had renounced his stance of noninvolvement in political struggles by publicly declaring his "empathy with the suppressed and exploited" during a Group 47 meeting at Princeton University.[19] The previous day he had participated in a Vietnam sit-in organized by students and professors—much to the irritation of colleagues like Günter Grass and Hans Werner Richter, who viewed such publicly demonstrated partisanship as an abuse of American hospitality (N I/491–92).

In the summer of 1966 Weiss published an article, "Vietnam!" in newspapers in Sweden and the GDR, documenting with facts and figures the increasing U.S. military involvement in South Vietnam and appealing for resistance against an America that "is continuing the tradition of Guernica, Lidice, and Maidanek among peoples of the 'third world.' "[20] At this time a "Song of the Devastators of Viet Nam" is mentioned in the notebooks (N I/519). The winter of 1966–67 was devoted mainly to working on this project, which was finished in late April 1967 and whose complete title is *Diskurs über die Vorgeschichte und den Verlauf des lang andauernden Befreiungskrieges in Viet Nam als Beispiel für die Notwendigkeit des bewaffneten Kampfes der Unterdrückten gegen ihre Unterdrücker sowie über die Versuche der Vereinigten Staaten von Amerika die Grundlagen der Revolution zu vernichten* (*Discourse on the Progress of the Prolonged War of Liberation in Viet Nam and the Events Leading up to It as Illustration of the Necessity for Armed Resistance against Oppression and on the Attempts of the United States of America to Destroy the Foundations of Revolution*). Its premiere took place in March 1968 in Frankfurt am Main.

The overly long title is program and polemic, indictment and condemnation. It formulates historical events and the protest against them; it encompasses the historically concrete as well as the general tendencies of the epoch. A title that is cumbersome and formless beyond all measure, thus drawing attention to the extraordinary efforts that had gone into finding an appropriate form not only for the title but for the play as well. The fact that Weiss had once before used an overly long title for his play about Marat and Sade does not sufficiently explain the title of the Vietnam play. As Brecht once noted, the key to understanding the choice of literary forms can be found in reality. In the mid-1960s reality was a rapidly expanding war in Southeast Asia that was played out daily in images of shocking immediacy on television screens. For someone who openly sided with the Vietnamese people, this reality tolerated no delay. American aggression had to be stopped immediately.

Viet Nam Discourse was conceived as a work that would intervene directly with reality. A concept that proved to be very difficult to execute and that inevitably had consequences for the form of the play. First, the urgency of events hardly permitted artistic elaboration. Secondly, the credo of bourgeois theater stipulates that art is unsuitable for direct intervention in political events and should not be used to this end. As a consequence, few artistic or literary tools had been developed for such a purpose. These difficulties led Weiss to an extreme solution. A few years after *Marat/Sade*, with its wealth of theatrical forms, and after the reduction of scenic means in *The Investigation* and of psychological means in *Song of the Lusitanian Bogey*, a radical aesthetic solution was found in *Viet Nam Discourse*. The play dispenses with all traditional means of the stage, with the creation of individual characters and plot, and with all theatrical opulence in set design, costumes, and props. If the text of *Lusitanian Bogey* was a kind of libretto for a music theater, *Viet Nam Discourse* reads like a blueprint for a sparse geometrical pantomime. Measured against the dramatic and technical means of the theater, there is an obvious impoverishment. The play about the Vietnam War is a Spartan "discourse" intended to convey facts; it is the prototype of the documentary theater of the 1960s and 1970s in the Federal Republic,[21] which to some extent includes Rolf Hochhuth's *The Deputy* (1963), and especially Heinar Kipphardt's *In the Matter of J. Robert Oppenheimer* (1964), Tankred Dorst's *Toller* (1968), Enzensberger's *The Havana Inquiry* of 1970, and Dieter Forte's *Martin Luther and Thomas Münzer* (1971).

Just like the two plays that preceded it, *Viet Nam Discourse* came out of Weiss's divine comedy project. The only reference to this origin that remains in the play, however, is the division (of each of its two parts) into eleven scenes, a structure that had already been used in *The Investigation* and *Song of the Lusitanian Bogey*. In *Viet Nam Discourse* these scenes are called "phases," a term associated with the natural sciences (phases of growth), with medicine (phases of a disease), but which a Marxist might also associate with Lenin's essay of 1916, "Imperialism as the Last Phase of Capitalism." It is in this latter sense that the term is used by Peter Weiss, whose knowledge of one of Lenin's best-known texts appears likely. The plan for the pacification of South Vietnam advocated by General Maxwell Taylor and Professor Eugene Staley in Phase 9 of the second half of the play (214)[22] illustrates in exemplary fashion Lenin's theses.

The play is divided into two parts. Part one renders the "Vorgeschichte" (prehistory—the word is omitted from the English version of the title) of the war of liberation, the more than 2,000-year history of Vietnam from 500 B.C. to late 1945. Part two presents the diplomatic intrigue of the imperialist powers and the increase in fighting from 1954 until 1964. Thus the play ends three years before the climax of the war.

Visually, the events onstage are organized according to their geographical locations. The foreword notes, "The figures move within the framework of the points of the compass," which largely correspond to the actual geography (68). For the spectator, upstage signifies north, downstage south, left signifies west and right is east. Weiss's painstaking adherence to the geographical reality holds great significance in a play that largely dispenses with concretization of events and individualization of characters. The high degree of abstraction in the form and content of *Viet Nam Discourse* creates a tendency toward idealist reflection removed from material reality. By dispensing with individually drawn figures, Weiss had foregone the possibility of presenting the historical process in terms of real individuals and their actual lives—"the world of bodies." The insistence on a depiction that was geographically as accurate as possible seems like a desperate attempt to try to anchor the play in material reality.

According to Weiss's aesthetic concept, the visual appearance of the figures is meant to signal that they are reduced to their historical function as "representatives of significant tendencies and interests" (67). They are mere embodiments of historical movements. The Vietnamese and Chinese wear "simple black costumes of uniform cut"; while the representatives of colonialism and imperialism, as well as Ngo Dinh Diem, their vassal in Saigon, wear identical white clothing (68). This division into black and white is the visual equivalent of Weiss's partisanship, a partisanship wherein "no conciliatory traits need be indicated in the aggressor, while full solidarity must be shown for the underdog," as Weiss had stated in his "Notes Towards a Definition of Documentary Theatre."[23] The dramatist considered objectivity as a barely veiled siding with the oppressor. Anyone insisting on objectivity would have to face the question of how, for instance, Auschwitz could be portrayed objectively (G/R 143). The vehemence of Weiss's arguments and the radicality of *Viet Nam Discourse* should be seen in their historical context. There was a war going on and the play was conceived as a weapon in that war. The operative effect of *Viet Nam Discourse* and its influence on the public debate about Vietnam in the FRG have been confirmed.[24]

As time goes by, however, the inadequacies of Weiss's black and white picture are becoming more apparent. Weiss himself found it necessary to insist that in no way should racial identities be suggested by the black and white costumes, that his concern was solely with the distinction between the oppressor and the oppressed, with "class differences" (G/R 137). Nevertheless, it remains unclear why, for instance, the *Chinese* colonialists are also dressed in black (70) while the *Japanese* conquerors, just like the Europeans and Americans, appear in white clothing (136). What kind of differences between Chinese and Japanese oppressors were to be expressed here? The *Vietnamese* rulers, such as the emperor Le Loi, the princes Trinh and Nguyen, and the emperor, Hue, also wear black clothing. Yet the play leaves no doubt that they exploit their own people—just like the foreign conquerors. Also, Ngo Dinh Diem, the dictatorial South Vietnamese ruler sponsored by the United States, is dressed in white, and rightly identified as an exploiter and oppressor. Diem and his clan embody a type of home-grown vassal government that often develops in Third World countries with the transition from colonialism to imperialism. (Other representatives of this type mentioned in the play are Syngman Rhee [South Korea], Ramón Magsaysay [Philippines], and Chiang Kai-shek [Taiwan]). The puppet character of such regimes is convincingly conveyed in the barely hidden disdain with which Diem is greeted on the occasion of his visit to New York. Without any attempt at diplomatic language, U.S. Secretary of State Dulles describes how vassal governments such as Diem's are used:

> It is up to us
> to see that governments are formed
> which when necessary
> will ask our help
> in preserving their neutrality (172).

These governments, made up of members of the small ruling oligarchies, were eventually assigned military control over their countries by the colonial powers. This changed little in the economic exploitation of the population of these countries. Nonetheless, the transference of power to the local upper classes is an important step along the route of Third World people toward self-determination. For the interests of these vassals—from Ngo Dinh Diem to the Panamanian General Noriega, who was arrested in 1990 by his own protector, the United States—are often to varying degrees in conflict with the imperialist powers who sponsor them. Diem, like many historical figures of his ilk, was a nationalist, and just as vigorously as he conducted the brutal repression of the Vietnamese socialist movement (the Viet Cong), he also pursued his country's independence from European and American imperialism.[25] This kind of complex and contradictory reality could not be conveyed in the black and white aesthetics of *Viet Nam Discourse.*

As these observations about the costumes show, Weiss's formal concept had consequences for the representation of history in *Viet Nam Discourse.* Where there had been progress, even along a meandering route, Weiss's play posits an image of an eternal return of the same:

> So it was in the year of the dragon
> So it was in the year of the serpent
> So it is now in the year of the rainbow (97).

This concept of history is reinforced by expressions such as "Again and again they rose up" (146), and the result of these uprisings, too, appears as an eternal repetition, "All that changed in thousands of years were / the names of the rulers" (146).

These passages in *Viet Nam Discourse* express a sense of fatalism about history that probably no effort by a director can overcome. The dialectical movement of history, which Weiss took such pains to bring to the stage, appears frozen. Millennia of history are reduced to nothing more than "prehistory," as the German title of the play suggests. It ends only with the fall of the monarchy "which had flourished / for thousands of years" (145). But the fall of the monarchy, as we now know, no more put an end to Vietnamese "prehistory" than did the withdrawal of the last Americans in 1975, or the withdrawal of Vietnamese troops from Cambodia at the beginning of the 1990s. The notion of historical events of the past as a "prehistory" implies a teleological goal toward which historical developments are moving, and this goal is usually the present, which consequently appears as the end and climax of history. (Already in Marx there is a reference to the "prehistory" of human society, the end of which coincides with the end of antagonistic social formations. To the extent that Marx regarded all history up to that utopian moment as prehistory, his concept needs to be critiqued.[26])

In Weiss's play the stage figures are conceived as "bearers of important tendencies and interests." While such a dramatic concept may appear impoverished in terms of the prevalent theater aesthetics of individually drawn figures, it allows the masses to appear as the subject of history. In the first part of *Viet Nam Discourse* the Vietnamese people are seen as making their own history. The individuals who rule them emerge from the people and even in their antagonism remain dialectically connected to them. That changes, however, in the second part of the play. The events of Stages 1–4 take place exclusively at the highest imperial level, at the level of the American president and the English prime minister and their closest advisers. Eisenhower, Dulles, Churchill, and Eden: *their* wishes and *their* goals, *their* arrogance, *their* greed for power, *their* avarice, and *their* unswerving anticommunism appear as the main force that determines the course of history. The American *people* in their material reality and real needs never appear as a major factor in the Vietnam War. Thus, the behavior of the United States toward Vietnam and other parts of the Third World seems largely determined by the will of a few powerful white males and their ideology. An ideology epitomized by the "domino theory" of the time, which held that a communist takeover in any one country would inevitably cause all the other countries of a region to fall to communism like dominoes. In the words of Secretary of State Dulles:

> If Vietnam falls
> Laos and Cambodia
> will also collapse
> We should lose
> Thailand Burma and Formosa
> and be forced back on Hawaii (150–51).

Against such an occurrence the great white men—women are not represented at this level of power—posit the concept of *containment*. The countries of the Third World, from Southeast Asia to the eastern borders of Europe, are to become U.S. client states, the strategy being "to build a chain of bases / around the Russia-China block" (150–51). Here, historically altogether fitting, the Vietnam War appears as an outgrowth of anticommunist hysteria. But where did this hysteria originate? As he had done in *The Investigation* and *Song of the Lusitanian Bogey*, Weiss points to the close links of the men of power with big business, and, once again, that proves revealing (161 ff.).

But Weiss has also been justly criticized for his caricature-like portrayal of the representatives of the highest levels of power, which does not go much beyond ascertaining their greed and lust for power.[27] Weiss's documentary theater had been intended to disseminate objective facts and it does so in *Viet Nam Discourse*, not least by using actual speeches and statements by leading politicians and military men of the United States and Great Britain. But this factual aspect of the play is at times overshadowed by the evil buffoons who appear to be determining the course of history. Weiss's insights into the systems of fascism (*The Investigation*) and of colonialism (*The Lusitanian Bogey*) are not matched in *Viet Nam Discourse* by a comparable analysis of postcolonialist imperialism.

Viet Nam Discourse was written in a time of intense struggle and its purpose was to intervene in this struggle. The shortcomings of the play, as attempted to be shown here, cannot be explained solely on the basis of Weiss's dramatic or ideological shortcomings. He did not have the leisure and distance that would have made possible a unified and well-rounded work of art. Among works of art, however, it is not just the ones that are unified and well-rounded that merit attention.

The Vietnam War left a profound imprint on the German cultural scene of the 1960s and 1970s (and directly gave rise to the student revolts of that period). One of the most important literary texts about Vietnam was Erich Fried's collection of poems, *und VIETNAM und*. Fried was Austrian and, like Weiss, of Jewish origin and a Marxist. He, too, had had to leave his homeland as a young man and, like his friend Weiss, had remained in permanent exile (in England). Another important text about Vietnam was also written in exile, even though not in antifascist exile; Uwe Johnson (1934–84), born in the GDR, had left his country when he was twenty-five years old, and subsequently lived in the Federal Republic, Italy, the United States, and England. Johnson, ideologically distant from Peter Weiss, also preserved the outrage and pain so many people felt about the U.S. war against Vietnam in his monumental novel *Jahrestage* (four volumes, 1970, 1971, 1973, and 1983).

For Peter Weiss his *Viet Nam Discourse* marked not the end but the beginning of a lasting commitment to the liberation struggle of the Vietnamese people. Scarcely a week after he finished the play, the dramatist took part in the Vietnam tribunal organized by the philosophers Bertrand Russell and Jean-Paul Sartre (2–10 May 1967; a second meeting took place 20 November–1 December 1967 in the Danish town of Roskilde).[28] From that time on, as the notebooks show, there was no period in Weiss's life when he was not intensely involved with events in Southeast Asia. From 15 May–21 June 1968, at the height of the American bombardments, he and his wife traveled to North Vietnam. Weiss later documented this trip in essays, journalistic reports, and interviews.[29]

With the official end of the Vietnam War in 1975, nothing was resolved for Weiss. Three years later he noted with bitterness, "The agitation against Vietnam continues."[30] He was referring to reactions to the conflict with the Khmer Rouge regime of Pol Pot in Cambodia, in which Vietnam, devastated and impoverished, was now involved. Many of those who had until then supported the Vietnamese struggle for liberation found themselves in an untenable position. The Vietnam movement disintegrated. Weiss, however, did not desist from his commitment, as numerous notations and newspaper articles attest (many of them are reprinted in the notebooks). After his trip there was no longer merely a political but also an emotional attachment to embattled Vietnam. Weiss acknowledged and validated this emotional tie. In a notation on 8 August 1978 he opposes the separation of politics from feelings. The notation concludes with words that today can be read as an epitaph to the Vietnam War: "At the thought of the faces of people we met in Vietnam, at the thought of the history and culture of this country, at the thought of the people's spiritual strength in the most extreme struggle, I can only view the present events there [Vietnam's intervention in Cambodia] with a trust which probably contradicts the cold and cynical judgment common in political life but which—if we want to avoid suspending humanity altogether—in this instance is appropriate" (N II/739).

NOTES

1. Oliver Clausen, "Weiss/Propagandist and Weiss/Playwright," *The New York Times Magazine* 2 October 1966: 132 (the interview was conducted in English in Stockholm).

2. Hans Magnus Enzensberger, "Europäische Peripherie," *Kursbuch* 2 (August 1965): 154–73.

3. See Peter Weiss, "Brief an H. M. Enzensberger" (1965), in Weiss, *Rapporte 2* (Frankfurt/Main: Suhrkamp, 1971) 35–44. (Originally published as "Enzensbergers Illusionen," *Kursbuch* 6 (July 1966): 165–70.) Concerning Weiss's dispute with Enzensberger see also David Bathrick, in his interpretation of *Song of the Lusitanian Bogey,* " 'The Theater of the White Revolution Is Over': The Third World in the Works of Peter Weiss and Heiner Müller," in Reinhold Grimm and Jost Hermand, eds., *Blacks and German Culture* (Madison: University of Wisconsin Press, 1986) 135–49.

4. Peter Weiss, "Antwort auf einen Offenen Brief von Wilhelm Girnus an den Autor in der Zeitung 'Neues Deutschland' " (1965), in Weiss, *Rapporte 2* 34.

5. See Rüdiger Sareika, "Peter Weiss' Engagement für die 'Dritte Welt.' 'Lusitanischer Popanz' und 'Viet Nam Diskurs,' " in Rainer Gerlach, ed., *Peter Weiss* (Frankfurt/Main: Suhrkamp, 1984) 256.

6. See Manfred Haiduk, "Peter Weiss' 'Gesang vom lusitanischen Popanz' " (1967), in Peter Weiss, *Gesang vom lusitanischen Popanz. Mit Materialien* (Frankfurt/Main: Suhrkamp, 1974) 79.

7. Henning Rischbieter, " 'Gesang vom lusitanischen Popanz' " (1967), in Volker Canaris, ed., *Über Peter Weiss* (Frankfurt/Main: Suhrkamp, 4th ed., 1976) 97, 104.

8. Manfred Haiduk, "Faschismuskritik als Imperialismuskritik im Werk von Peter Weiss. Thesenhafte Bemerkungen zu einem Forschungsgegenstand," in Jens Peter Lund Nielsen et al., eds., *Antifaschismus in deutscher und skandinavischer Literatur* (Aarhus: Arkona, 1983) 134.

9. Parenthetical page numbers refer to Peter Weiss, *Song of the Lusitanian Bogey* (*Gesang vom lusitanischen Popanz*, 1967), trans. Lee Baxandall. Weiss, *Two Plays* (New York: Atheneum, 1970).

10. For an account of the history of Angola, the takeover by Diego Cão, and especially the struggle for independence from 1961 to the beginning of the 1980s, see Jean Ziegler, "Staatslogik gegen Klassenlogik," in Ziegler, *Gegen die Ordnung der Welt. Befreiungsbewegungen in Afrika und Lateinamerika* (*Les Rebelles / Contre l'ordre du monde*, 1983), trans. Elke Hammer (Wuppertal: Hammer, 2d ed., 1986) 263–322.

11. See Peter Weiss, *The Investigation* (*Die Ermittlung*, 1964), trans. Jon Swan and Ulu Grosbard (New York: Atheneum, 1966) 216ff.

12. See Frantz Fanon, *Die Verdammten dieser Erde* (*Les damnés de la terre*, 1961), trans. Traugott König (Frankfurt/Main: Suhrkamp, 1981). Concerning the "animalization" of colonized peoples by colonists, see 35.

13. See Weiss, "Brief an H. M. Enzensberger" 35; see also N I/429, 501, 594, 613.

14. See Weiss, "Brief an H. M. Enzensberger" 41.

15. Weiss, "Brief an H. M. Enzensberger" 43.

16. Bertolt Brecht, *Herr Puntila und sein Knecht Matti* (1940), in Brecht, *Werke,* annotated Berlin and Frankfurt edition (Frankfurt/Main: Suhrkamp, 1989) 6:301.

17. Karl Marx, "Thesen über Feuerbach" (1845), in *Marx Engels Werke* (Berlin: Dietz, 1956–) 3:6.

18. Unless otherwise indicated, information about the Vietnam War comes from the book by James S. Olson and Randy Roberts, *Where the Domino Fell. America and Vietnam, 1945 to 1990* (New York: St. Martin's, 1991).

19. Peter Weiss, "I Come Out of My Hiding Place" (written by Weiss in English), *The Nation* 30 May 1966: 652, 655.

20. Peter Weiss, "Vietnam!" (2 August 1966), in Weiss, *Rapporte 2* 61.

21. See Peter Weiss, "The Material and the Models. Notes Towards a Definition of Documentary Theatre" ("Notizen zum dokumentarischen Theater," 1968), trans. Heinz Bernard, *Theatre Quarterly* 1, no. 1 (January–March 1971): 41–43.

22. Page numbers in parentheses refer to Peter Weiss, *Discourse on the Progress of the Prolonged War of Liberation in Viet Nam and the Events Leading up to It as Illustration of the Necessity for Armed Resistance against Oppression and on the Attempts of the United States of America to Destroy the Foundations of the Revolution* (1968), trans. Geoffrey Skelton, in Weiss, *Two Plays* (New York: Atheneum, 1970).

23. Weiss, "The Material and the Models" 42.

24. See Manfred Haiduk, *Der Dramatiker Peter Weiss* (East Berlin: Henschelverlag, 1977) 192.

25. On Diem, see Olson and Roberts 60ff.

26. Karl Marx, "Zur Kritik der politischen Ökonomie. Vorwort," in *Marx Engels Werke* 13:9.

27. See Bernd Jürgen Warneken, "Kritik am 'Viet Nam Diskurs' " (1970), in Volker Canaris, ed., *Über Peter Weiss* (Frankfurt/Main: Suhrkamp, 4th ed., 1976) 121.

28. On the Russell Tribunal, see John Duffett, ed., *Against the Crime of Silence. Proceedings of the Russell International War Crimes Tribunal* (New York: O'Hare Books, 1968). See also the book edited by Peter Weiss in collaboration with Peter Limqueco, *Prevent the Crime of Silence. Reports from the Sessions of the International War Crimes Tribunal Founded by Bertrand Russell* (London, 1971).

29. See G/R 239–42. In the footnotes to the various conversations about Vietnam there are further references to Weiss's publications.

30. See Peter Weiss, "Die Hetze gegen Vietnam geht weiter," *Deutsche Volkszeitung* 50 (14 December 1978).

CHAPTER SEVEN

Intellectuals and Artists in the Revolution

The literary career of Peter Weiss reveals the contradictions of a socialist writer, and an internationally successful one at that, in bourgeois-capitalist society. His works are good business, so business is done; the culture industry celebrates him—and then again it does not. In 1963 Peter Weiss had been awarded the Charles Veillon literary prize by the Swiss city of Lausanne, and in 1965 he was awarded the Lessing Prize. He also received literary awards in Sweden. In 1966 he was awarded the Heinrich Mann Prize of the German Democratic Republic. This honor resulted in his not receiving any other awards in the Federal Republic for ten years: until he was honored with the Thomas Dehler Prize in 1978. He was now prominent, yet increasingly shunned, as he did not hesitate to take a public stand on controversial issues. Following the Six-Day War in 1967 between Israel and its neighboring countries the author of *The Investigation* accused the Israeli government and army of having assumed the "mentality of a master race" toward the Arab population.[1] In a public letter to the Czechoslovakian writers' association, Weiss, who always emphasized his solidarity with the socialist countries, criticized the lack of free speech. Not mincing his words, he rejected the "choking off" of much needed cultural debates "through Stalinism."[2] Little liked or trusted by the powers that be, both in capitalist and in socialist countries, Weiss never desisted from speaking out against them. It was a difficult position.

A few weeks after the Vietnam tribunal in Stockholm, Weiss and Gunilla Palmstierna-Weiss visited Cuba, 16 July–20 August 1967. Weiss was overwhelmed by the contrast between revolutionary Cuba and those Central American "banana republics" he had studied while working on *Song of the Lusitanian Bogey* (N I/548). He discussed *Marat/Sade* with Fidel Castro; a planned meeting with Che Guevara (1928–67) did not take place, as the physician and revolutionary was in Bolivia.

That summer, 1967, in Sweden, Weiss's thoughts continued to revolve around the Third World, which, he maintained, should be called the first world, as it was where the forces of change and the future could be found.[3] The Third World increasingly became the focus of the West German New Left. That same summer of 1967 in West Berlin thousands took to the streets in opposition to the visit by the shah of Iran who, with the support of his secret police and capitalist countries, was plundering and terrorizing his own people. In clashes with the police, the student Benno Ohnesorg was shot and killed. The incident gave rise to the student movement of 1968, whose long march through the institutions would lead to profound changes in West German society.

Another death occurred during this time: in October 1967 Che Guevara was murdered by the Bolivian army. More than Mao Tse-tung, Ho Chi Minh, or the North Vietnamese General Giap, Guevara had become a role model for student activists in the Federal Republic and elsewhere. From him one had learned that the fight against the exploitation of the Third World had to be brought to the first world. Peter Weiss, living in exile in Sweden and belonging to a different generation, expressed in words what so many, primarily younger people in the Federal Republic, felt about the death of Guevara: "When we heard about Che's death, our first thought was: had he to die just now, when he was needed more than ever?" (N I/555).

In November 1967 Weiss took part in the second meeting of the Vietnam tribunal, in the Danish town of Roskilde. On 17 February 1968, along with the student leader Rudi Dutschke (1940–79), the Austrian poet Erich Fried, who was living in exile in England, the philosopher Günther Anders, and the Belgian Trotskyite Ernest Mandel, Weiss spoke at a Vietnam congress in West Berlin. The premiere of *Viet Nam Discourse* took place in March. In April Dutschke was wounded in an assassination attempt, the long-term consequences of which eventually caused his death. That same year Martin Luther King, Jr., and Robert Kennedy were murdered: an obliteration of bearers of hope for millions of people. On 15 May Peter Weiss and Gunilla Palmstierna-Weiss arrived for a several-week stay in North Vietnam, a country devastated by U.S. bombing raids. The following day the premiere of a new play by Weiss took place in the Landestheater of Hanover: *Wie dem Herrn Mockinpott das Leiden ausgetrieben wird* (*How Mr. Mockinpott Was Cured of His Sufferings*), a grotesque comedy, a slapstick blend of Chaplin and the Marx brothers.

How Mr. Mockinpott Was Cured of His Sufferings

The new play appears as a complete turnaround from Weiss's writings of that time. After *Viet Nam Discourse* and the polemical essays on Israel and Che Guevara, now came the playfulness of a Punch and Judy show. Was this a relapse into prepolitical artistic praxis or a return to the true world of the artist Weiss? An artistic oeuvre does not develop in a linear way, its nature is not continuity or a logical development toward a goal known in advance. It is not what has just been completed that determines the next work but desire for the new, for change, for experiment.

Weiss had written most of the play about Mr. Mockinpott's sufferings in 1963, that same productive year during which he had already created *Night with Guests* and a first version of *Marat/Sade*. Now, four years later, a much changed Peter Weiss decided to complete this work.

Up to the events depicted in *How Mr. Mockinpott Was Cured of His Sufferings*, the title character had been a minor employee whose activity consisted solely in verifying the contents of crates on the basis of certificates. After work he used to sit in his easy chair in his cozy home and, by the light of the lamp, read the newspaper aloud to his wife. For no apparent reason he is one day arrested, and at the beginning of the play he is in jail. In order to get out he must bribe lawyers and officials, and he thus loses all his savings. On the street Mockinpott encounters one Jack Pudding (Hans Wurst), who becomes his companion. His wife, meanwhile, has taken a lover and throws Mockinpott out of the house. His employer pretends not to recognize him, and Mockinpott's job has been given to someone else. At the doctor's office Mockinpott's skull is opened up and treated; and his heart, which has fallen into his pants, is again implanted in the right place. Not knowing where to turn, Mockinpott goes to the government, which turns him away with bland banalities. Finally, he encounters the good Lord, who lacks any insight into the causes of Mockinpott's sufferings. Mockinpott recognizes that he must take his fate into his own hands, that only he can bring about his liberation.

The original impetus for this play about the sufferings of the petit bourgeoisie clearly came once again from Weiss's own life and his continuing need for (self-)liberation from enduring constraints. But rather than as introspection, the eleven scenes succeed through their playful and imaginative use of theatrical elements and through their creative answers to some of Weiss's artistic influences, such as Kafka, Beckett, and even Goethe's *Faust*. As in *Night with Guests*, Weiss uses elements of the Punch and Judy show and the farce and of folk theater with stiff doggerel. And, as in the early play *Die Versicherung* (The Insurance, 1952), the abundance of theatrical means serves to expose to satirical laughter the pillars of society, the magistrate, the employer, the doctor, and ultimately the good Lord.

The opening scene recalls the beginning of Kafka's *The Trial:* Mockinpott is arrested without being aware of any guilt, and no guilt is ever proven. The similarity to Beckett's *Waiting for Godot* extends into the details of the characters and the action: Mockinpott and Pudding appear as variants of Vladimir and Estragon, particularly in Mockinpott's pantomime with his shoes, a kind of running gag that continues throughout the play. The end of the play seems like a reversal of the ending of *Waiting for Godot*. In Beckett's play Godot will never arrive, and waiting for him becomes an image of existential hopelessness and abandonment. In earlier works Weiss had already created his own response to Beckett's ending. In *The Shadow of the Coachman's Body*, as well as in the play *Die Versicherung,* his characters do not wait entirely in vain. The coachman and the anarchist revolutionary Leo may be lightweight, secular, and ersatz-redeemer figures with nowhere near the mystical power of Godot, but at least they show up. A messianic bearer of hope is also mentioned in *Night with Guests,* but the "red" Peter Wright never appears onstage. In *Mockinpott* Peter Weiss brings the good Lord himself onstage: a capitalist wearing a fur coat and top hat, puffing on a fat cigar, and addressed by Pudding as "Mr. Manager" (208).[4] This manager has lost control over his business and he is no longer able to track profits and expenses, investments and bribe money. He is as little able to answer Pudding's casuistic question, "How many choirs of angels have you on balance" (208), as Mockinpott's sly "why if things are / they are as they are / and how it would be / if they were arranged differently" (207). Crushed, the good Lord leaves the scene; evidently redemption is not his domain. Mockinpott has to provide his own answer:

> I once thought that sufferings had their reward
> in heaven but I see now my good Lord
> that injustices when they befall
> the likes of us mean nothing to you at all
> but I can tell you and I hope I'm understood
> I've done with the swindle now for good (210).

He takes his fate in his own hands. The shoes that he has been wearing on the wrong feet since the second scene he now puts on properly and walks off cheerfully. This outcome of the play was signaled from the beginning by the name Mockinpott. The repeated mispronunciations of this name inevitably lead to that point at the end of the play where the good Lord by mistake calls the ill-treated little man "Hopping*god*" (209, emphasis added).

Undoubtedly, in the course of the play Mockinpott comes increasingly closer to understanding the "riddle of the universe" (198). From the beginning that had been the goal of his Faustian quest: "how it all ties up I'd like to know / and find an end to my tale of woe'' (174), and later, ''Oh the in-justice in this world . . . / I wish I knew what it all meant'' (181). Already for Goethe's Faust the answer lay in this world, in the active life. With Peter Weiss the answer is given a Marxist-materialist slant: Mockinpott's sufferings are directly related to the fact that he has no money (189) and has lost his job to someone else. Whereupon Pudding slyly comments, ''Clearly it can't have been *your* job in any case / if there's another man now filling your place'' (189, original emphasis). Thus, Mockinpott learns who really owns his job. Finally, a government official enlightens him on what really holds the world together at its core: ''Again and again we make a point of it / that nothing is more important than profit'' (201).

Is this a mere harlequinade? On closer inspection, the seemingly crude play about Mockinpott and Jack Pudding proves to be a workable concept, equally suited for a response to literary works and experimenting with the-atrical forms as for a critique of capitalism. That may be what prompted Peter Weiss, more than four years after its inception, to complete this play. Ap-parently, for the dramatist all that was necessary was to slightly strengthen the social criticism; otherwise the original version remained unchanged. But the rough-hewn design of the characters and events also place limits on *Mock-inpott*. Critics rightly pointed out that the play provides no analysis for social conditions, that it does not present causes but only effects.[5] What may remain of this play has been accurately formulated by Manfred Karnick: a ''delight-ful theatrical joke . . . with a deeper meaning which is at the same time de-structively revealing and constructively innovative.''[6]

Trotsky in Exile

Not until eight years after its premiere in the West German city of Hanover did *Mockinpott* have its first performance in the GDR, in Rostock, in No-vember 1976, which is surprising, for since the advent of *Marat/Sade*, Weiss's plays were usually presented in the GDR simultaneously with the Federal Republic. In the German Democratic Republic Weiss was considered an important socialist author, and his works were promoted there, especially at the Volkstheater in Rostock. The director, Hanns Anselm Perten, and his staff had created productions significantly different from those in the Federal Republic, and these stagings had an important influence on Weiss's artistic as well as his ideological development. But Weiss was also aware of the fra-gility of his position in the GDR. That same year, 1968, when he publicly committed himself to communism by joining the Communist Party of Sweden (VPK), there is yet another passage in the notebooks about the lack of free speech in the GDR, where, Weiss felt, he could speak openly only with "Christa [Wolf] and Stephan [Hermlin]." Weiss adds, "If I lived here [in the GDR], I would long have been caught between a rock and a hard place" (N I/577). This is precisely what was to happen to him with his next work.

On 21 August 1968 troops of the Warsaw Pact countries, under the leadership of the Soviet Union, invaded Czechoslovakia. They crushed the attempt that had begun a few months earlier by party secretary Alexander Dubček and other Czech communists to reform socialism. The very next day a protest by Weiss was published in the Swedish daily newspaper, *Dagens Nyheter*. The man who had so vehemently rejected the brutal suppression of Vietnamese self-determination by the United States now turned just as vehemently against the use of force by the USSR. In debates, newspaper articles, and radio interviews Weiss made his protest public.[7] It must have become clear to him, though, that public statements and journalistic interventions were not enough; the events in Czechoslovakia demanded a more profound analysis of the Stalinist deformation of socialism.

As always in that period of his life, when Peter Weiss attempted to give literary form to an idea, he returned to his divine comedy project. Purgatory was now to be the realm wherein socialism would be depicted, with its *"contradictions"* and *"stagnations"* ranging from the positions of Stalin and Trotsky to the "occupation of the CSSR" (N I/598, original emphasis). Once again, Weiss was unable to construct a work in the manner of Dante's epic poem, but once again this effort eventually yielded the solution. In December 1968 Weiss started work on a play whose title had already been determined: *Trotzki im Exil (Trotsky in Exile)*. Nine months earlier, in March 1968, Weiss's most important theoretical essay on the theater had been published: the politically outspoken "Notes Towards a Definition of Documentary Theatre."[8] This text turned out to be not so much a program for the future than an artistic accounting for Weiss's work of the past years. He now began to turn away from some of the more rigid concepts of the documentary theater. In the new play (as well as in the one that followed it) there is again a plot, there are again individually drawn characters, and there is again an individual hero.

Lev Davidovich Bronstein (1879–1940), writer and revolutionary, son of a Jewish peasant from Ukraine, had decided in 1902 to call himself Trotsky. At times an opponent of Lenin (1870–1924), but after October 1917 Lenin's closest ally and the founder of the Red Army, Trotsky became after Lenin's death an embittered opponent of Stalin (1879–1953). He was forced into exile by Stalin in 1928 and murdered in Mexico in 1940 at the Soviet dictator's behest. But that was not enough for Stalin; Trotsky's entire family, into the third generation, was eliminated and Trotsky's name was expunged from Soviet historiography. He had never existed. This manipulation of history did not change, even after Khrushchev's famous secret address at the 1956 party congress in which Stalin's crimes were officially acknowledged.

This distortion, suppression, and denial of reality in socialist countries seemed to Weiss contrary to the thinking of Marx and Lenin.[9] The new play was intended to reverse this process of lies and distortions. The time had come, or so thought Weiss. The countries of the Eastern bloc were preparing to celebrate the one-hundredth anniversary of Lenin's birth. It was, the dramatist decided, a chance to restore just historical proportions, especially as Weiss's new play was not intended in any way to be anti-Soviet or anticommunist but only anti-Stalinist. In July 1969 Weiss was still confident that *Trotsky in Exile* would be performed in the Soviet Union and the GDR (G/R 181–82). A short time later, however—copies of the not yet published manuscript had just been sent to various theaters—Weiss noted in his notebooks: "Vehement reactions from Rostock. Telegram: how could I carry out anti-Soviet agitation and spread Trotskyite ideology in the year of Lenin's anniversary. . . . The rupture is beginning" (N I/655–56).

The play that brought about this rupture resembles a "station drama" in the tradition that leads from Baroque theater to German expressionism. In two acts and fifteen scenes, events from Trotsky's life are recreated onstage, starting with his first banishment, under the reign of the czar, to the Siberian town of Verkholensk in 1901, and ending with his assassination in Coyoacán, a suburb of Mexico City. These stations, however, are not presented chronologically but from a historical moment that is understood as a turning point in the title character's biography. *Trotsky in Exile* begins on 16 January 1928, the day of the final break between Stalin and Trotsky. On this date Trotsky was banished to Alma-Ata, a city in central Asia. Twelve months later he was forced to leave the Soviet Union. There followed stations of exile in Turkey, France, Norway, and, finally, Mexico. From the date of 16 January 1928— the present time of the play—the stations of Trotsky's life are presented in flashbacks. But time also moves forward in the present time, from January 1928 to August 1940; thus, the flashbacks occur at different moments during Trotsky's exile odyssey. This progression of time on two levels develops an inexorable movement toward a third time level: the present time of the author—with its worldwide student revolts and its anticolonialist struggles in Third World countries. Critics in the East and in the West, focusing on the political provocation of the play, have hardly taken note of this complex structure of *Trotsky in Exile*. During the ensuing debates over the play's content and ideological tendency, its form was, at best, dispatched in passing remarks: "quick and facile montage," "conventional historical drama," and a "thoroughly conventional concept of reality and truth."[10] But it is precisely this "truth" of *Trotsky in Exile* that cannot be understood without an appreciation of the play's complex aesthetics.

This is underscored by the efforts of some critics to map out the temporal and spatial structure of the play. A helpful endeavor, for those unfamiliar with the historical events will not easily find their way through *Trotsky in Exile*. But these efforts at shedding light on the play's structure only tended to strengthen the impression that *Trotsky in Exile* might be nothing more than artfully constructed historiography. An impression that, in the course of the work, is progressively undermined, for instance, when Trotsky says to the dying Lenin, "When you died, all that remained was the struggle for power" (86).[11] How could Trotsky know that at this time? How can he use the past tense in speaking to Lenin who is still alive? In scene 13, Trotsky, in exile in Norway (June 1935 to late 1936), is visited by a physician. Then, in a thoroughly filmic process, the scene shifts from Norway to the Moscow show trials. The three historic trials in which most of the closest collaborators of Lenin were sentenced to death (and subsequently executed) by Stalin's court took place in 1936, 1937, and 1938. In *Trotsky in Exile* they are merged into one single trial, which in the temporal structure of the play appears not as a flashback but rather as a kind of flash-forward to that future moment when Trotsky would learn about the trial. But this interpretation of the temporal sequence cannot be maintained, for at the end of the scene Trotsky is still standing in his home in Norway, shirt in hand, the way the physician had left him. Moreover, in the middle of the Moscow legal proceedings, Trotsky (in Norway) leaps up and refutes the defamations made against him in Moscow without having his interjections noticed by the trial participants. This leads one to assume that Trotsky's impassioned speeches take place only in his imagination. But how could Trotsky in 1936 possibly know about the show trials when they had not yet begun? The time continuum as well as the geographical logic of the plot, already veiled by the structure of the play, tend toward dissolution. This is made clear in the same scene when Trotsky, contradicting the accused, Pyatakov, asserts, "I live two hours away from Oslo, not thirty minutes" (107). The present tense clearly refers to the years 1935–36. At the time when Pyatakov appeared before Stalin's court (late January 1937), however, Trotsky was already living in Mexico.

Such obvious disregard for the time-space continuum indicates a logic different from that of historiography. Here artistic or, more accurately, dramatic necessities determine the sequence of events. At the emotional climax of the play when, in the show trials, that moment has been reached when all the lies, distortions, and defamations about him are being broadcast to the world, Trotsky, contrary to all historic reality, had to be given the opportunity to defend himself and to refute his accusers, to posit *his* truth against what was, in the communist world, to become the historic canon.

Trotsky in Exile presents an important period in the communist movement, but not according to the rules of the science of history—not objectively; rather, according to the rules of art, subjectively. This is signaled in a subtle way right at the beginning: "Trotsky, seated at the desk, is reading a manuscript, pen in hand" (11). This scene is repeated several times (14, 35), and the plays ends with it (122). Occasionally, the title figure is called by his nickname, "the pen" (20), the alias under which the historical Trotsky published articles. At one point a fellow prisoner deprecatingly says to Trotsky and his friends, "You're still literati" (16).[12] The pejorative undertone notwithstanding, that is what Trotsky undoubtedly was; and the many thousands of pages of his works attest to it. Trotsky the author was prevented by the revolution from his real calling, from his literary and theoretical work:

As if the battle of ideas were more important to me than revolutionary activity. The writing, the printed impression of my thoughts more real than the actions outside. (35)

Weiss had long been interested in this type of character, the Sade type (also the Hölderlin type, as will be shown), who prefers to work out social contradictions in literature rather than in reality—for example, by writing a play about the assassination of Marat. *Trotsky in Exile* is, in fact, in several ways a continuation of *Marat/Sade*. Both plays deal with revolutions: *Marat/Sade* with the bourgeois, *Trotsky in Exile* with the socialist revolution. Both plays have writers as principal protagonists and both end with the murder (of one) of the protagonists. Both plays aim to correct the lies that later were disseminated about the revolutionaries by those who had carried the revolutions: by the bourgeoisie about Marat and by socialists about Trotsky (N I/696). Both plays deal with attempts by their protagonists to work out through dialogue their place in the ongoing class struggles: Sade in his disputes with Marat, Trotsky in his discussions with Lenin (and all of them serve Peter Weiss in trying to find *his* place within the struggles of his own time). There is one other compelling analogy: just as the play about the assassination of Marat takes place in Sade's head, *Trotsky in Exile* takes place in Trotsky's head.

The play, as Weiss noted in the notebooks, arises "from the interior monologue of someone condemned to exile" (N I/718). The someone, of course, being Trotsky, but probably also the author of the Trotsky play, who was himself in exile since 1934. *Trotsky in Exile* is "a structure made up of recollections, surveys, fragments of conversations, of figures appearing and disappearing, reflections of historical situations, references to decisive events and passionate disputes, it is a fabric easily torn, subjected to sudden vacillations and leaps, *more dream than reality*" (N I/717–18, emphasis added). Rarely did Peter Weiss describe his poetological method, from *Marat/Sade* to *The Aesthetics of Resistance,* with more accuracy.

The impression that the play takes place inside Trotsky's head grows stronger as a consequence of ever new reports of the horrific fates that befall the members of his family as they are systematically exterminated by the Stalinist police or commit suicide. To none of these personal tragedies does Trotsky react with any display of emotion; after the report about his second son's execution he stands motionless. The effect that the ever increasing horror of his family's fate may have on him remains locked within him, which adds to the surreal sense of the spectators that they may be reliving Trotsky's dreams, or rather his nightmares.

The distancing, the oneiric (dreamlike) aspect of events is further heightened by the use of language: telegram-like, abbreviated sentences often lacking subject or predicate, with articles omitted. Many sentences consist of merely one word. This should not be seen, however, as a return to the overheated, artificial language of German expressionist drama but rather as an attempt to convey, through language, the restlessness of the Russian revolutionaries, a restlessness that tolerated no delays, no interruptions, and no distractions. "Next," an impatient Lenin repeatedly urges, "Next, next."[13] This idiosyncrasy, however, which so accurately captures the essence of Lenin and the October Revolution, was not invented by Peter Weiss; it is authentic and frequently recurs in the speeches and writings of the historic Lenin (hence the Soviet author Mikhail Shatrov gave his play about Lenin, published in 1988, the title *Next . . . Next . . . Next*).

This detail shows how inextricably creative artistic liberty and obsessive fidelity to facts are interwoven by the author of *The Investigation* and *Viet Nam Discourse*. There has been no extensive research on the degree to which

Trotsky in Exile adheres to historical fact; but even a cursory comparison reveals the extent of Weiss's fidelity to documented facts. All figures in the play are based on historic persons, and they apparently say or do nothing that their historic models did not also say or do—or at least could have said or done. "Tatsachenphantasie" (fantasy of facts) is what Weiss's literary treatment of historical figures has come to be called.[14] After completing *The Aesthetics of Resistance,* Weiss himself summed up this method as follows: "They [the figures] . . . are historical, just as all locations and events are also authentic—and yet, everything is treated liberally. . . . I have tried to ascribe nothing to them that they could not have done or said" (N II/926–27).

What the figures in *Trotsky in Exile* say was often lifted almost verbatim from historical sources—from Trotsky's bitter refutation of Lenin ("When Lenin says dictatorship of the proletariat, he means dictatorship over the proletariat" [29]) to his speech in the czarist court ("Yes, my lord judges" [34]), as well as the address by Father Gapon and Lenin's "We must form a government. What shall we call ourselves?" (59).[15] Lenin's address before the all-Russian congress (67–68) is likewise assembled from original texts, as are his last thoughts expressed to Stalin and Trotsky.[16] The numbers given at the beginning of the second part about animals slaughtered by the Kulaks (72) are based on historical fact,[17] and Trotsky's lyrical words about the beauty of nature and his love for his companion Natalia Sedova, expressed a few minutes before his assassination, can be found almost literally in his will.[18]

All these painstakingly researched facts are molded into a surreal, oneiric, and aesthetic concept. This unresolvable contradiction is at the core of most of Weiss's literary works. It forms the basis for any interpretation of *Trotsky in Exile.* Weiss's play is a fantasy offered up to reason as well as to the imagination, the fears, anxieties, and obsessions of the audience—especially to the socialists among them. A fabric easily torn, from which no simple truth emerges that can readily be taken home. It is an unsettling work that produces doubts, questions, and, most of all, encourages the readers and spectators to call into question that which has so long been considered historic truth and not to ignore in their own present time those developments that may lead to a more just society and also to more imaginative lives, enriched by a multitude of artistic forms of expression.

With *Trotsky in Exile* the concept that sociopolitical revolutions must be linked with and accompanied by revolutions in the arts became a focus of Weiss's thinking. Researching Lenin's biography, a minor item stirred his imagination: from early 1916 to April 1917 Lenin had lived in Zurich, on the narrow and steep Spiegelgasse, occasionally visited by his close collaborators, among them probably Trotsky. In February 1916 when Lenin had just arrived in Zurich, an artists pub, Cabaret Voltaire, opened on Spiegelgasse, less than 100 yards from Lenin's apartment.

The Cabaret Voltaire became a meeting place for artists exiled from the warring countries. Among them, Hugo Ball and Emmy Hennings, Jean Arp, Marcel Janco, Tristan Tzara, and Richard Huelsenbeck. Soon after it opened, a name was found for the new kind of art or, more accurately, anti-art and antiwar art that was being created at the Cabaret Voltaire: Dada. Whether Lenin (or Trotsky) frequented the nearby pub, or had any discussions with Dada artists, has not been conclusively established. What appears likely is that the two groups knew of one another. There were connections, for instance, via the politically radical Zurich psychiatrist and physician Fritz Brupbacher. Also, the antibourgeois artists from the Cabaret Voltaire were very much politically aware. Ball, Hennings, Huelsenbeck, and others publicly supported an anarchist socialism in the tradition of Bakunin;[19] on the other hand, many of the Bolsheviks, in particular Trotsky and Karl Radek, were interested in literature and the arts.

From these facts and from the temporal and spatial proximity of the two groups, Peter Weiss once again created onstage what had not taken place in reality. In scene 7 of *Trotsky in Exile* the debate between the protagonists of artistic renewal and the protagonists of social renewal becomes a confrontation between the irrational and enlightened reason, between fantasy and plan, between antibourgeois art and anticapitalist revolution. For the Dadaists, too, were an "international," as Tzara confidently reminds the Bolsheviks, adding, "We'll go down in history too, like you" (47). And Hugo Ball beseeches the exiled revolutionaries, "You must join hands with us . . . or our revolution will trickle away into the sand" (47–48).

The revolutionary artists and the technicians of the revolution did not join hands. The movement that was founded with revolutionary élan in the Cabaret Voltaire subsequently trickled away into the sand; after 1933 the Nazis would call it "degenerate art." The revolutionary artists in the Soviet Union fared no better. That, too, is recalled in the Cabaret Voltaire scene, when Christian Rakovsky enumerates the names of great Soviet artists: Malevich, Kandinsky, Chagall, Tatlin, El Lissitzky, Blok, Mayakovsky, Meyerhold, Vakhtangov, and Tairov (50). We now know what Rakovsky could not have known at the time: all these artists would soon thereafter either leave their country or languish under Stalinism, commit suicide, or be executed.

The idea of presenting onstage the unequal innovators from the Spiegelgasse is not unique to Peter Weiss. In *Travesties,* a farce by the English dramatist Tom Stoppard which is set in Zurich during World War I and had its premiere in 1974, there is also a scene where Lenin debates Tristan Tzara, and there is an appearance by yet another prominent Zurich exile of the time, James Joyce. For Weiss himself, the possibilities of that historic constellation were not exhausted with the Cabaret Voltaire scene in *Trotsky in Exile*. In the second volume of *The Aesthetics of Resistance* the encounter between Dadaists and Bolsheviks is recreated once again: as an "emblem of the violent dual revolution, one real, the other a visionary dream."[20]

Peter Weiss was, in a number of ways, a forerunner of the 1968 student movement: in his turn toward Marxism, in his preoccupation with the fascist German past, in his radical critique of capitalism, and in his support of liberation movements of the Third World. But, unlike Marcuse or Adorno, Weiss was no father figure of the student movement. (The Frankfurt School, by the way, had no noticeable influence on Weiss's work). Rather, he was its father and its pupil at the same time. He repeatedly debated with leftist students, especially with the budding writers among them, as an equal among equals. Communication, however, proved to be difficult. There was too much that separated the older writer living in permanent exile in Sweden from the young German left. In the company of the brothers Peter and Michael Schneider, Hans-Christoph Buch, or Hermann Peter Piwitt, Peter Weiss thought he sensed condescension (N I/602). For his part, he noted ironically that these revolutionaries lived on their parents' money (N I/603). After a fruitless attempt to collaborate with a student group's theater project, there was the disheartened conclusion, "I am constantly reminded that I come from someplace completely different" (N I/607). A notation shortly before the completion of work on *Trotsky in Exile* states that the student movement was "the best thing" that happened in the year 1968, but Weiss also notes that it was no more than a bourgeois revolution (N I/650). The ambivalence toward the young radicals was not to be overcome. Eventually, the negative aspects of the student movement caught up with Weiss.

On 19 January 1970, the day before the premiere of *Trotsky in Exile,* there was a scandal in the Düsseldorf Schauspielhaus. Oppositional and rowdy leftist students forced an interruption of the final rehearsal. For Peter Weiss the evening turned into an unfathomable catastrophe. It was to affect him physically, as will be seen. The first notations after that final rehearsal reflect anger and bitterness. A few weeks later, in March 1970, there follows a longer text in which Weiss, without rage and passion, tries to understand what had happened that night at the Düsseldorf Schauspielhaus. The few pages of prose, inconspicuously inserted into the notebooks (N I/697–721), are among the most beautiful he ever wrote. Dialectical and critical toward himself, tolerant toward the young people who destroyed his work that evening, and prophetic in his ideas about the meaning of art and the relationship of art and the masses, but also undeterred in his adherence to socialism and to solidarity with the socialist countries.

The next one to two years must be considered the low point of Weiss's existence as a writer. The easily torn fabric of *Trotsky in Exile* had not been able to withstand the intense attacks from the left and from the right. In the Federal Republic, where a few years earlier *The Investigation* had premiered on more than a dozen stages simultaneously, *Trotsky in Exile* was staged only twice. In Weiss's relationship with the GDR, where the play would never be staged, the low point was reached at the beginning of November 1971. When Weiss, as he had on numerous occasions in the past, wanted to cross the Berlin border into the GDR, he was turned back at the train station at checkpoint Friedrichstrasse. He was no longer welcome in socialist East Germany. His sense, expressed earlier in the notebooks, that if he were a citizen of the GDR he might one day be caught between a rock and a hard place had proven prescient. However, a few weeks later friends in the GDR, including Perten, Haiduk, and the film director Konrad Wolf, were able to make Weiss welcome again. In late November 1971 (Weiss's next play, *Hölderlin,* had already had its premiere in the FRG) these friends arranged a meeting in East Berlin between Weiss and leading party officials, Kurt Hager and Alexander Abusch. Weiss has described this meeting in detail in the notebooks (N I/24–28). The dramatist rejected as unreasonable the demand that he disavow his play and insisted that it continue to be available as a book. He agreed, however, not to permit any further stagings of *Trotsky in Exile,* since it did seem to him that it contained not only "dramatic weaknesses but also shortcomings in terms of content" (N II/26). After this meeting the collaboration with theaters in the GDR that was so important to Peter Weiss again became possible.

On 16 June 1973 Hager and Abusch showed up in Rostock for the GDR premiere of Weiss's next play, thereby officially ending the Trotsky affair. Reservations remained, however: from Peter Weiss toward the GDR cultural bureaucrats (N I/816–20) and from the cultural bureaucrats toward Peter Weiss. *The Aesthetics of Resistance,* Weiss's magnum opus, would be published in the GDR only after a delay of several years.

Hölderlin

"Our illnesses are mostly political illnesses. When our breathing stops, when the blood clots in the veins, the heart fails, then our weariness has settled in the organism, and we react with our whole person as a unit, as a natural process, react definitively to a situation that can no longer be dealt with rationally.'' This perceptive description of a psychosomatic illness appears in the notations in which Peter Weiss tried to come to terms with the defeat he suffered with his play about Trotsky (N I/719). What made him write down these thoughts at the time? What did he know? What kind of sensibility, what kind of intuition guided him? And, assuming that for some time he had been aware of his poor general health (N I/617–19), how could he have known that a few weeks after these notes, on 6 June 1970, his breathing would stop, the blood would clot in his veins, and his heart would fail? The following day, in the hospital, he noted that his cardiac arrest had occurred ''incredibly suddenly, absolutely unexpectedly'' (N I/734).

Our illnesses are mostly political illnesses. Artists seem particularly at risk for these kinds of illnesses. One need only remember the list contained in a famous letter by the novelist Anna Seghers to Georg Lukács in their dispute over realism in literature: ''Kleist died in 1811 from suicide, Lenz died insane in 1791, Bürger was mentally ill at the time of his death in 1794, Günderode died a suicide, etc.''[21] Lenz's mental illness, Kleist's suicide: were they the result of political conditions? Was Hölderlin's insanity a ''political illness''?

The book in which Peter Weiss found such an interpretation of the great German poet Hölderlin's malady was published in 1969: Pierre Bertaux, *Hölderlin und die Französische Revolution* (Hölderlin and the French Revolution), a painstakingly researched and elegantly written study in which the French Germanist turns Friedrich Hölderlin (1770–1843) back on his feet. Thereby the pious and ecstatic poet of a mythological ancient Greece revered by Nazi ideologues becomes a radical Jacobin whose thinking was profoundly influenced by events in France. Hölderlin's works, supposedly removed from the lowly concerns of the realities of his time, appear saturated with the ideas of the French Revolution—ideas of freedom, equality, brotherhood, and even of tyrannicide.[22] Bertaux's insights had not received a lot of attention in the Federal Republic. Since the end of the war there had been no major effort to correct the image of Hölderlin promoted by the Nazis. The important essay on Hölderlin by Georg Lukács[23] had had no impact, and neither had the research on Hölderlin by Germanists in the GDR.[24] Only when Weiss's *Hölderlin,* equally indebted to Bertaux's study and to Lukács's essay, was presented in theaters in the FRG could the distorted image of Hölderlin no longer be maintained.

Although still reeling from the ''Trotsky defeat'' (G/R 186), Weiss began working on the Hölderlin material. It brought back childhood memories.

In 1928 twelve-year-old Peter Weiss had spent several months in the southern German city of Tübingen, where he stayed with an aunt who was married to a lawyer by the name of Autenrieth. Their house was located on the banks of the Neckar River, directly beside the tower in which, 100 years earlier, the mentally ill poet had spent the last 40 years of his life. The uncle Autenrieth, as Weiss became aware of only much later, was a descendant of the infamous Professor Autenrieth who had so much badgered Hölderlin in the name of science. Like almost everything connected with his childhood and youth, Weiss recalled his stay in Tübingen as a time of pain (N I/820–22; G/R 227).

The tower as a place of confinement and oppression had already been the topic of Weiss's first play, *The Tower* (1948). At the time it was a metaphor for a traumatic childhood; now it became the place where a great poet had languished for decades into his old age. Starting with this image, Weiss drafted a play in the spring of 1970; on 22 May he was already reading parts of it to his publisher Siegfried Unseld. After the heart attack, work continued in the hospital, and by mid-June the order of the scenes had been determined. When Peter Weiss was able to leave the hospital in late July, however, it became clear to him that he did not yet have the strength to carry out such intense work. Instead, he starting writing an extensive diary, in which he once again tried to come to an understanding of the pain and the obsessions of his life and oeuvre, his miserable youth, and his stay with the Autenrieths, as well as of issues such as the relationship between art and society, the Third World, the depressing experiences with *Trotsky in Exile,* being a member of the communist party, and various other topics. What is apparent in these important notes, which were for the first time published in their entirety in 1991,[25] is the revalidation of the unconscious, of fantasies, dreams, visions, and hallucinations for the artistic work. This side of the human experience had been the focus of Weiss's artistic production for many years. In the 1960s the needs of the documentary theater and Weiss's growing sensitivity to the political demands of the day had pushed him away from these preoccupations. Now, however, with the renewed awareness of the fragility of his own body and with the awareness of how easily and permanently everything could have ended, he began to revalidate the irrational, the emotional.

Gradually, in the fall of 1970, work on *Hölderlin* was resumed, and in late 1970 a first version was sent to the publisher and to writer-colleague Martin Walser (N I/840). Criticism and suggestions by Walser, as well as by Joachim Bernhard, a Germanist from Rostock (N I/845, N II/33), were assimilated into the work, and the manuscript was sent to various theaters. On

18 September 1971 the premiere took place in Stuttgart under the direction of Peter Palitzsch, and was followed by stagings in the FRG, Switzerland, and the GDR.

With *Hölderlin* two very different groups of spectators (or readers) found themselves confronted with two very different issues. One group, lead by philologists, especially their more conservative representatives, turned their attention toward the difference between the traditional image of Hölderlin and the character created by Peter Weiss. Had Weiss interpreted the facts irresponsibly? Was the historical Hölderlin being misrepresented? The second group, leftists familiar with Marxist theory, was interested in the importance Weiss ascribed to the attitude of writers and intellectuals such as Hölderlin, Hegel, Schelling, and Goethe in influencing the course of history. Had Weiss overstated the ability of such figures to affect change in the material basis of society? Was Weiss lapsing from Marxist materialist positions into an idealism and voluntarism of the kind he himself criticized in the play, particularly in the figure of Schiller?

For a better understanding of these issues one must once again look at Weiss's aesthetics, as well as at his themes and obsessions.

Like *Trotsky in Exile, Hölderlin* presents a biography of the title figure as a two-act station drama, divided here into a prologue, eight scenes, and an epilogue. Scenes 1–7 dramatize events from Hölderlin's life in the period from 1793–1807. Scene 8 sums up the remaining almost forty years until Hölderlin's death. In contrast to *Trotsky in Exile,* however, Weiss here maintains the chronological sequence of events, with a herald announcing the time and place at the beginning of each scene. There is also a renewed opulence of theatrical means: choirs, song and dance, a singing herald, and dreamlike and nightmarish scenes, as well as a short play within the play. As a theater of the senses *Hölderlin* is a successor to *Marat/Sade,* which can be taken quite literally: *Hölderlin* begins where *Marat/Sade* ends, on 14 July 1793, the day after the death of Jean-Paul Marat whose murder is gloatingly announced at the beginning of *Hölderlin* by Duke Karl Eugen von Württemberg. The play's vicinity to *Marat/Sade* is underscored also in the obsessive portrayal of scenes of torture and ecstasy that once again serve as a reminder that, as the Marquis de Sade put it, this is a "world of bodies." Scenes of torture recur repeatedly in *Hölderlin:* for instance, when the rebellious student Sinclair is given a thrashing while Hölderlin weeps (scene 1); when Hölderlin is brought forth in a straightjacket and face mask and force-fed (scene 7); or when he conjures up that horrible image of crossing the Vendée:

where the earth screamed of corpses
and with each step in the field
I bumped against skulls and bones (384).[26]

Here is, once again, that image of horror Weiss had first created in the 1946 drawing "Adam, Eva und Kain" (Adam, Eve, and Cain), and which he had later used in *Conversation of the Three Wayfarers,* as well as in *Marat/Sade.*

The ecstasy of the body is conjured up in the scene where the emancipated Wilhelmine Kirms opens her dress and challenges Hölderlin to an erotic encounter. In that time, however, liberated sexuality was as little to be had as equality of women. Startled, Hölderlin declines. Having pined away in a hopeless and Platonic love for Susette Gontard, who is wasting away as the wife of a Frankfurt banker, he is unable to become an equal partner to the self-confident Kirms, to her combative feminism and her contempt for this weakly "sex / along with everything / they have between the legs" (297). Under the taboos of the bourgeoisie, the ecstasy of the body turns into unbearable torment. Which was, of course, Weiss's own issue, his early life having revolved around this torment; he had re-created it over and over in his early work. In *Hölderlin* the torment is expressed in the suffering of young Fritz von Kalb. For nights on end Hölderlin must watch over him to prevent him from succumbing to his "vice" (297). It is an agonizing duty, since Hölderlin himself is being tormented by the taboos of society, by the "ice-cold zones of the prevailing order" (315). Sobbing hysterically, he starts slapping Fritz, who is masturbating (305).

The repression and oppression that permeate scenes like these are not restricted to sexuality. In a disturbingly believable scene both Hölderlin and Fritz beat themselves (299, 304): an expression of the self-hatred that has always characterized the victims of repression—and has always benefited the oppressors. A painful image, and one that Weiss had used once before, in *Leavetaking,* where the maid, Augusta, humiliated by the narrator's mother, slaps herself in the face.[27]

Thus there is in *Hölderlin* an abundance of theatrical means, sensuous theater, and a "world of bodies," as in *Marat/Sade.* At the same time the earlier concepts are expanded so that the emotional and irrational moments in *Hölderlin* do not distract from but rather serve to emphasize the critique of social and political issues.

From today's perspective the polemics provoked by *Hölderlin* among some traditionalist Germanists about the "correct" Hölderlin[28] appear like a rearguard action. Weiss's play alone cannot explain the intensity of the debate.

Hölderlin was part of the new thinking, especially in the humanities, that had developed in the Federal Republic after 1968. Weiss was by no means the only writer who at the time undertook to correct the antiquated image of the great poet. In 1970, a year before *Hölderlin* first opened, a biographical radio play about Hölderlin by GDR author Stephan Hermlin, entitled *Scardanelli,* was broadcast in East Germany. Also in the GDR, in 1976, Gerhard Wolf's *Der arme Hölderlin* was published; that same year Peter Härtling's biographical novel *Hölderlin,* in which Peter Weiss is mentioned as one of the sources, appeared in the Federal Republic.

Those struggling to preserve the "correct" Hölderlin were particularly unconvincing in accusing Weiss of feigning "historical truth."[29] Historical truth is not revealed by merely conveying the facts; it requires interpretation. An interpretation may be more or less convincing, but it cannot be criticized for feigning the truth. What Weiss's critics probably meant was that Weiss was feigning historical *reality*—that he emphasized the factuality of his drama and tried to hide its fictional aspects. That, however, is precisely what Weiss did not do.

Unlike *Viet Nam Discourse* or a play like Heinar Kipphardt's *In the Matter of J. Robert Oppenheimer, Hölderlin* is not and does not pretend to be documentary theater. The free treatment of the material is signaled from the very beginning when Hölderlin speaks about himself in the third person (268) in a manner recalling Brechtian alienation. The figure of the herald, the abundance of theatrical means, the surreal scenes of ecstasy and of torture, Hölderlin's visionary fantasies (scene 7), and the meeting with Marx, which was invented by Weiss, all point toward fiction, as does the complex weaving of time levels, particularly in Hölderlin's play within a play about Empedocles. All of these aesthetic and dramatic devices, themes, and motifs remove Weiss's play from a merely historiographical representation of reality. Yet these diverse forms of fictionalization were not used to force the facts of Hölderlin's life into a context alien to them. Peter Weiss, in fact, went the opposite way. He projected the problems of a writer and intellectual *of his own time* onto the epoch of Hölderlin[30]—a method that precluded neither fidelity to the sources nor "historical truth."

Therein, however, lies the difficulty with the figures in Hölderlin—or in *Trotsky in Exile* or *The Aesthetics of Resistance.* Weiss's literary figures are intended to be both identical and nonidentical with their historical models. Weiss even changed the degree of fictionalization from work to work and from figure to figure—a contradictory poetic method that the dramatist himself was never completely able to explain, a method that hardly permits statements of a general nature about Weiss's treatment of reality. It can be ascertained about the Hölderlin figure of the play that all the facts of his life correspond to the facts about the historical Hölderlin. Nonetheless, onstage one is confronted with a character created by Peter Weiss, which he accurately summed up in the following words: "I wanted to describe something of the conflict that arises in a person who suffers to the point of madness from the injustices, the humiliations in his society, who completely supports the revolutionary upheavals, and yet does not find the praxis with which the misery can be remedied, who is ground down between his poetic vision and a reality of class separation, state power, military force" (N I/826)—a self-portrait of Weiss, undoubtedly. At the same time it is a portrait of Hölderlin that coincides with the findings of Lukács, Bertaux, and others. The interpretation of Hölderlin's life in the tower—the last thirty-six years of the poet's life—however, remains Weiss's own contribution to Hölderlin research. Here he parts with Bertaux, who, in a later book, described Hölderlin's existence after his withdrawal into illness as a petit bourgeois idyll. In a lengthy notation in 1979 Weiss criticizes Bertaux's interpretation as trivializing and repeats his own hypothesis, which also constitutes the basis of his play: Hölderlin's condition was the consequence of his hypersensitive reaction to a "hostile and sick environment" (N II/800). The kind of illness, in other words, about which Weiss, after his *Trotsky* defeat, had noted: "Our illnesses are mostly political illnesses."

Had Weiss, with *Hölderlin,* relapsed into idealist positions? The Marxist Weiss scholar, Manfred Haiduk, argues as follows: Weiss, by according so much significance to the positions of Goethe, Schiller, and Hegel, to their insistence on the status quo, or at best, their cautiously reformist attitude, may create the impression that these poets and thinkers were primarily responsible for the lack of a revolution in Germany. The explanation for the "teutsche Misere" (the misery of German history, 328) would thus be seen as the failure of the intelligentsia.[31] From this can be drawn the analogous conclusion that social upheavals depend on the will of a few important individuals. Such an emphasis on the importance of the individual puts Weiss in opposition to one of the basic tenets of historical materialism, which holds that history is decided by the consciousness and ultimately by the actions of society as a whole. *Hölderlin* shows that Peter Weiss was aware of this problem. He took a number of steps to make an idealistic interpretation of his play more difficult. In scene 4, for instance, the chances for a revolution in Germany appear to depend entirely on the position of one individual, the Jena philosopher Johann Gottlieb Fichte (1762–1814). In his lecture Fichte initially insists on the "right to revolution" as a "human right" (318), but then, under pressure from reactionary fraternity students, he begins to retract his ideas and ultimately permits the arrest of Hölderlin and Hölderlin's friends. Does this change of heart make it his fault that the revolutionary forces are once again defeated?

At this point the herald reminds the spectators somewhat cryptically that "This play puts mainly up for view / Philosophers and poets in the super-structure" (327). In the superstructure? The term refers to Marx's famous model wherein he distinguishes between the *basis* of human society and its *superstructure*. The basis consists of the material conditions of an epoch, foremost among them its economic conditions, as well as the working masses who produce and reproduce these conditions. The superstructure consists of the legal, political, religious, artistic, and philosophical values and relations; in short, its ideological manifestations. In Marx's model, social change al-ways originates from contradictions at the basis, which find conflicting ex-pression in the ideological systems of the superstructure and hence in the minds of the individuals.[32]

To the extent that the individuals lack insight into the importance of events at the basis—in the economy, in the conditions of the laboring masses—the importance of their own ability to influence events will appear exaggerated. This was the case with the representatives of German idealism, who in Weiss's play are Goethe, Hegel, Fichte, and especially Schiller. The last men-tioned, at least in his youth, had been just as passionate a revolutionary as Hölderlin, and in 1792 even had been made an honorary citizen of the French republic. In his dispute with Hölderlin in Jena in November 1794 the philo-sophical idealist Schiller has not turned completely against his former belief in the necessity of social change. Schiller insists, however:

> Before the structure of society
> can be changed
> first the human being
> must be changed (324).

Schiller's idealism is strongly refuted by Hölderlin's materialist thinking:

> No
> First everything must be turned around
> from the bottom up
> before something new
> can come into being (324).

Which means that without the preceding changes at the basis, human beings will not change. Later, in a discussion with his friend Siegfried Schmid in the garden of the Adlerflychthof, the country house of the Gontards, Hölderlin makes clear which change he mainly has in mind:

> Foremost
> the cause of the whole evil
> the holy right to private acquisition
> must be swept away (343).

Once again Weiss repeats the ironic formula of the "holy right" to private acquisition, which he had previously used in *Marat/Sade* and in *Song of the Lusitanian Bogey.*

The bottom line, in other words, is economics. This is one of the issues Weiss emphasizes in order to provide his play with a materialist foundation. Economics is the topic of scene 5, that rapid sequence of short conversations between businessmen and financiers in the garden of the Adlerflychthof. Gontard, Gogel, Bethmann, and Schellenberg are representatives of rapidly evolving capitalism and colonialism and, thus, representatives of the main tendency of the epoch. Compared to these figures of power, the poets and philosophers who are also present at Gontard's country house, whether inclined toward revolution or toward affirmation of the existing order, seem nothing more than harmless court jesters. The powers that be like to adorn themselves with men such as these, but the thinking and intentions of these writers and intellectuals clearly do not have much impact on either their own fate or on the fate of Germany.

Another way in which Weiss draws the spectators' and readers' attention to the basis that supports the entire superstructure is through the various brief appearances and comments by laborers, domestics, and gardeners. They are the foundation of society, as Weiss says in the afterword in *Hölderlin* (614). Without their labor it would not be possible for either conformist or revolutionary poets and philosophers to spend their lives reflecting about models of human coexistence. Without them the visions of a more just society remain just that.

This is the topic of "Grund des Empedokles," the play within a play that Hölderlin performs for his friends in Homburg in 1799. In *Hölderlin* Empedocles is once again the type of messianic bearer of hope that recurs frequently in Weiss's work. More clearly than ever before, Weiss uses the figure of a redeemer for the purpose of making the oppressed and exploited aware of their own strength and responsibility. Since, in Hölderlin's play, the Agrigentians become all too dependent on Empedocles, the wise leader takes the ultimate step: he gives up his life for his people—a messiah whose sacrificial death is intended to make people not into objects of a heavenly power but into subjects of history. That had already been the theme of Brecht's poem from the 1930s "Der Schuh des Empedokles" (The Shoe of Empedocles), where, after Empedocles' disappearance, it is said about the Agrigentians, "Still some of them postponed their questions until his [Empedocles'] return, while already others / tried to find the solution themselves."[33] The same thought is expressed by Weiss's Hölderlin, who suggests to a laborer the following meaning of his drama:

> Do not expect
> that you are to be helped
> if you don't even help yourselves. (372)

These words were taken almost verbatim from the real Hölderlin's first version of *Empedokles:* "You cannot / be helped if you yourselves do not help yourselves."[34]

Idealism? Too little emphasis on the basis? Haiduk's objection cannot be entirely refuted, but it should be kept in mind that the importance of processes in the superstructure—and of the intellectuals and artists who carry them in agreement and in contradiction—should not be undervalued. In *Hölderlin* it is ultimately Marx himself who emphasizes the importance of contributions by artists and intellectuals, and hence the importance of processes in the superstructure, in the preparation of profound social change. In doing so the young philosopher places the contributions of the artists—here, Hölderlin's "visionary shaping / of deepest personal experience"—on a par with his own "analysis of the concrete / historical situation" (410). With these words by the young Karl Marx, Weiss once again conjures up the alliance between revolutionary artists and social revolutionaries that never materialized in Zurich's Spiegelgasse in *Trotsky in Exile.*

Solely at issue, however, in the struggles of artists and philosophers in the superstructure—as Weiss's Marx clearly stipulates—is the *preparation* of social upheavals. The upheavals themselves remain the task of the basis.

NOTES

1. Peter Weiss, "Der Sieg, der sich selbst bedroht" (1967), in Weiss, *Rapporte 2* (Frankfurt/ Main: Suhrkamp, 1971) 71.

2. Peter Weiss, "Offener Brief an den Tschechoslowakischen Schriftstellerverband" (10 September 1967), in Weiss, *Rapporte 2* 80.

3. See Peter Weiss, "Che Guevara!", N I/558 (the text is in English in the notebooks).

4. The page numbers refer to Peter Weiss, *How Mr. Mockinpott Was Cured of His Sufferings (Wie dem Herrn Mockinpott das Leiden ausgetrieben wird*, 1963–68), trans. Christopher Holmes, in Michael Roloff, ed., *The Contemporary German Theater* (New York: Avon, 1972).

5. See Henning Rischbieter, "Peter Weiss. 'Wie dem Herrn Mockinpott das Leiden ausgetrieben wird,' " in Peter Weiss, *Wie dem Herrn Mockinpott das Leiden ausgetrieben wird* (Stuttgart: Ernst Klett, 1983) 81.

6. Manfred Karnick, "Peter Weiss' dramatische Collagen. Vom Traumspiel zur Agitation," in Rainer Gerlach, ed., *Peter Weiss* (Frankfurt/Main: Suhrkamp, 1984) 214.

7. For Weiss's activities in connection with the Soviet invasion of Czechoslovakia, see G/R 170–80, esp. n. 1.

8. See Peter Weiss, "The Material and the Models. Notes Towards a Definition of Documentary Theatre" ("Notizen zum dokumentarischen Theater," 1968), trans. Heinz Bernard, *Theatre Quarterly* 1, no. 1 (January–March 1971): 41–43.

9. See Peter Weiss, "Offener Brief an die 'Literaturnaja Gaseta,' Moskau" (Letter to Lew Ginsburg of 4 April 1970), in Weiss, *Rapporte 2* 142.

10. See (in the order of the quotations) Marcel Reich-Ranicki, "Die zerredete Revolution. Peter Weiss: 'Trotzki im Exil,' " in Reich-Ranicki, *Lauter Verrisse* (Munich: Piper, 1970) 150; Manfred Durzak, "Zurücknahme einer Illusion: 'Trotzki im Exil,' " in Durzak, *Dürrenmatt Frisch Weiss* (Stuttgart: Philipp Reclam jr., 2d ed., 1973) 320; and Heinrich Vormweg, *Peter Weiss* (Munich: Beck, 1981) 106.

11. The page numbers in parentheses refer to Peter Weiss, *Trotsky in Exile (Trotzki im Exil)*, trans. Geoffrey Skelton (New York: Atheneum, 1972).

12. Thus the literal translation. Skelton translates as, "You're still intellectuals."

13. Translated by Skelton both as "further" (67, 68) and as "next" (79).

14. See Robert Cohen, "Tatsachenphantasie," in Cohen, *Versuche über Weiss' 'Ästhetik des Widerstands'* (Bern: Peter Lang, 1989) 70–77.

15. For the first three quotations, see Harry Wilde, *Trotzki* (Reinbek b. Hamburg: Rowohlt-Bildmonographie, 1979) 46, 64–65, 51–53. For the quotation from Lenin, see Hermann Weber, *Lenin* (Reinbek b. Hamburg: Rowohlt-Bildmonographie, 1978) 124–25.

16. See V. I. Lenin, *Ausgewählte Werke*, 6 vols. (East Berlin: Dietz, 1970 onward), 4:6ff., 6:639ff.

17. See Wilde 178.

18. See Isaac Deutscher, *The Prophet Outcast* (vol. 3 of Deutscher's biography of Trotsky) (London: Oxford University Press, 1963) 479.

19. On the Cabaret Voltaire, on Brupbacher, and on the political positions of the Dadaists, see Raimund Meyer, *Dada in Zürich. Die Akteure, die Schauplätze* (Frankfurt/Main: Luchterhand, 1990) 19–27.

20. Peter Weiss, *Die Ästhetik des Widerstands* (Frankfurt/Main: Suhrkamp, 2d ed., 1986) 2:59.

21. Anna Seghers, Correspondence with Georg Lukács (1938–39), in Georg Lukács, *Essays über Realismus, Werke* 4 (Neuwied: Luchterhand, 1971): 346.

22. See Pierre Bertaux, *Hölderlin und die Französische Revolution* (1969) (Frankfurt/Main: Suhrkamp, 5th ed., 1980) 127ff.

23. See Georg Lukács, "Hölderlins Hyperion" (1934), in Lukács, *Deutsche Literatur in zwei Jahrhunderten, Werke* 7 (Neuwied: Luchterhand, 1964): 164–84.

24. See Manfred Haiduk, *Der Dramatiker Peter Weiss* (East Berlin: Henschelverlag, 1977) 212 and n. 20.

25. See Peter Weiss, "Rekonvaleszenz," in *Peter Weiss. Werke in sechs Bänden,* ed. Suhrkamp Verlag in cooperation with Gunilla Palmstierna-Weiss (Frankfurt/Main: Suhrkamp, 1991) 2:345–546.

26. The page numbers refer to Peter Weiss, "Hölderlin," revised version, December 1971–April 1972, in Weiss, *Stücke II/2* (Frankfurt/Main: Suhrkamp, 1977) 265–416, and the appended remarks 608–17.

27. See Peter Weiss, *Leavetaking (Abschied von den Eltern),* trans. E. B. Garside, Alastair Hamilton, and Christopher Levenson, in Weiss, *Exile* (New York: Delacorte, 1968) 10.

28. For an example of the traditionalist approach, see Otto F. Best, "O Marx und Business," *Basis* 3 (1972): 238–44; and see Benno von Wiese, "Peter Weiss' 'Hölderlin.' Ein kritisches Essay," in Thomas Beckermann and Volker Canaris, eds., *Der andere Hölderlin. Materialien zum "Hölderlin"-Stück von Peter Weiss* (Frankfurt/Main: Suhrkamp, 1972) 217–46.

29. von Wiese 221.

30. See Klaus L. Berghahn, " 'Wenn ich so singend fiele. . .' Dichter und Revolutionär, gestern und heute, Hölderlin und Weiss," in Beckermann and Canaris 173.

31. See Haiduk 215.

32. The most succinct formulation of this model is found in Karl Marx, "Zur Kritik der politischen Ökonomie. Vorwort," *Marx Engels Werke* (Berlin: Dietz, 1956–) 13:7–9.

33. See Bertolt Brecht, "Der Schuh des Empedokles," in Brecht, *Werke,* annotated Berlin and Frankfurt edition (Frankfurt/Main: Suhrkamp, 1988) 12:31.

34. Friedrich Hölderlin, "Der Tod des Empedokles. Erste Fassung," in Hölderlin, *Werke. Briefe. Dokumente,* based on the text established by Friedrich Beissner for the smaller Stuttgart Hölderlin edition. Selected, annotated, and with an afterword by Pierre Bertaux (Munich: Winkler, 1977) 426.

CHAPTER EIGHT

Magnum Opus: *The Aesthetics of Resistance*

The 1970s were to prove favorable for attempts to overcome the Federal Republic's "helpless anti-fascism" (Wolfgang Fritz Haug) through literature. The Social Democratic Party (SPD), in a coalition with the small liberal party (FDP), had come to power in October 1969. The chancellor was a former exile; Willy Brandt (1913–92) had spent part of his exile years in Sweden—like Peter Weiss. What conservative administrations had neglected since the founding of the Federal Republic was now made up for in the FRG's relations with the countries of Eastern Europe. Treaties were signed with the Soviet Union, Poland, Czechoslovakia, and eventually with the GDR, improving the situation of uneasy coexistence that had lasted since World War II. On both sides the rigidities of the cold war were beginning to loosen. As a consequence, in 1973 both German states became members of the United Nations. In 1971 Chancellor Brandt was awarded the Nobel Peace Prize for his foreign policy.

But the development of the Federal Republic was marked by contradictions. The student rebellion against the inertia of society had initially brought about only few changes. A tiny number of young idealists began to take up terrorist activities. There were bomb attacks and deaths; but were these actions a threat to peace and order in the entire country? The Social Democratic government reacted sharply: more power and better weaponry were provided for the police, and changes were made in the law of the Republic, including the infamous *Radikalenerlass* (decree concerning radicals): radicals—which generally meant radicals of the left—were to be excluded from civil service, particularly as teachers.

Relations remained difficult between the two German states. The GDR had placed a spy in the immediate vicinity of Willy Brandt, even though Brandt's policy of détente was welcomed by most citizens of East Germany. The spy was discovered, Brandt resigned in May 1974, and was succeeded by Helmut Schmidt. One image, in particular, remains from Brandt's chancellorship: a photograph showing him kneeling in the rain in front of the memorial to the Warsaw ghetto. Finally, a representative of the Federal Republic had found a way to express in an appropriate and moving way that ability which, in the 1960s, had been expressly denied the Germans, the ability to mourn.

Mourning is also the underlying tone of several major novels from the 1970s dealing with the epoch of German fascism: mourning for all the destruction and killing; for all the missed opportunities and for the lesser or greater complicity: of the figures in the novels, as well as of their authors. Alfred Andersch's *Winterspelt* (1974), Christa Wolf's *Kindheitsmuster (Patterns of Childhood)* (1976), Stephan Hermlin's slim volume *Abendlicht* (1979), and, in a different way, Uwe Johnson's *Jahrestage* (1970–83) are examples of this kind of literature. There was no attempt on the part of these authors to put the past behind them once and for all, and there certainly was no invocation of the "mercy of having been born later" (in the inappropriate words of Chancellor Helmut Kohl, who succeeded Schmidt in 1982). There were only attempts to finally break the silence about the recent German past, efforts to finally speak the truth (including the truth about the authors' present time), as, for instance, in Wolf's *Patterns of Childhood*. It is hardly surprising that Peter Weiss, too, was working on an antifascist novel in the 1970s.

Ever since *Marat/Sade,* Weiss had written works dealing with some of the main questions of his time. His preoccupations eventually led to an epic novel about fascism and the fight against it. As Haug and Maase have stated, it became a *Jahrhundertbuch* (book of the century).[1] The label implies not only the incommensurability of the work but also the breadth and depth of an undertaking in which an entire (European) epoch and its historical background were re-created.

The Aesthetics of Resistance deals with a time out of joint:[2] the defeat of Germany at the end of the World War I and the attempt at a German revolution in November 1918; labor's struggles against economic exploitation and against the decline of the Weimar Republic; struggles also within the left, between Social Democrats and communists; in the Soviet Union the deformation of socialism under the Stalinist system; in 1933 German capitulation to fascism, with the known consequences—World War II, destruction of a continent, and Auschwitz; and the increasingly hopeless resistance of the left against fascism, ending with the death of the resistance fighters. All of this Weiss had lived through, all of this had touched his life in major ways (of which he had at the time remained largely unaware), and all of this, in defiance of all probability, he had survived.

His own life once again provided the impetus for a literary work: a 1,000-page novel, begun in July 1972 and completed in August 1980. The author of *Song of the Lusitanian Bogey, Viet Nam Discourse,* and *How Mr. Mockinpott Was Cured of His Sufferings* had, of course, long turned away from tortured introspections and subtle, psychological self-revelations. The facts of his existence now served only as source of material based upon which an entirely different biography could be constructed, namely, a biography that the author—who meanwhile professed communism and solidarity with the exploited and oppressed—did not have but that he would have liked to have. Weiss conceived of it as a kind of intellectual experiment: "What would I have become, how would I have developed if I had come from a proletarian home instead of a bourgeois-petit-bourgeois milieu" (G/R 27). Instead of the isolated, almost autistic youth of an artist far removed from the real world, the protagonist would be a worker's son who participates actively and with solidarity in the struggles of his era.

A *Wunschautobiographie* (wished-for autobiography) was how Weiss himself on occasion characterized his concept (G/R 27). This strongly irritated some established West German critics. Their irritation can hardly be explained by Weiss's free treatment of the facts of his own life. Literature contains many examples of an imaginative and fictionalized treatment of the author's own biography. In this case, however, someone from an obviously well-to-do bourgeois background insisted on writing for himself a proletarian past, of all things. The irritation this concept created was obviously of an ideological nature. But it also revealed the difficulty of interpreting a literary work that mixed fact and fiction, even from Weiss's own life, with a radicality that went beyond anything in Weiss's previous literary oeuvre.

As shown in *Hölderlin,* Weiss's literary figures are intended to be at the same time identical and not identical with their historical models. The first-person narrator of *The Aesthetics of Resistance* is born on the same day as Peter Weiss; his father comes from Hungary and is a Czech national, just like Weiss's father; and the first-person narrator grew up in Bremen and lives in Berlin, in 1937 he spends time with his parents in the Czech town of Varnsdorf, at the outbreak of the war he goes into Swedish exile, all of which is true of Peter Weiss. The narrator has friends such as Jacques Ayschmann and Max Hodann and a girlfriend named Rosalinde von Ossietzky, just like Weiss, and he wants to become a writer.

The differences between the young first-person narrator and young Peter Weiss, however, are equally important: the narrator is a worker and a class-conscious proletarian and his parents are socialists. In fascist Germany he works illegally against the Nazis. During the Spanish Civil War he fights on the side of the loyalists against the Franco troops. He meets the Soviet writer Ilya Ehrenburg, Brecht, and the Swedish author Karin Boye, as well as Willi Münzenberg, who in the Weimar Republic headed a giant communist media conglomerate, and Herbert Wehner (who was to become one of the leading Social Democratic politicians in the Federal Republic), and many other historical figures. In Sweden he continues to be active in the antifascist underground and, at age twenty-three, becomes a member of the Communist Party (III/95).[3] None of that is true of Weiss. The fact that Weiss and the narrator are born on the same day is true and also not true: the first-person narrator is born on 8 November 1917—one year to the day after Weiss—on that historical day when the population of St. Petersburg unleashed the Russian Revolution by storming the Winter Palace. Thus the first-person narrator literally becomes a child of the Russian Revolution.

But if the autobiographical references to Weiss's life provided the impetus for *The Aesthetics of Resistance,* they are not at all its focus. And the first-person narrator is by no means its main character. In fact, he at times completely disappears behind the events he is relating. He is a chronicler, an almost anonymous voice that narrates the text—a text that can neither be summarized nor retold. *The Aesthetics of Resistance* has no plot that can be related in a few or even in many sentences. The events do not occur in a temporally circumscribed epoch; they unfold neither chronologically nor logically in terms of a plot; and the novel does not focus on any particular figure, such as the first-person narrator. He is, in fact, absent at the culmination of the novel, which occurs in the second part of the third volume. As in earlier works by Weiss there is once again no attempt to elaborate on the characters' psychology, much less on their age or clothing. The motifs and themes of this novel cannot be treated separately from one another: their significance and their meaning are yielded only from their complex interrelation with all other motifs and themes. A retelling of the events can in no way convey anything from which readers would recognize their own experiences in reading this book. In view of all these difficulties it may be useful to approach this text from without, starting with a few observations concerning its appearance.

The first impression while leafing through these 1,000 pages is of their hermetic appearance. There are large blocks of text with no paragraphs, as in Weiss's early, pre-Marxist texts, including *Leavetaking* and *Vanishing Point.* This aesthetic concept was retained, as well as the practice of dispensing with punctuation except for the comma and period. Dispensed with also was the unstressed ''e'' (elision). All of which leads to a very dense text, uniform and forbidding in appearance, a text that refuses all emphasis and interpretive aid; which certainly exacerbates its difficulties, as Weiss was well aware (G/R 280–81). But he could not do otherwise. He was not free in choosing the form of his text, as he explained on occasion by referring to his life as a painter, "A painter whose style is cubist can paint only in this very specific manner. . . . It is a kind of compulsion."[4] And upon publication of volume III he explained, "It is a tradition from my time as a painter: I want to see a complete, unbroken image" (G/R 280). The structure of the text, down to the use of syntax, is determined by the visual appearance of the printed page: a unique occurrence in literary prose, as was pointed out in the discussion of *Leavetaking*.

Weiss did not try to explain these large blocks of text solely on the basis of an aesthetic continuity. In the novel itself the young narrator, who wants to become a writer, reflects on the question, "How could all this be described" (I/130). What he is relating time and again seems to defy description, for no literary form seems available for events such as these. Thus, a little later the narrator asks himself, "And how should writing be at all possible for us, I asked myself . . . , how, could this thin, fragmented material, which can be got at only piece by piece, be conveyed in printed form with any claim on continuity" (I/135). Still obsessed with the need to find a literary expression for the death and destruction all around him, the narrator, now working with Wehner in the Swedish underground, notes in the third volume, "I [saw] everything I was dealing with as one sole related effort to overcome obstacles" (III/113). To the discontinuity of the events he juxtaposes the only continuity that still has validity, the solidarity of the resistance. That is what, in the face of all this fragmentation, provides the events with a "unity" (III/113) that is tirelessly invoked by the narrator and that is used as a protective wall against fascism. The large blocks of text, the visual appearance of *The Aesthetics of Resistance*, must be seen within this context. As a visual expression of what is one of the main topics of the novel: the unified effort, the unity of the resistance. The hermetic appearance of the printed page becomes a protective wall against an all-powerful enemy.

This concept of renouncing any emphasis or dramatization of events also led Weiss to avoid describing events directly. Instead, they are the subject of narrations, reports, and discussions by the figures in the novel. These narrations are, in turn, related by the first-person narrator. Thus the text becomes a multilayered narrative that creates distance and protects the reader from being overwhelmed. As the notebooks show, Weiss himself was increasingly afraid of being overwhelmed by the events he was writing about. They had a maelstrom effect on him that he was ever less able to resist. For his own protection Weiss developed a kind of theory of feelinglessness that was to prevent him from succumbing to the horror of the events. This theory is included in the novel. The narrator's young comrade, Heilmann, speaks of "anaesthesia" (I/83) that creates a psychological wall between the artist and the events. For hundreds of pages Weiss sustained this narration by means of anaesthesia. At the very end, however, when after more than eight years of work there came the time to describe the extermination of the Schulze-Boysen and Harnack resistance group, this distancing narrative technique could no longer be maintained. Events are now related without any distance and without even the mediating function of the first-person narrator. There is no more wall made of aesthetic form distancing the author from the description of the execution of members of the resistance (III/210–20). The author opened himself up to these events without any defenses, and the readers, too, are defenselessly confronted with them. What is done to the human body is rendered in obsessive, surreal detail. Having for hundreds of pages described all the battles, the small victories, and the final defeat of the antifascist resistance, Weiss is once again faced with the ultimate truth: that this is "a world of bodies" (as Sade remarks in *Marat/Sade*). Thus it had been in *The Investigation,* in *Song of the Lusitanian Bogey,* and in *Hölderlin.* In the novel, however, there is nothing left of the marquis's irrationality and secret pleasure in sadistic-masochistic torture. Weiss's minute description of the execution of the men and women of the Schulze-Boysen and Harnack organization is intended to create insights into how a rationally organized state could and did produce such horrors.

The passage becomes a "walk through Hades," as Weiss noted more than once (N II/661, 761). With this turn of phrase the reader is once again referred to Dante in the final part of Weiss's novel. The *Divina Commedia,* with which Weiss had been involved for so long, became for the last time the point of departure for an attempt to express in words that which, as Christa Wolf wrote in *Accident (Störfall),* has gone beyond the boundaries of prose. Lotte Bischoff's trip to fascist Germany, and her stay in a Berlin as it is going up in flames is modeled after Dante's *Inferno* in a variety of ways.[5] Based on the Dante model and an unbearably precise description, Weiss has created one of the great moments in the literature of our time, a moment that will long endure with the readers of *The Aesthetics of Resistance.*

Three figures are introduced in the first pages of the novel: a fifteen-year-old high school student named Heilmann and two young workers, one a Siemens apprentice by the name of Coppi, the other the first-person narrator, an assistant mechanic whose name is never mentioned and who works in a warehouse. The novel opens on 22 September 1937 in fascist Berlin with long conversations among the three friends about art and politics. A few days later the narrator travels to Spain. When the defeat of the Spanish republic is imminent, he goes to Paris. Several months before the start of World War II he escapes to Sweden, where he continues to participate in the illegal resistance against fascism. All this time Heilmann and Coppi remain in Germany; hardly anything is heard of them for hundreds of pages: they seem no longer to have any part in the course of events. Near the end of the novel, however, in the second part of the third volume, they reappear. The events are set in Berlin in 1942. Heilmann and Coppi are members of a resistance movement that is directed by German communists residing illegally in Sweden, one of whom is the first-person narrator. This resistance movement, which actually existed, was called *Rote Kapelle* (Red Orchestra) in childish Nazi jargon. It has become known, especially through Weiss's novel, as the Schulze-Boysen and Harnack Organization, after the names of two of its leading members. By now what the reader may have suspected throughout the novel has become clear: Horst Heilmann, by then nineteen years old, and the worker Hans Coppi, actually lived, and, together with the other members of the Schulze-Boysen and Harnack Organization they actually died in the way described in the novel. After having been captured and tortured, they were executed by the Nazis on 27 November 1942 in Berlin Plötzensee prison: the men were hung, the women beheaded. Hans Coppi's wife Hilde was allowed to remain alive until she gave birth to her baby: then she, too, was beheaded.

Why is it that most readers from the Federal Republic did not know about the Schulze-Boysen and Harnack Organization until *The Aesthetics of Resistance* came out? Another resistance group, which had attempted to assassinate Hitler on 20 July 1944, was quite well known. This group, unlike the *Rote Kapelle*, was made up mostly of officers and descendants of Prussian nobility. Also known was the resistance of those young idealistic students led by the Scholl siblings. There is no intention here to minimize in any way the struggle of these groups and the sacrifice they made. The fact remains, however, that the largest resistance movements, those of the left, and especially the resistance of the communists, was largely ignored or discredited by the helpless antifascism of the Federal Republic.[6] Fascism, to be sure, was finally conquered, but the ideology of the victors was now anticommunist, and not even the dead were secure from this thinking. Just like leftist politicians and cultural innovators from the Weimar Republic, the leftist resistance fighters were to a large extent excluded from the canon of names worth preserving. After all, wasn't it true that groups like the Schulze-Boysen and Harnack Organization had gone so far as to pass along information to the Soviet Union? The fact that the USSR had at the time been an ally of the Western powers was conveniently overlooked. Thus, during the cold war the activities of people like Heilmann, Coppi, and the other members of the Red Orchestra came to represent treason, rather than heroism.

The Aesthetics of Resistance is a "counterarchive" (Burkhardt Lindner),[7] in which the names of so many who perished are preserved. And there are many, though few of them may be familiar to readers in Germany (and even fewer to non-German readers).[8] This seemed of no concern to the arrogant author, or so one of Weiss's critics suggested.[9] Weiss's arrogance apparently consisted of presuming that readers would not just passively receive the text but would be willing to interrupt their reading, their aesthetic pleasure, and that they would collaborate with the text by informing themselves about the names in the novel. In addition, Weiss's critics in the FRG overlooked the fact that the novel, like all of Peter Weiss's works since *Marat/Sade,* was also intended for readers in the GDR who might indeed be familiar with many of these names. At the same time, however, the readers in the GDR might be unfamiliar with a number of names: those of anti-Stalinist communists, men and women who had lost their lives under the regime of the Soviet dictator.

The need to write *The Aesthetics of Resistance* as a counterarchive to the prevailing version of history, and, at the same time, to create an artistic form in which to preserve so many names, led to a stylistic device in the novel that may appear paradoxical:

> Brecht, Piscator, Dudow, Ihering, Jessner and Busch, Grosz, Dix, Kollwitz and Heartfield, Feuchtwanger, Döblin, Toller, Tucholsky, Ossietsky, Kisch, Becher, Seghers and Renn, Gorki, Gladkow and Ehrenburg, Dreiser, Shaw, Sinclair, Nexö, Barbusse and Rolland, Gropius, Taut and van der Rohe, Kerr and Jacobsohn, Pechstein, Muche, Hofer and Klee, Einstein and Freud (I/159)

or

> Groener, Hindenburg and Seeckt, . . . Stinnes and Hugenberg, and Kapp, Sklarz and Tamschik, and Lüttwitz, Epp and Escherisch [correct spelling: Escherich], and Erhard, Lettow Vorbeck and Hülsen (I/115)

or

> Dimitroff, Marty, Pieck, Florin, Ulbricht, Thorez, Cachin, Smeral, Andersen Nexö, Pasionaria and Mao Tse Tung (II/240).

Mere lists, no aesthetic transformation, no literarization. Which is precisely why these lists become part of a work of fiction, of literature. In a history book these names would have been commented on and explained, dates would have been given, information about these peoples' lives, important events of their biographies, and their important writings. Peter Weiss did nothing of the sort. "Only enumeration of names," as stated in the notebooks (N II/554); a formal asceticism that was deplored by some reviewers as a "dry catalogue," a "dry protocol style"[10] that, it was maintained, had nothing to do with the art of literary narration. Similar arguments had been used earlier to critique Weiss's spartan renunciation of theatrical opulence in *Viet Nam Discourse*. Such criticism notwithstanding, the unadorned enumeration of names and genealogies is one of the oldest narrative elements in any story, going back to at least the *Iliad* and the Bible.

In Weiss's work this literary practice is by no means new: in *Vanishing Point* there were already mere lists of names.[11] In *The Aesthetics of Resistance* this stylistic device serves as a challenge to readers to enlarge the traditional canon of memorable names by including the names of ruthless politicians (such as Groener, Hindenburg, and Seeckt) and right-wing murderers (such as Epp and Escherich), but mostly by including the names of resistance fighters—a number of them artists and intellectuals—all the men and women who ultimately had nothing left to oppose the existing order with but their bodies. It is *their* names that fill the lists in *The Aesthetics of Resistance:* lists of intellectuals on the side of the Spanish republic (I/224); lists of Soviet writers, artists, and journalists who became victims of Stalinism (I/265; there was a similar list in *Trotsky in Exile*); and finally, the list of the resistance fighters who were executed at Plötzensee prison in Berlin (III/231).

Writing as *"memory work*, wrested from the pain about the countless victims," as Thomas Metscher has said.[12] Memory is the secret engine that drives Weiss's imagination in *The Aesthetics of Resistance*. In the words of the young student, Heilmann: "All of art, he [Heilmann] continued, all of literature is present in us under the one goddess we can still accept, Mnemosyne. She, the mother of the arts, is called recollection" (I/77). The old concept of Greek mythology, that memory, recollection, is the mother of all muses, is taken literally in *The Aesthetics of Resistance*.

It is, however, by no means necessary to be familiar with all or even with many of the names in Weiss's novel in order to become involved in *The Aesthetics of Resistance*. After completing work on the novel Weiss emphatically pointed out that the authentic figures were not identical with the figures in his text (N II/927). He had used the historical persons who lent their names and biographies to his figures merely as "ciphers" (N II/117). Weiss used this term in various ways in his attempts to shed light on his concept. Cipher meant, first of all, that aspect of the individual which transcends his or her uniqueness, his or her character, and his or her individual psychology—the human being as a historic creature; as the "ensemble of social relations," in a phrase by the young Karl Marx quoted earlier;[13] and a creature through whom the forces and tendencies of an era are expressed. Stage characters conceived as ciphers had appeared earlier in Weiss's oeuvre, for instance, in *The Investigation,* in *Song of the Lusitanian Bogey,* and especially in *Viet Nam Discourse.* But in *The Aesthetics of Resistance* there was further reason why the personnel should consist of such almost anonymous ciphers. Most of the historical figures whose names are used in the novel had after 1933 lived illegal existences in the underground, in constant fear of being discovered, frequently changing their place of residence, and frequently changing countries. They had long since set aside their bourgeois identity and their real names, using only "ciphers, aliases" (III/265). The ones who worked most closely with one another knew the least about each another (so there was nothing to betray to the Gestapo under torture). As stated in a key passage of the novel, these people "were not even in possession of their own names. . . . If I [the narrator] would describe what happened to me among them, they would retain this shadowy aspect," and " I would give back their true names to them, the furtive ones" (III/265–66).

Weiss has carried out the young narrator's intentions. He has returned their actual names to these people: Horst Heilmann, Hans and Hilde Coppi, Lotte Bischoff, John Sieg, Erika von Brockdorff, Mildred Harnack, Walter Husemann, Oda Schotmüller, and countless others. What's more, he has given them back traces of their identity. Thus, for instance, Heilmann, confronted with imminent death, is given back his obsession with the figure of Heracles and his feelings for Libertas Schulze-Boysen, a fellow member of the group who is herself about to be beheaded. Even the most ephemeral of party bureaucrats, Rosner, Funk (Herbert Wehner's alias), or the undaunted party warrior Stahlmann (Richard Illner's alias) retain some small, unmistakable individual traits: Rosner likes to sing, Funk grows flowers, and about Stahlmann there is this enigmatic comment: "He abandoned himself to a petrified female dancer" (III/122). But such individualization is kept within bounds. Most of the figures' first names are never mentioned. The "shadowy aspect" of their existence is preserved.

This is also true of the women. It might not be inappropriate to view the women as the main figures of the novel: Marcauer, Boye, Rosalinde von Ossietzky, and especially Lotte Bischoff and the narrator's mother. They are the sum of all of Weiss's earlier attempts at creating female figures, such as Lily

Tofler in *The Investigation,* or Ana in *Song of the Lusitanian Bogey.* Their combative humanism is broader and deeper than that of the men. They oppose male power games, even those played by their own side, as in Marcauer's unrelenting critique of the "man's world" that is reflected in the Stalinist show trials (I/293). Lotte Bischoff, the main figure of the third volume (and possibly of the whole novel)—who willingly places her life in the service of the Communist Party, and who in the middle of the war illegally returns to Berlin and becomes a witness to the extermination of all her fellow conspirators—even Lotte Bischoff harbors no illusions: "The party, however, despite Rosa [Luxemburg], despite [Klara] Zetkin, was led by men. Not a single woman was on the Central Committee" (III/80): a man's world. Even a figure like Bertolt Brecht (one of the protagonists of the second volume), fully recognizing the necessity of changing existing conditions, persists in his atavistic and authoritarian patriarchy.

Weiss's women figures are the most radical in refusing to conform in a time that is out of joint, and they pay the highest price. That holds true even for Karin Boye, the lesbian Swedish writer who at times succumbs to the aesthetic magic of fascism: equally horrified by the terror unleashed by the Nazis and by how easily she had been seduced by them, she commits suicide. Marcauer, who does not desist in her criticism of the man's world of Stalinism, is arrested and presumably executed in Spain by her own comrades. Rosalinde von Ossietzky, the daughter of the German journalist and Nobel Peace Prize winner Carl von Ossietzky who was tortured to death by the Nazis, becomes mentally disturbed in her Swedish exile. The narrator's mother, fleeing with her husband from the Nazis, witnesses the execution of Jews, men, women, and children in Poland. Having found exile in Sweden, she refuses to speak, then refuses to eat. Her death becomes the ultimate expression of protest. In the words of her son, "If a scream could be awakened in her, no living person could endure it" (III/16).

The only survivor of the fascist carnage is Lotte Bischoff, who may be one of the great female figures in European literature.

On Thursday, 22 June 1971, in a meeting in East Berlin, the real Lotte Bischoff told her memories to Peter Weiss (N I/99).

The Aesthetics of Resistance is a book about the left, about socialists and communists, and about the labor movement in Germany, in the Soviet Union, in Spain, in Sweden, and elsewhere. It is about the battles and the defeats of the oppressed against their oppressors over the course of more than 2,000 years, leading up to the struggle against fascism, which ends with the annihilation of the antifascist resistance and much of the European left. The forces of progress and humanity had once again proved to be weak. But long before the fascists set about systematically eliminating the forces of the left, these forces had already become weakened, disintegrating into numerous splinter groups fighting each other with increased bitterness.

In the first volume of *The Aesthetics of Resistance* Peter Weiss tries to reveal some of the causes of this disintegration through long debates between the narrator and his father. In the kitchen of his parents' apartment in the city of Varnsdorf in Czechoslovakia, where they live in exile, the two men talk about the breakup of the German labor movement at the end of 1918, with the founding of the German Communist Party by Rosa Luxemburg, Karl Liebknecht, Klara Zetkin, Franz Mehring, and others. The narrator's father, a Social Democrat, is as reluctant to join this new party as he is to make a commitment to the Social Democrats, whom he sees as increasingly inclined toward compromise with the bourgeoisie. When revolutionary upheavals break out all over Germany in November 1918, they are bloodily suppressed by the Social Democratic government that had just been elected. There was revolutionary activity in the port city of Bremen, too, where the narrator had spent the first years of his life—just like Peter Weiss, who had written once before about his childhood memories of those revolutionary days, in the autobiographical novel *Leavetaking*.[14]

Disgusted by the politics of the Social Democrats, the father now becomes a member of a leftist splinter party, the USPD. When this party is dissolved at the end of 1920, the father, despite all his reservations, returns to the Social Democrats. "I again joined the [Social Democratic] party, he [the father] said, because here I was able to adopt the critical position that would have been denied me in the communist party" (I/121). Within his party he actively pushes for a merger with the communists and opposes currying favor with the bourgeoisie. But his efforts meet with no success. Unity remains elusive during the years of the Weimar Republic. In the early 1930s the Stalin-dominated Communist International (Comintern) proclaims that the main enemies of communism are not the Nazis (who are rapidly gaining power) but the Social Democrats—a historical error for which communists as well as Social Democrats would soon have to pay a terrible price.

How can readers of the novel find their way through such a tangle of often obscure and remote historical events? *The Aesthetics of Resistance,* it should be kept in mind, is not a history book, it is not concerned primarily with historical truth (even though it painstakingly adheres to it) but with artistic truth. In the figure of the narrator's father Weiss has created a type that could be found by the millions in Germany during the 1920s: the politically aware and self-assured worker. People like him, men and women, found themselves in an economic and political struggle for survival, a struggle that threatened their material and—with the growth of fascism—physical existence. In a society that was starting to break up under the pressure of radical forces, they had to choose between various parties, movements and groups whose policies and goals became increasingly puzzling to them. With the greatest efforts these workers tried to make themselves into the subjects of history, to determine their own fate. How they tried and how they failed is the topic of Weiss's novel. Like the antifascist novels of Wolf, Andersch, or Hermlin, it is about the descent of a highly developed and civilized society into barbarity.

In the fight against fascism the first defeat took place in Spain before the beginning of World War II. With the support of German and Italian armed forces and bombers, the legal Spanish republic was overthrown in a putsch headed by the fascist General Franco. To many contemporaries the Spanish Civil War seemed like a last opportunity to contain German and international fascism. International brigades made up of volunteers from all over the world fought on the side of the Spanish republic. There was support also from the Soviet Union. In contrast, the democratic governments of the Western world did nothing. The Spanish republic was defeated and the consequences are well known.

In *The Aesthetics of Resistance* Peter Weiss sends his narrator to Spain in the fall of 1937, but not to the front, since that would have contradicted the antidramatic concept of the novel. The narrator works behind the front lines as a medical orderly in a convalescent home for wounded soldiers. His superior is the physician Max Hodann who, in real life, had been a father figure to Peter Weiss in Swedish exile, and who had already been memorialized under the name Hoderer in *Vanishing Point*.

In Spain the narrator, Hodann, and their comrades find themselves in a situation similar to that of the narrator's father in the Weimar Republic. Their organizations are divided and fighting each other; the war against fascism is growing steadily worse, defeat is foreseeable. Rumors are flying, and there are intrigues and incomprehensible commands. The anarchists, who are courageously fighting against Franco's troops, are decimated by the communists. Soon it will suffice to merely be suspected of being an anarchist to find oneself in an untenable situation. Stalin's long arm is behind everything.

The loyalty of the novel's figures is subjected to an unbearable strain. Stalin, the leader of that party to which most of them belong or are in solidarity with, declares Lenin's former closest collaborators—the erstwhile most courageous and capable leaders of the Russian Revolution—traitors who should be executed. From the radio in the Spanish hospital ward of Denia, the first-person narrator, Hodann, the Norwegian writer Nordahl Grieg and his girlfriend, the journalist Lise Lindbaek, the anarchist Marcauer, and others follow the trials taking place in Moscow. In this situation Weiss is not interested in assigning blame after the fact, to sort out his figures according to whether they took a stand for or against Stalinist policy. Rather, he shows the extreme efforts undertaken by them in order to determine the truth. They all had come to Spain to lay down their lives in the deadly struggle against the deformed system called fascism. Now these volunteers had to confront the deformations within their own ranks. How did they react? What kinds of choices were available to them, assuming they wanted to hold on to their socialist convictions and continue their unconditional resistance against fascism?

Mourning, as mentioned earlier, is the underlying tone of the antifascist novels of the 1970s. Mourning about all that had been brought into the world by German fascism. Mourning about the inability of the left to resist the growing deformation of its own theory and praxis, and about its inability to oppose fascism by providing a compelling alternative. The fact that Grieg and the young narrator stand by their commitment to the Soviet Union, despite the events in Moscow, while Marcauer denounces the trials as an expression of male power struggles, is by no means the main point of the debates about Stalinism in Weiss's novel. What is conveyed foremost is the historical situation in which countless people found themselves at that time; a situation which could not be conclusively dealt with, a situation which demanded decisions that tore people apart and in many cases cost them their lives. Marcauer was executed, Grieg later lost his life during World War II, while Hodann eventually committed suicide. All these deaths are in some way related to the issues presented in the passages about the Moscow trials.

The numerous and prolonged debates in *The Aesthetics of Resistance* about the creation of an antifascist people's front; the narration on the Swedish peasant uprisings in the late middle ages (which the Brecht figure wants to turn into a play); the extensive passages on the history of the Swedish labor movement; the debates about socialism and communism, about the effect of the German-Soviet nonaggression pact; the narration on the strategy and tactics of the antifascist resistance—all the great passages of *The Aesthetics of Resistance* are based on the same narrative *gestus:* that the questions are more important than the answers, the discussions more important than the results. Also important are the contradictions. Each participant in these discussions and debates, from the dogmatic communist bureaucrat Mewis to Rosalinde von Ossietzky who radically rejects communism, is given equal space to express his or her opinions. Therein lies the essence of this work and this democratic narrator Peter Weiss. The socialist-communist positions are not presupposed in *The Aesthetics of Resistance*. They may be gleaned from the sum of all the questions, doubts, and contradictions.

The Aesthetics of Resistance opens with a now famous and much analyzed passage: a description of the Pergamon altar, an immense 2,000-year-old stone relief from Asia Minor depicting the battle between gods and half-gods. Discovered toward the end of the nineteenth century by a German explorer, the sculpture was subsequently removed piece by piece and reassembled in the Pergamon Museum in Berlin, where it still stands today. The powerful description of the relief is followed by a rambling interpretation; in thorough detail the prehistory and history of the Pergamon Empire is related up to the time of its decline and the rediscovery of the relief and its shipment to Germany. This description alone covers the first 50 pages. This is not what one might expect in an antifascist novel.

In the third volume there is a comparable set piece in the broadly executed description of the ancient temples at Angkor Wat and Angkor Thom in present-day Cambodia. The description of the Asian temple sculpture is provided by Stahlmann, the carefree communist warrior who had once visited Angkor (as had the real Stahlmann, as well as Peter Weiss on his trip to North Vietnam in 1968). On his way to a conspiratorial meeting in Stockholm in the year 1941, Stahlmann describes the Cambodian temples to the narrator who has just become a member of the Communist Party. (One is reminded of the novel's complex fabric.)

Following the passages about the Pergamon sculpture in *The Aesthetics of Resistance*, there are discussions of Courbet, Millet, and other nineteenth-century French painters, about Soviet "socialist realism," Dante's *Divine Comedy*, and Piero della Francesca. Shortly before he leaves for Spain, the narrator studies Brueghel's paintings and reflects on the possible references between Kafka's novel, *The Castle*, and a novel by Klaus Neukrantz, a working-class novelist of the Weimar Republic who has hardly left a trace in the canon of German literature. The narrator's first impression upon arriving in Spain, which is engulfed in civil war, is also determined by a work of art: in Barcelona he visits the Sagrada Familia Cathedral, an incomparable structure by the strange Spanish architect Antonio Gaudi y Cornet (1852–1926). The first volume ends with a long conversation between the narrator and

Ayschmann about Picasso's famous painting "Guernica" of the destruction of that Spanish city by fascist bombs.

Like the first volume, the second volume of *The Aesthetics of Resistance* opens with the description and interpretation of a work of art that extends over several dozen pages: the huge painting, *Raft of the Medusa,* created in 1819 by Géricault. Later there are also references to surrealism and dadaism, Russian nineteenth-century painting, Dürer, Joyce, Klee, Schönberg, and to well-known and little known painters and writers of all centuries—from the German sculptor of the late Middle Ages, Tilmann Riemenschneider, to Goya, Delacroix, Munch, and Sue, to Sassetta, Meissonnier, and Menzel.

"If we want to understand art and literature, we must interpret it against the grain," says the young worker Coppi, in a turn of phrase recalling Walter Benjamin (I/41). "We . . . us": the pronouns refer to the working masses, those for whom art was not intended and from whom it was usually withheld. At the core of all passages about art in *The Aesthetics of Resistance* lies the same impetus: to interpret anew the great works of art of (mainly) European culture for working people, for whom a higher education and aesthetic training have not been accessible. In addition, Weiss wants to turn the attention of the working class toward those aspects of art that had hardly aroused interest among the representatives of mainstream art history, but which might interest the working class themselves: the enormous sacrifices made by the slaves and workers who had dragged and piled up the stones in Pergamon or Angkor. He points out that these works of art were ordered and paid for by the ruling few and were intended for them, thus glorifying the high-born and ignoring or depicting in a degrading manner the low-born. Weiss draws attention to the traces that, against all odds, the low-born have left in the great works: as craftsmen, for example, without whose strength and skill these works could not have been created. Coppi discerns in the faces of the lesser figures of the Pergamon sculpture a deep humanity he associates with the working masses and compared to which the facial features of the gods appear stiff and cold (I/49). In Millet's painting of peasant figures the three friends find a "dignity that they [the peasants] had fought for" (I/62). Heilmann, Coppi, and the narrator read Kafka's novel *The Castle,* unencumbered by the metaphysical walls an elitist circle of cognoscenti had erected around it, but also unconcerned about the narrow-minded critique of Kafka by communist cultural bureaucrats. In their reading the novel is revealed to be a description of the likes of them: the debased and the weak, helplessly subjected to an anonymous power—a "proletarian novel" (I/179).

The giant Pergamon frieze, as is stated in the opening sentence of *The Aesthetics of Resistance,* consists of fragments, broken and scruffy bits and pieces of stone, and empty spaces, a confusing chaos of only partially preserved figures, and remnants of weapons, faces, and limbs. The three young viewers, approaching this work in an exemplary creative manner, an equal mixture of precise observation and imagination, recreate the Pergamon altar from its ruins. There is one figure, however, that they seek in vain, a figure that was once part of the sculpture but of which nothing remains except the "paw of a lion's skin which he had worn as a cape" (I/11). That figure is Heracles, the only mortal among the gods. This Heracles, in Coppi's opinion, had been one of them, and since he was missing they themselves would have to create an image of him. This the three young comrades repeatedly attempt in the course of the novel. The story of Heracles' life and deeds is told near the beginning (I/18–25) as part of the long opening passage on the Pergamon relief. In Heracles' endless vacillations between the low-born and the gods, Heilmann tries to make visible a development that eventually led the Greek hero to the "side of the enslaved" (I/25). A year later, in the summer of 1938, the narrator in Spain receives a long letter from Heilmann: a rambling reinterpretation of Heracles (I/314–20). Heilmann has come to doubt the Greek hero. The myth of Heracles as a "helper in need" (I/315) had been intended to make the oppressed seek solace in the "divine abilities" of a redeemer, rather than in their own strength. Such a myth, Heilmann concludes, could only profit those in power.

The last part of *The Aesthetics of Resistance* opens with an appeal to Heracles: "O Heracles, said Heilmann, how should we be able to assert ourselves without your presence" (III/169). It is the beginning of the "walk through Hades," which is what Berlin had become as a result of the Allied bombings. Coppi refutes Heilmann's hopes for a redeemer: "in us is the one who fell from the frieze of the gods, we need no guiding star, we do not need the myths that want only to make us smaller, we are all we need" (III/169). But a short time before his execution, in the farewell letter he writes from his death cell to the narrator, the nineteen-year-old Heilmann calls out one more time to the savior who will not come: "O Heracles . . . O Heracles" (III/203, 210).

Many years after the war, with his comrades long dead, the narrator imagines how some day he would again visit the Pergamon frieze. The space of Heracles would still be empty. There is no hope for a messiah. From *The Shadow of the Coachman's Body* and *Die Versicherung* to *Night with Guests,*

Mockinpott (where God himself makes an appearance), and *Hölderlin,* Weiss had repeatedly created redeemer figures, until a completely secular concept of this myth was arrived at. With *Mockinpott* and especially with the Empedocles fragment in *Hölderlin,* it became clear that any concept of a messianic bearer of hope would only prevent the masses from ever taking their fate into their own hands. *The Aesthetics of Resistance* ends with this thought. Heracles' place in the Pergamon frieze remains empty. The first-person narrator comprehends that nobody will ever come to fill it. The poor, the exploited, and the oppressed "would have to empower themselves, would have to seize this broad and vibrant movement with which they would finally be able to sweep away the terrible pressure weighing them down" (III/268). The novel ends with this sentence.

This is, indeed, a difficult book.

Critic Heinrich Vormweg called *The Aesthetics of Resistance* monstrous, adding these perceptive thoughts: "Has it not been true again and again throughout history that those works have appeared monstrous to the *Zeitgeist* which have made it recognize its own deformations with particular clarity?"[15] In a first approach, the form and content of *The Aesthetics of Resistance* might be understood as the result of Peter Weiss's attempt to give expression, through literature, to that monstrosity which in the twentieth century hindered and defeated the struggles of the masses for their liberation.

Weiss himself stated that the novel was the result "of an incredibly strenuous labor," adding, "the readers . . . will have to repeat this achievement, this effort" (G/R 281). Labor, achievement, effort: terms that, through the struggle for survival under real existing capitalism, have acquired mostly negative connotations. Yet the demands it makes upon the reader did not stop *The Aesthetics of Resistance* from becoming a best-seller in the late 1980s, even after the conservative *Tendenzwende* (change of trend) under Chancellor Kohl.[16] Apparently, there is a kind of labor that does not lead to fatigue and accommodation but brings about a lively stubbornness. There is a kind of achievement that is not to the detriment of others but for the benefit of all. There is a kind of effort that does not cost one's leisure but serves everyone's liberation. Beyond all the difficulties, the involvement with *The Aesthetics of Resistance* is of this kind.

The first volume of the novel was published in the fall of 1975. There was only a small edition, for what could the publisher expect from this book, which was considered difficult and, what's more, which was written by a communist about communists. The interest in Marx and in the causes of fascism, in Vietnam, and in antibourgeois art that had been spawned by the student movement of 1968 had faded. The Vietnam War had ended in the spring of 1975. In the Federal Republic, Social Democrat Helmut Schmidt had succeeded his party comrade Willy Brandt, who had resigned as chancellor. Since 1968 students had tried to bring "fantasy into power," according to a slogan of the movement. Under Willy Brandt there had been a few beginnings. Now, power once again ruled without any fantasy.

That there would be a second volume of *The Aesthetics of Resistance* only became clear to Weiss in the course of his work on the first volume. The work on this second volume led to more research. Shortly before its completion in February 1978, it turned out that it would be followed by a third volume, an epilogue (N II/661). The enormous work left Weiss little opportunity to involve himself in the events of the 1970s. One opportunity, however, arose from an international meeting of writers scheduled for the summer of 1977 in the Bulgarian capital, Sofia, which Weiss planned to attend. He learned that dissident Czechoslovak writer Pavel Kohout was not to be allowed to participate, even though Kohout insisted that he was "not an enemy of socialism." Kohout informed Weiss about his plight in an open letter published in the FRG in the *Frankfurter Allgemeine Zeitung* (N II/574–76). Weiss answered, also in an open letter. It was "absolutely necessary," he wrote, that critical people like Kohout be given the opportunity to express their opinion within the framework of the meeting in Sofia—provided they did not misuse the event for "antisocialist purposes" (N II/577–78). When it became clear that despite Weiss's plea Kohout would not be allowed to attend, Weiss withdrew (N II/583–86, 590–96).

Weiss's support of the People's Republic of Vietnam continued throughout this period. The official end of the Vietnam War had not brought peace to that part of the world. Especially in Cambodia there were new, terrible struggles that brought Vietnam into an untenable situation, as has been shown at the end of chapter six.

In addition to these activities, the notebooks document Weiss's concerns about his wife's health. Gunilla Palmstierna-Weiss suffered from an eye disease that was difficult to cure and that required numerous medical consultations and several operations. Nadja Weiss, Peter and Gunilla's daughter, born November 1972, is also a frequent topic in the notebooks. These entries by the fifty-six-year-old father are very moving.

The second volume of *The Aesthetics of Resistance* was published in the fall of 1978. Only after a period of several months, however, was the writing of the final volume begun, in December 1978. Weiss's energy was waning, as the notebooks show. At times he doubted whether he would be able to complete the novel at all. For the moment had now come to write the passage from which he had shied away since the beginning of the project: the description of the execution of the men and women of the antifascist resistance. During work on these chapters Weiss notes "almost constant visions of death" (N II/896). Work on *The Aesthetics of Resistance* was completed on 28 August 1980 (N II/926). The notebooks also end on this date. Peter Weiss spent the rest of the year on corrections and preparation of the text for publication. The final volume of *The Aesthetics of Resistance* was published in 1981.

NOTES

1. Wolfgang Fritz Haug and Kaspar Maase, "Vorwort," in Haug and Maase, eds., *Materialistische Kulturtheorie und Alltagskultur* (Berlin: Argument, 1980) 4.

2. Since I have already presented in book form my interpretation of *The Aesthetics of Resistance,* I refrain here from presenting the extensive source material for a second time. For this information, see Robert Cohen, *Versuche über Weiss' "Ästhetik des Widerstands"* (Bern: Peter Lang, 1989). For detailed information on all aspects of the novel, see also Robert Cohen, *Bio-bibliographisches Handbuch zu Weiss' "Ästhetik des Widerstands"* (Berlin: Argument, 1989).

3. The parenthetical numbers refer to the volume and the page of Peter Weiss, *Die Ästhetik des Widerstands* I (1975), II (1978), III (1981), single volume ed. (Frankfurt/Main: Suhrkamp, 2d ed., 1986) (the pagination in all Suhrkamp editions is identical). Although the novel has not yet been translated into English, for easier reading the English translation of the title is used throughout.

4. Jürgen Lodemann, "Jeder Mensch, der denken kann, kann auch weiterdenken. Jürgen Lodemann im Gespräch mit Peter Weiss," *Deutsche Volkszeitung* 38 (17 September 1981).

5. On the many ways in which the final part of *The Aesthetics of Resistance* refers to Dante's *Inferno,* see Robert Cohen, "Der Gesang von Plötzensee: Zur Darstellung des antifaschistischen Widerstands in Peter Weiss' 'Ästhetik des Widerstands,' " in Helmut Pfanner, ed., *Der Zweite Weltkrieg und die Exilanten* (Bonn: Bouvier 1991) 203–4.

6. See Cohen, "Der Gesang von Plötzensee" 197–98.

7. Burkhardt Lindner, "Halluzinatorischer Realismus. Die 'Ästhetik des Widerstands,' die 'Notizbücher' und die Todeszonen der Kunst," in Alexander Stephan, ed., *Die Ästhetik des Widerstands* Frankfurt/Main: Suhrkamp, 1983) 164.

8. For short biographies of the figures in *The Aesthetics of Resistance,* see Cohen, *Bio-bibliographisches Handbuch.*

9. See Fritz J. Raddatz, "Abschied von den Söhnen? Kein Fresko, sondern ein Flickerlteppich: Zum Abschluss der Roman-Trilogie. Peter Weiss: 'Ästhetik des Widerstands,' " *Die Zeit* 8 May 1981.

10. Hans Christoph Buch, "Seine Rede ist Ja ja, nein nein. Hans Christoph Buch über Peter Weiss' 'Die Ästhetik des Widerstands,' " *Der Spiegel* 47 (20 November 1978): 260; and Franz Schonauer, "Heldenlegende vor düsterem Hintergrund. Zur Fortsetzung von Peter Weiss' Roman 'Die Ästhetik des Widerstands,' " *Der Tagesspiegel* (Berlin) 25 March 1979.

11. See Peter Weiss, *Vanishing Point (Fluchtpunkt,* 1960–61), trans. E. B. Garside, Alastair Hamilton, and Christopher Levenson, in Weiss, *Exile* (New York: Delacorte, 1968) 102, 130–31, 240.

12. "Avantgarde—Arbeiterklasse—Erbe. Gespräch zu Peter Weiss' 'Die Ästhetik des Widerstands,' " *Sinn und Form* 36, no. 1 (1984): 78 (emphasis in the original).

13. Karl Marx, "Thesen über Feuerbach" (1845), in *Marx Engels Werke* (Berlin: Dietz, 1956) 3:6. See also chap. 7 above.

14. See Peter Weiss, *Leavetaking* (*Abschied von den Eltern*, 1960), trans. E. B. Garside, Alastair Hamilton, and Christopher Levenson, in Weiss, *Exile* 8.

15. Heinrich Vormweg, "Ein grosser Entwurf gegen den Zeitgeist. Peter Weiss hat 'Die Ästhetik des Widerstands' abgeschlossen," *Süddeutsche Zeitung* 20 May 1981.

16. See Cohen, *Bio-bibliographisches Handbuch* 7.

CHAPTER NINE

After Kafka: Interpretations
and Dramatizations

Weiss and Kafka: this topic has been touched upon here repeatedly. How could a young artist with a tortured, at times almost unlivable youth, half-Jewish, German-speaking, a Czech national, stranded in Prague in 1937 by anonymous, unfathomable powers, a foreigner who did not belong there or anywhere else—how could Peter Weiss help being deeply affected by the Jewish writer from Prague whose fictional characters are exposed to anonymous powers, aliens in an alienated world, abandoned, tortured, and ultimately killed like dogs? The young painter's attention had first been drawn to Kafka's works by his friend at the Prague Academy of Art, Peter Kien. But not until several years later when an exile in Sweden, in the middle of the war, did Weiss begin to focus on the works of the author of *The Trial* and *The Castle*. The young exile was overwhelmed by what he read, if one is to accept the description of the narrator's encounter with Kafka's work in the autobiographical novel of 1961, *Leavetaking*: "All that I had read previously receded into the background." The narrator continues, "So now, while reading *The Trial* I became keenly aware of the trial in which I myself was entrapped."[1] Reading Kafka was self-therapy; and thus began an involvement with Kafka that was to last until Weiss's death.

Traces of a more objective appropriation of Kafka appear in Weiss's first postwar texts: in *Von Insel zu Insel* (written in 1944) where an "execution machine" is described; and in the 1947 "Reportagen aus Deutschland," in which the factory-like extermination of people is perceived as "reality's answer to Kafka's visions."[2] Kafka's influence is found in many of Weiss's prose texts and dramas of the early literary oeuvre. It is most obvious in *The Shadow of the Coachman's Body*: in the narrative tone of a pedantic and laconic registering of a small, shabby, and miserable world, similar to the world of Kafka's *The Castle;* in the father-son conflict of the family residing in the boarding house; and even in the surreal and archaic vocabulary—hired man, housekeeper, coachman, garrison town. In the mid-1960s there was Weiss's investigation of Auschwitz—a work that would have been inconceivable without Kafka (as well as Dante). Kafka's influence is also in evidence in the farce about Mr. Mockinpott, who one day finds himself arrested without reason.

In *The Aesthetics of Resistance* a major passage is devoted to the narrator's interpretation of Kafka's *The Castle*. Considering the young worker's communist convictions, this is rather surprising. The narrator recalls correctly that Georg Lukács, possibly the most important Marxist cultural philosopher of the century, was in the forefront of Marxist intellectuals who rejected Kafka. The author of *The Castle* was considered "decadent" (I/177), not in any vulgar meaning of the word but in a Marxist-philosophical sense: a representative of the capitalist system in its decline. But it is also true that Lukács, at least in his later works, acknowledged Kafka's realism.[3] A worthy opponent indeed, Lukács was fully aware of Kafka's genius and of the "profound and deeply moving truth" of Kafka's world.[4] More important, however, Lukács's rigidly theoretical rejection of Kafka had little effect on the critical reception of Kafka in the West, and was subject to shifting fates even in communist countries. Of greater and more enduring importance for an understanding of Kafka are the texts of several other thinkers influenced by Marx: Walter Benjamin, Theodor Adorno, Günther Anders, and Ernst Fischer; especially Fischer, a communist intellectual who, like Kafka, had been born in the Austro-Hungarian Empire, has maintained that the truth of the Prague poet cannot be found in that speculative heaven where his texts are considered timeless depictions of the human condition that need to be interpreted theologically but rather in Kafka's re-creation of the historical reality of the Habsburg monarchy. "Kafka's novels are not unfounded dreams of anxiety, they contain a reality, in eerily-satirical distortion, that was experienced by millions."[5]

A reality experienced by millions. This is the aspect of the novel brought out, in *The Aesthetics of Resistance*, by the narrator's interpretation. The young worker is struck by Kafka's minute descriptions, in *The Castle*, of the lowest-born, most miserable, most insignificant of human beings: peasants, barkeepers, stable-boys, farmhands, domestics, and cleaning women. Where, indeed, in twentieth-century European literature, has the suffering of the lowest class been portrayed with greater truth than in the words with which the cleaning woman, Pepi, describes her life? Or in that passage where K., demoted from being a surveyor to being a janitor in a school, and Frieda, freezing and weeping, cower on a straw sack in the unheated gymnasium of the village school? In Kafka's text not the smallest nuance of class differences and master-servant relationships is lost. This is exemplified in the description of the barkeeper, a "man carefully bred through his association with far more highly placed people," who, despite his apparent politeness, "never ceased to be the employer dealing with an employee" while talking with the barmaid

Frieda.[6] *The Castle* can indeed be read as a "proletarian novel," as the narrator of *The Aesthetics of Resistance* notes (I/179).

Nonetheless, the narrator's reading of *The Castle* is too narrow. What he does not see, what he is not able to relate to, except in the very last sentence (I/180), are the elements of dream, vision, and fantasy on which Kafka's art feeds (and Peter Weiss's as well). What the narrator does not see is the enigma at the center of all of Kafka's work. In *The Castle,* the surveyor K. formulates this enigma as follows: "Someone who is blindfolded can be encouraged ever so strongly to look through the cloth, but he still will never see anything; he can see only if the cloth is removed"[7]—an image that provides occasion for endless questions, but they are never posed by Weiss's narrator.

Der Prozess

Weiss had just completed the first part of volume I of *The Aesthetics of Resistance,* which contains the passages on *The Castle,* when, on 5 February 1974, he received a proposal from the Swedish film and theater director, Ingmar Bergman, to write an adaption of Kafka's *Trial* for the stage. Bergman's offer was promptly accepted; in the passage in *The Aesthetics of Resistance* Weiss had apparently not said everything he had to say about Kafka. Work on the novel was interrupted, as is shown by the numerous entries in the notebooks on *Der Prozess* (The Trial) (N II/255). After working on this project for six weeks, Weiss noted, "Am giving . . . up work on *Der Prozess*" (N II/273). He had come to the conclusion that the extremely subjective, dreamlike vision of Kafka's Josef K[8] could not be transposed into the more objective form of a stage play.

There may have been another reason for abandoning the project. What Bergman may have expected of this adaption—for which its author had already received partial payment—seems to have irritated and impeded Weiss. He promptly returned the honorarium—then continued work on the project. Free of Bergman's expectations, he was now able to finish the project (N II/274). By mid-April 1974 the dramatization of *The Trial,* in two acts and eighteen scenes, was sent off to the Dramatic Theater in Stockholm.

Bergman rejected it. The director, as Weiss notes, had expected something different, "a 'bold experiment,' a 'personal interpretation' " (N II/328). Weiss had never been able to react calmly to his critics. He now had bitter words for directors such as Bergman who regarded Kafka's texts merely as source material for their own ambitions. Why didn't they write their own plays? Weiss maintained that the only way to remain true to Kafka was to follow the text closely, for "it contains everything that can be said about the topic" (N II/331).

They were both wrong: Bergman by insisting that Weiss's treatment lacked a "personal interpretation," and Weiss by claiming that he had adhered closely to the text (522).[9] While this may be true in terms of plot, Weiss clearly plays down the extent to which his adaption was determined by his own personal interpretation. What needs to be examined is the degree to which Weiss's very personal reading is rooted in themes and motifs already present in Kafka's text.[10]

The novel, *The Trial,* which Kafka began writing in August 1914, tells the story of Josef K, a bank clerk who is arrested on his thirtieth birthday by servants of an anonymous, mysterious court. Since he is unaware of any guilt and since he is allowed to continue his life and his occupation as before, K does not take the arrest seriously. Only during the course of several months does he become interested in the proceedings against him. But all the measures that he now undertakes come too late, and apparently would have been pointless anyway. On the day of his thirty-first birthday K is stabbed to death by two myrmidons of the court. Even though this tale has the characteristics of a parable, it is by no means set outside of any specific time or place. The society Kafka describes, with its representatives of the upper and lower middle class and its proletariat, the world of bureaucrats and their bureaucracy has all the traits of the bourgeois-capitalist society of the prewar era in a big city of the Habsburg empire, such as Kafka's Prague.

In his adaption Weiss precisely placed the time of the events described in *The Trial.* Kafka's thirtieth birthday was on 3 July 1913. Weiss's play begins with this date and ends on 2 July 1914. July 1913 falls within the period of the second Balkan War, in which the Balkan countries fought the expansionist ambitions of the Habsburg empire—a final rehearsal for the coming World War. This historical constellation is referred to at the beginning of the play when Weiss's figure of the army captain announces that "there is war" (529). When the captain repeats these words at the end of the play, shortly before K's execution, there is an ominous hint that K's death prefigures the coming slaughter of millions. Like them, K is innocent and, like them, he had done nothing to prevent this imminent catastrophe.

Incidentally, Weiss considered the possibility of a very different form of historicization. "Understanding for Kafka awakened by the Moscow trials," he noted in mid-May 1973 (N II/212). Toward the end of 1974, the dramatization of *Der Prozess* having been completed, Weiss was working on the passage about the Moscow trials of 1936–38 in *The Aesthetics of Resistance.*

The notebooks show that he returned to the idea of linking the two trials. But the Stalinist proceedings, which had not been held by a secret court in a dingy loft but rather in front of the whole world, no longer seem to have much in common with the trial described by Kafka. Comparing the two trials, Weiss notes that Kafka's text deals "with something completely different" (N II/ 391)—as is indeed the case.

The Balkan War, which was already under way in July 1913, had direct effects on the economy in the Austro-Hungarian monarchy. The first tremors of the impending World War, too, were being registered by the control centers of economic processes, the banks. In one of them K works as a head clerk, a position not without influence. This context, which was laid out in Kafka's novel, is emphasized in Weiss's dramatization. Unlike in the novel, however, in the play K's attitude toward the business dealings of his bank are a major factor in his "case." At one point K's superior, the deputy director, formulates the bank's policy that no consideration must be given to the uneasiness of the small savers. In view of the danger of war, even small loans were to be rejected. On the other hand, for the big manufacturer looking for investment opportunities for his capital, war turns out to be a boon: the deputy director enthusiastically recommends that the manufacturer invest his money in weapons, "There you will get the highest dividends!" (571). K is present at both events, but both times he remains indifferent to the banker's decisions. He is preoccupied with his court case. In these scenes there is a growing sense that K, nonpolitical and indifferent to the injustices that surround him and for which he bears part of the responsibility, is indeed guilty. Therein Weiss's play reflects a thinking radically opposed to Kafka's concept of an existential guilt a priori.

K's guilt through indifference is also brought out elsewhere in the play. For instance, there are at all times "customers and petitioners" waiting in front of K's office in the bank. If the slightly senile director happens to pass by, they bow humbly. At the court, too, there are at all times people waiting humbly and patiently, "in a similar arrangement as the customers and petitioners at the bank" (557). All these lowly people are either ignored or kept waiting and probably never received. Even though K is himself the object of such treatment, he is completely oblivious to this humiliation. He lets his customers and petitioners wait, as seems to be customary for a person in his position. He cooperates with an inhuman system—as did so many in Nazi Germany. A parallel that was obviously intended by the author of *The Investigation*.

"What struck me in rereading the book," Weiss wrote in the preface to *Der Prozess*, "was that the forces that pull K down and finally destroy him, are the forces of the petty bourgeoisie" (523). The most obvious representative of this class is K himself. He remains almost anonymous, a "cipher" (589) in the world of the rulers, only noticed by his superiors when he, for the first time in five years, arrives late for work, and is easily mistaken for someone else by the courts. Insignificant, replaceable; yet as a head clerk K has reached the social status where he risks attracting the attention of the court. The members of the working class know nothing of the court and, for its part, the court seems not to notice them either. They are too slight to be worthy of an indictment. As one of the accused, K has a very low status compared to, say, a "customs director," a "wholesaler," or "civil service executive" (561). In reaction to his tenuous position between the working class and the upper class, K has developed certain useful characteristics, such as adaptability, submissiveness, and that highest virtue of his class, inconspicuousness. Far more than about the trial itself, K is worried about the possibility that his superiors might find out about it. When the two servants of the court, Franz and Willem, are administered a thrashing in a hidden corner of K's office and when his uncle visits him in the boarding house to discuss his case with him, K is always consumed by a single idea: not to attract attention, not to be noticed. Which is also why he treats those in a socially lower position exactly the way the socially higher placed treat him. K's arrogance and contempt are displayed not only in his interactions with the petitioners in the bank but also with his subordinates, Rabensteiner, Kullich, and Kaminer; and when Miss Bürstner is forced to cancel a talk desired by K, she is promptly put in her place on the social ladder—"Typist" (553). A different, more humane behavior would apparently be conspicuous in this society. Weiss's K unwaveringly adheres to the advice he had already received in Kafka's novel: "The right thing to do was to conform to existing conditions."[11]

K's opportunistic and servile behavior is similar to that of Diederich Hessling, in Heinrich Mann's famous novel *Der Untertan* (*The Little Superman*). Mann's novel was written in 1914, barely a year before Kafka's *Trial*. Both are great satirical works about the petty bourgeoisie of the prewar era for whom nothing is more important than to adapt as completely as possible to the system: "to become one with the larger whole!" as Diederich Hessling so longingly desires.[12] K and Hessling belong to a class that loyally adheres to the maxim Günther Anders defined as guiding Kafka's figures: *"Always carry out with precision the duties you do not understand!"*[13] In the words of the brute who administers the thrashing to Franz and Willem, "I am hired to give thrashings, so I give thrashings" (555). This line of dialogue in Weiss's dramatization was lifted verbatim from the novel.[14] Weiss, however, made an inconspicuous change in the instrument of punishment. In Kafka's novel, Franz and Willem are thrashed with a switch,[15] in the play with a *bundle* of switches (554, 556): the symbol of power of ancient Rome (Latin, *fascis*), which became the emblem of fascism in Italy in the 1920s and gave the movement its name.[16]

That there is a connection between the realm of Kafka's *Trial* and the Third Reich has been emphasized by Anders and especially by Adorno.[17] Weiss, too, emphasizes this connection. In a dialogue not found in the novel, prosecutor Hasterer calls K's attention to the emergence of forces outside of the prevailing order: "Something is groping around, the masses are rising up . . . something grave, something powerful is starting here" (544). But K is unable to grasp what is happening, what kind of court this is that he, for a long time, has not taken seriously and with which, too late, he tries to ingratiate himself. He is told by the painter Titorelli that there has never been an acquittal. Eventually, K comes to realize that the court might as well be replaced by henchmen (578)—which was to happen in Germany twenty-five years later. The court chaplain informs K that the court has the right to even take away his name, to identify him by a "cipher." This, too, would come to pass with the branding of numbers into the skin of the inmates of the concentration camps. K finally begins to understand: "That means they take away my right to live" (589). Kafka, who died in 1924, could not have foreseen the Nazi extermination camps, but he described certain developments of his own time with a precision that went far beyond the reality perceived by most of his contemporaries. This is brought out by a dramatization that never loses sight of the result of these developments.

Kafka did not know a way out of the horrors that threatened him in his time. The events were unfathomable to him, and his characters find themselves confronted by an enigma. In *The Castle* they stare in vain through the cloth that blindfolds them. In the "cathedral" chapter of Kafka's *Trial* the court chaplain tells the distraught K the parable of the "man from the country," who one day appears before the law and desires entry but is told by the gatekeeper to wait outside the open gate. For years the man waits, and just as he is about to die the gatekeeper tells him that this entrance to the law had been meant only for him and that now it would be closed. This parable is usually regarded as the key to the interpretation of the novel. Kafka, however, defied all efforts by his readers to gain possession of this key by letting the chaplain himself provide an endless series of contradictory interpretations. The enigma was not meant to be solved.

Weiss was not interested in this enigma (no more than the young worker in *The Aesthetics of Resistance* is interested in the enigma in *The Castle*). In Weiss's dramatization the chaplain's tale is reduced to a few lines. There is no longer talk of a "man from the country"; the chaplain applies the parable directly to K (589). Weiss's intention "to read Kafka against the grain" (N II/255) is characterized far more by his choice to disregard the enigmatic, the metaphysical, and the mystical in Kafka's work than by any partisan socialist and antifascist reading of *The Trial*. A Marxist reading of Kafka, however, as the essays by Anders, Adorno, Fischer, and others show, need by no means share Weiss's disinterest in an essential aspect of Kafka's oeuvre. Doubts about and distance toward the mystical and metaphysical elements in Kafka's texts may, on the contrary, lead to a heightened interested in those elements. For they can be perceived as a nonrealistic expression of a very real deficit: of an anxiety caused by a world that appears unfathomable and by social conditions that appear beyond one's control. This anxiety did not have its origin solely in Kafka's personal biography or in his artistry but in historical reality: in the disintegrating Habsburg monarchy. This disintegration behind a shiny facade, and the ominous mood it created throughout the empire, is also the subject of great literary works by Karl Kraus, Robert Musil, Joseph Roth, and others.

In Weiss's dramatization Kafka's unfathomable metaphors of an unfathomable world are dismissed almost derisively. Are we unable to see the truth because we are blindfolded? Then we should remove the blindfold. Does someone want to enter the law? He need not concern himself with a lowly gatekeeper's regulations. In Weiss's play there are no endless conjectures about the difficulties of the problem posed, certainly there is no humble abeyance by any rules (decreed by whom?). To paraphrase the young Marx: the apparently unfathomable social reality need not be endlessly reinterpreted, it should be changed. What is needed is a kind of thinking that is constantly in the process of turning into practice.

There is a spokesperson for this Marxist position in Weiss's *Prozess:* the helper. The figure is based on that apparition, in Kafka's *Trial*, which, immediately prior to K's execution, becomes visible behind a brightly lit window. It produces in K a flash of recognition of humanity and solidarity at the moment of his death: "Who was it? A friend? A good person? Someone who participated? Someone who wanted to help? Was it a lone person? Was it everybody?"[18] In his dramatization Weiss answered all these questions in the affirmative. His helper[19] is a relation to those class-conscious workers he was at the time writing about in *The Aesthetics of Resistance*. When K is arrested at the beginning of the play, the helper (also called THE MAN) encourages him not to heed the incomprehensible rules set up by unknown judicial powers:

THE MAN *turns to K:* Just walk out, Mr. Head Clerk. Don't pay any attention to them. They can't do anything to you. (530)

But Weiss's K is not amenable to such advice. He is imbued with the idea that everything may yet take a turn for the better as long as he is willing to accept the incomprehensibility of his situation. He clings to the enigma like a drowning person to a sinking ship. The helper is as little in a position to redeem K as God was able to cure the petty bourgeois Mockinpott from his suffering in Weiss's earlier play. The helper is the last in a long series of messianic redeemer figures in Weiss's literary work. He is portrayed as having no extraworldly powers. All he has to offer is a clear understanding of the prevailing order and an ability to ask the right questions:

THE MAN [to K]: Who, then, is giving you orders? Who dominates you in this way? . . . You don't defend yourself? (591)

He is a representative of the working class who tries to deter the petit bourgeois K from his self-destructive ingratiation with those in power and who tries to lead him to the side of the proletariat. In this he fails; as indeed the historic attempts at an alliance between the proletariat and lower middle class have failed.

With these reflections prompted by Weiss's play, we have seemingly moved far beyond Kafka's *Trial*. Yet Weiss repeatedly insisted that his dramatization adhered closely to the text—and certainly Bergman had thought so. But Weiss had also decided from the beginning to read Kafka against the grain. An ambivalent attitude, which led to a productive and creative rereading of an over-canonized and over-interpreted text.

Der neue Prozess

The premiere of *Der Prozess* took place on 28 May 1975 in Bremen. Weiss, always easily hurt and angered by negative criticism, experienced the critical response as an "execution" (N II/429). Those who earlier had attacked him for his treatment of Hölderlin now deemed the way he dealt with Kafka equally unacceptable.[20] However, Weiss confined his reactions to the notebooks. His interest had long since returned to the main business at hand, his work on *The Aesthetics of Resistance*. Revisions for the third and final volume were completed in late 1980.

The exhausted writer immediately began a new work. In early 1981 he wrote the play *Der neue Prozess* (The New Trial) within a few weeks. Once again Weiss tries to come to terms with Kafka, once again he tells the story of Josef K on his thirtieth birthday, and of his life at the boarding house with its lodgers, who, as in the earlier *Der Prozess* of 1975, remind one of the bizarre personnel of the micro-novel, *The Shadow of the Coachman's Body* of 1952. Once again K works in a vast office with an obscure hierarchy. Once again there are the secret meetings in a "suburb," "past a freight depot" (33)—the scenery of Weiss's childhood.[21] And once again, on the day before his thirty-first birthday, there is K's execution. And yet, one wonders: why this insistence on the connection to Kafka's novel? Why the title *Der neue Prozess*? In Weiss's play K is neither arrested at the beginning nor at any time during the course of the play. There are no lesser or greater lawyers whom K needs to call on, for there is no court that could put him on trial, let alone sentence him to death. The basic constellation of Kafka's novel is missing.

In a brief text written for the premiere of the play in Stockholm (on 12 March 1982) Weiss himself called attention to the difference between Kafka's novel and *Der neue Prozess.* There was, according to Weiss, nothing more than a sense of kinship; the names of Kafka's figures and his locations were being used, but not the trial itself. So, why the title? Weiss might have been equally justified in calling his play *The New Divine Comedy.* For he had once again returned to the structure of Dante's epic poem with which he had been obsessed for so long. The three-act *Der neue Prozess* is divided into thirty-three scenes—like the three parts of the *Divina Commedia:* an intimation of Dante, a sense of kinship, nothing more (in contrast to works like *The Investigation* or the last part of *The Aesthetics of Resistance,* which are inconceivable without Dante). *Der neue Prozess* uses elements of Kafka's novel that are fitted into the structure of Dante's *Divine Comedy.* In terms of these literary references, the play appears over defined. Two of the greatest works of European culture weight it down like millstones. Which is all the more remarkable since Weiss has on occasion called *Der neue Prozess* "the most spontaneous and personal" play he ever wrote (109).

In Kafka's novel the reader finds out hardly anything about the private life of Josef K or of any of the other characters. Whatever individuality they may possess is defined by their occupation or their social function. They are "abstract people," as Günther Anders has said, they exist only as practitioners of an occupation, an activity: as clerks, for example, or as flogsters. It is precisely this conceptualization of his figures that, according to Anders, makes Kafka a realist, since the modern world has brought about the identification of the person with his or her occupation.[22]

In *Der neue Prozess,* in contrast, the reader learns almost too much about Josef K and his family situation. There are his wealthy parents: a sick father and a recently blinded mother who in his childhood forbade him to play with children from the poor people's district; and there are his siblings. K has broken off all relations with his family, because family life for him had been "an endless calamity" (47)—as had been true for Weiss (as well as for Kafka). Weiss's K finds refuge from his family with another family. The Grubachs, in whose boarding house he has been living for years, become a substitute family. At one point Mrs. Grubach reminds K of how he wept when her husband died, as though Mr. Grubach had been K's own father. At times, the spectator or reader learns, K had felt like a brother toward the captain who is Mrs. Grubach's nephew. Often K experiences an urge to call Mrs. Grubach "Mother Grubach" (47), which is what she ultimately becomes in the moments before K's death. K exists within an excess of family ties, old and new, that reproduce not only the family ties in Kafka's novel but also conjure up Kafka's and Weiss's own complex and painful relations with their own families. Yet all of this information about K's private life, his real and substitute families, contributes little to a clearer understanding of the character.

K is an intellectual; he is interested in art, he is himself an artist type, as is made clear at the beginning of the play, in the scene showing K's room. It is filled with reproductions of paintings from Bosch to Picasso, with portraits of Don Quixote and Dante, with Greek statues, sculptures by Degas and Gauguin, stacks of books, and piles of newspapers: an entire room of bric-a-brac of Western culture. On the desk in K's office there are additional objects "similar to those in K's room" (18). Prosecutor Hasterer reminds K that even as a child K wanted to become an artist. On another occasion Hasterer confirms that K was able to formulate well, his monthly reports were of high moral value, "I'd almost like to say they [K's monthly reports] are like poetry" (33).

K is an idealist, a do-gooder and a political activist. His office coworker, Rabensteiner, reproaches him for his incessant talk about how to improve people's lives and combat misery. But K also acts on his convictions: he collects information about "student groups, associations, political parties" (20), he works in a "united society for the common good" (42), and he is a former member of the "freedom party" and the "equality party" (62). At the beginning of the play he also is a member of the "progress party," from which he receives letters and telephone calls to his office, and at whose meetings he participates (Scene 10). Later he will also participate in meetings of the revolutionary party (Scene 17). On Sundays and even on weekdays at 7:00 A.M. K can be found at political meetings. There he hears speakers such as the representative of the Progress Party who praises his party because it "includes people from all classes of the population," and it represents "not just any one group or class" but "all who are no longer willing to accept the prevailing conditions," from the worker to the future director. The speaker also insists that renewal can only come about if it fits the wishes and needs of all, emphasizing again that everyone can become a member of the Progress Party and that no distinctions are made between "poor or rich" (41–42).

What K hears at these meetings are clichés, distortions, and lies. In *Der neue Prozess* all politics are equally suspicious. The speakers' perorations amount to nothing more than an affirmation of the status quo, the political parties are worth nothing. No exception is made for the left. Thus, one learns that the politics of the Revolutionary Party are bankrupt (41) and that the party has broken up (62). K, however, is not dissuaded by the endless gabble of the political parties. He even considers it powerfully "subversive" (63). He never quits. He can't help his empathy with people's suffering for he is an incurable do-gooder.

This makes K the ideal employee in his firm, an insurance company, which is itself part of a huge financial conglomerate that includes banks dealing in real estate, transportation systems, and construction, and that is eventually able to establish itself on the world market. The goal of this enterprise is colonization, "an economic colonization" (57), which for the time being is to be achieved without the use of force. Weiss has emphasized the scope and unlimited power of this conglomerate by adding new characters to the personnel of Kafka's novel. The directorate of the firm now includes the American ambassador as well as a general. The firm's director is also the minister of economics, its general manager also the prosecutor. Thus, the concept of K's firm as a large industrial-military-political-judicial complex becomes more pronounced than in *Der Prozess* of 1975. Further emphasis is also put on the cynicism of the managers of the company: their use of words such as democracy, tolerance, and humanity is intended merely to distract from the relentless international expansion of the company. A lot of effort is expended, however, to convince the working masses to believe in these clichés. For that purpose the company has hired a spokesman who still believes in them and who can use them without cynicism. This spokesman who is behind the times (9), a "museum piece" (52), is Josef K.

Thus, Josef K, the idealist, the sympathizer, and the do-gooder, is chosen for a career in this exploitative capitalist conglomerate inimical to the working people and, not least of all to women (as Miss Bürstner's fate demonstrates). Starting out as a young lawyer in the legal department, K, who unwittingly embodies the "humanity" and "tolerance" of the company, is eventually made a director. But now the company decides to change its strategy. It rescinds its "concept of equality" (98). The silent appearance of the general, decked out in his uniform covered with ribbons and medals, at the end of Scene 21, reveals the means by which the company's expansion will from now on be achieved. It will be pushed through by violent thugs such as Franz and Willem who, in Weiss's own words, represent the foundation of fascism (128). After the huge financial conglomerate decides to openly use violence to pursue its goals, it drops all pretense at capitalism with a human face. At this point there is no longer any need for Josef K. In the war unleashed by the power brokers of the firm, K is shot, apparently at their command.[23]

There had been no lack of warnings to K. In particular, Leni tries to make him see the real interests behind the seemingly humanitarian stands of politicians and political parties. She also warns him about his status within the company. He had been hired and was regularly being promoted because his honest beliefs in justice and morality had been useful to the company. In its inhuman activities, of which K had not been aware, the company had been able to hide behind *his* uprightness and innocence. The company had put a human face on power, and it had been K's face (95).

Leni is the only figure in *Der neue Prozess* who sees through the system. Although the painter Titorelli also opposes the world of the conglomerate, his resistance remains rather ineffective. He believes the world to be unknowable. In his works it appears as a place of horror: "For me it is filth. Scum, monstrous offspring of suffering. Everything bleeding. Guts, Muck, that's what it is" (71). K, the art enthusiast, has been appointed head of the company's art department. Charged with finding suitable paintings for the firm's soon-to-be-opened showplace building, he suggests Titorelli's paintings, which are bought by the company and exhibited at the opening of the new building. The American ambassador is "stirred, shattered" by Titorelli's works (88), even though the intoxicated painter announces that he painted them not *for* but *against* the company. To which the director responds, "But after they hang in *our* space they lend expression to *our* essence!" (88, emphasis added). As indeed they do for everyone except the general, who expresses suspicion that these paintings contain "explosive material" (88).

This scene reveals the contradictory process by which art is appropriated by those who pay for it. Even Titorelli cannot escape the realization that the impact of his paintings is distorted and to some degree canceled by the fact that they are shown at a bank. Art does not exist in a vacuum. The impact Titorelli's paintings may have on the viewer is influenced by the place in which they are shown—just as the effect of Weiss's plays is influenced by the place in which they are performed. This had been brought home to Weiss in traumatic fashion with the scandal that surrounded the premiere of *Trotsky in Exile* in the new and ultra expensive Düsseldorf Schauspielhaus. That bitter experience is reflected in the figure of the painter Titorelli and the fate that befalls his paintings.

Much in evidence in Titorelli's paintings is the world of the paintings and early writings of Peter Weiss, as the dramatist himself has pointed out (G/R 327). In an interview about *Der neue Prozess,* conducted a few weeks before his death, Weiss called reality "absurd" (G/R 327)—a view of the human condition that is present in much of his work as a painter as well as in his early literary works. After his turn toward Marxism Weiss had no longer perceived the world as absurd but rather as governed by recognizable laws that could be changed. In *Der neue Prozess,* however, the forces of change are either sharply criticized or ignored. Neither the working class nor any perceptive spokesman, such as the helper, in *Der Prozess* of 1975, make an appearance. The "family" that repeatedly turns up in the course of the play and eventually sets up housekeeping in K's room embodies the "lumpen" proletariat, rather than a class-conscious working class. There is no longer mention of a student movement that had appeared as bearer of social changes in *Trotsky in Exile.* At most, resistance comes from individuals like Leni and, in a smaller measure, from Titorelli and Miss Montag, but not from K.

To a higher degree than Weiss may have intended, K appears as an accomplice of an inhumane system. He is not merely a moralist and do-gooder who allows himself to be misused by the company (123). From the beginning of the play, K has doubts about his work for the company, doubts that are reinforced by Leni and Titorelli as well as by his own experiences. Nonetheless, after some feeble protest he lets himself be promoted to the position of director. He is in complicity with those who abuse his genuine idealism and who eventually bring about a fascist war. K's entirely preventable career does not lead him to any real insights. The spectators or readers cannot learn anything from his attitude, which constantly vacillates between wanting to understand and refusing to understand. In his refusal to draw the necessary conclusions from the world around him, and in his refusal to learn from experience, K may have been modeled after Brecht's Mother Courage, in the play by the same name. Mother Courage, however, in her stubborn resistance to changing her ways, no matter what the costs, encourages the spectators to consider alternatives.

But if Weiss's protagonist is not conceived in the manner of Brecht's Mother Courage, neither is he a Tui, which is what Weiss labeled him, borrowing another Brechtian concept (111). Tui was the name Brecht invented for those intellectuals who let themselves be bought by those in power; who knowingly collaborate with the system by producing and disseminating those daily lies, distortions, and half truths through which capitalism maintains its hegemony. K, however, is no perfidious mouthpiece but rather a stubborn idealist and do-gooder who continues to harbor doubts about the system, as becomes ever clearer in the play.

Finally, the central assumption of the play, namely that a multinational conglomerate might need a humanistic figurehead like K in order to veil its inhuman machinations, seems no longer plausible today. Where might that occur in reality? Which large corporations, from Exxon to Nestlé, from the weapons manufacturers to the national and international financial corporations that fill the news with their illegal activities, have any need for such figureheads? These questions point toward that which is lacking in *Der neue Prozess* but which was present in Weiss's first dramatization of Kafka's novel: historic concretization. In *Der Prozess* of 1975 the plot was clearly situated in the year 1913–14, the last year before the start of the First World War. The depiction of the social forces of that period, the condition of the various classes, and of people's sense of themselves and the world can be verified. Thus defined, the events onstage allow the spectators to draw parallels to their own epoch.

Which epoch is meant in *Der neue Prozess* or which corporation? (In his earlier plays, *The Investigation,* and *Song of the Lusitanian Bogey,* Weiss had insisted on naming names.) Which war is being orchestrated by which forces and for what reasons? "For a long time now profit has no longer been our concern," says Rabensteiner, the company representative, at the beginning of the war. For which worldwide enterprise is that supposed to be true? Since *Marat/Sade* Weiss had seen "the holy right of enrichment" as the essence of capitalism. Was that no longer valid? Was a change of mind being sounded in *Der neue Prozess?* The play seems to express Weiss's nascent doubts, at the beginning of the 1980s, that either the Eastern bloc countries or the leftist political parties in the West still represented the future of socialism. In obvious contrast to all of his works since *The Investigation, Der neue Prozess* is informed not so much by a socialist as by an anticapitalist stance. This is more than a nuance. In spite of his many criticisms of the socialist system of Eastern Europe, Weiss had always maintained his loyalty to and his belief in its goals. Now for the first time doubts and distance prevail. Seen from today, these doubts, which so strongly inform the play, appear to anticipate historic developments. Less than ten years after *Der neue Prozess* was written the communism of formerly socialist countries, controlled from above and administered bureaucratically, was everywhere in the process of dissolution. Capitalism, on the other hand, whose cynicism and inhumanity *Der neue Prozess* indicts in a tone of bitter hopelessness, appears unstoppable.

Least to be expected of Weiss (and hardly noticed to date) is the fact that *Der neue Prozess* begins with an enigma, with an intimation of that unfathomable, mystical, and religious element that Weiss had so insistently rejected in *The Aesthetics of Resistance* and in his earlier adaption of *The Trial*. For quite some time K has been noticing a scarcely audible disturbance in his room, a "humming" that keeps him awake at night (10). In response to his request, Franz, Willem, and the engineer, Kaminer, arrive with measuring instruments. According to K the disturbance comes from the ventilator, which has been glued shut with a piece of cardboard. The measuring instruments register nothing. The disturbance is mentioned again when, in order to explain his arriving late at the office, K insists that the humming noise, "for which actually the company is responsible," had kept him awake the whole night. Shortly before the end of the play, however, as the violence begins, Franz and Willem appear in K's room with a ladder. They lean the ladder against the wall next to the ventilator. Franz climbs up and tears away the piece of cardboard: "A strong stream of air immediately comes from the ventilator" (110). That is all.

K was probably more perceptive than might be assumed. He felt the approach of the storm at a time when the measuring instruments registered not the slightest movement. The forces that were gathering were, of course, not meant to be noticed, which is why the ventilation had been covered with cardboard. Now that the fascist storm has broken out, the cardboard is superfluous. K's exceptional sensibility enabled him to notice the disturbance earlier than others. It remains his guilt not to have done anything about it.

The impact of Weiss's big novel began to make itself felt in the months following publication of the third volume of *The Aesthetics of Resistance*. Weiss had already been awarded the Thomas Dehler Prize in 1978. In the Federal Republic he now received one literary award after the other: in

September 1981 the prize of the SWF literature magazine (awarded annually by the TV station Südwestfunk); in October 1981 the literature prize of the city of Cologne; and in January 1982 the literature prize of Bremen, the city of Weiss's childhood. He had not, however, received the most coveted literature prize of the Federal Republic, the Georg Büchner Prize, a fact which the world famous dramatist of *Marat/Sade* and *The Investigation* had already noted in the 1970s, adding that this award was denied him "for obviously political reasons" (N II/221). In the spring of 1982 it was finally decided that Weiss would receive the Büchner Prize. But there was no longer any need to fear an uncomfortable address of the kind the dramatist had written for the Dehler Prize. Shortly before the announcement of the prizewinner Peter Weiss had died, on 10 May 1982, at the age of sixty-five.

NOTES

1. Peter Weiss, *Vanishing Point (Fluchtpunkt,* 1960–61), trans. E. B. Garside, Alastair Hamilton, and Christopher Levenson, in Weiss, *Exile* (New York: Delacorte, 1968) 131.

2. See chap. 3 above.

3. See Georg Lukács, "Franz Kafka oder Thomas Mann" (1957), in Lukács, *Essays über Realismus, Werke* 4 (Neuwied: Luchterhand, 1971): 501, 505ff.

4. Georg Lukács, "Vorwort zu Band 6" (1964), in Lukács, *Der historische Roman, Werke* 6 (Neuwied: Luchterhand, 1965): 9.

5. Ernst Fischer, "Franz Kafka," in Fischer, *Von Grillparzer zu Kafka* (Frankfurt/Main: Suhrkamp, 1975) 366.

6. See Franz Kafka, *Das Schloss,* novel in the version of the handwritten manuscript, ed. Malcolm Pasley (Frankfurt/Main: Fischer, 1982) 456ff., 195ff., 67, respectively.

7. Kafka, *Das Schloss* 291.

8. Kafka puts a period after the initial, but from here on I will follow Weiss's practice of omitting the period.

9. The parenthetical page numbers refer to Peter Weiss, *Der Prozess. Stück in zwei Akten* (1974), in Weiss *Stücke II/2* (Frankfurt/Main: Suhrkamp, 1977) 519–94 (preface 522–25).

10. For a monograph investigating Weiss's adaptions of Kafka's *The Trial,* see Ulrike Zimmermann, *Die dramatische Bearbeitung von Kafkas "Prozess" durch Peter Weiss* (Frankfurt/ Main: Peter Lang, 1990). See also Burkhardt Lindner, "Entzifferung Kafkas auf der Schaubühne" (1982), in Rainer Gerlach, ed., *Peter Weiss* (Frankfurt/Main: Suhrkamp, 1984) 294–301; and see Manfred Haiduk, "Identifikation und Distanz. Aspekte der Kafka-Rezeption bei Peter Weiss," *Weimarer Beiträge* 6 (1984): 916–25.

11. Franz Kafka, *Der Process,* ed. Malcolm Pasley (Frankfurt/Main: Fischer, 1990) 160.

12. Heinrich Mann, *Der Untertan* (Munich: dtv, 20th ed., 1980) 37.

13. Günther Anders, "Kafka, pro und contra. 'Die Prozess-Unterlagen' " (1951), in Anders, *Mensch ohne Welt. Schriften zur Kunst und Literatur* (Munich: Beck, 1984) 102. Emphasis in the original.

14. Kafka, *Der Process* 112.

15. See Kafka, *Der Process* 109.

16. See Manfred Haiduk, *Der Dramatiker Peter Weiss* (East Berlin: Henschelverlag, 1977) 234.

17. See Anders 103. See Theodor W. Adorno, "Aufzeichnungen zu Kafka" (1942–53), in Adorno, *Prismen* (Frankfurt/Main: Suhrkamp, 3d ed., 1987) 267–69. See also Zimmermann 122.

18. Kafka, *Der Process* 312.

19. On Weiss's concept of this figure, see also Haiduk *Der Dramatiker Peter Weiss* 235.

20. On the critical reception of Weiss's *Prozess*, see Zimmerman 149ff.

21. In Weiss's *Prozess* of 1975 the location of the legal building was described in almost precisely the same words; see Weiss, *Der Prozess* 545. The page numbers in parentheses refer to Peter Weiss, *Der neue Prozess* (The New Trial) (Frankfurt/Main: Suhrkamp, 1984). This edition is readily available and contains useful additional material. It should be noted, however, that the conclusion of scene 31, as well as the short scenes 32 and 33, which end the play, are missing. For an adequate evaluation of *Der neue Prozess* one needs to consult the first edition: Peter Weiss, "Der neue Prozess. Stück in drei Akten," *Spectaculum 35. Sechs moderne Theaterstücke* (Frankfurt/Main: Suhrkamp, 1982) 219–78. Quotations from this edition are indentified as such. The complete text is now also available in *Peter Weiss. Werke in sechs Bänden,* ed. Suhrkamp, in cooperation with Gunilla Palmstierna-Weiss (Frankfurt/Main: Suhrkamp, 1991) 6:337–407, 424–26.

22. Anders 77ff.

23. See *Spectaculum* 278. Rather than investigating the discrepancy between the various allusions to this conclusion and the fact that it is missing in the Suhrkamp edition of 1984, Zimmerman simply explains it away. Her interpretation, therefore, remains inadequate, even though it does contain useful information. See Zimmermann 160–61.

AFTERWORD

Whoever becomes involved with the oeuvre of Peter Weiss, it was stated in the preface, is always closer to hell than to paradise. Weiss's paintings, films, and texts are an expression of the dark times in which they were created. Should the question now arise as to whether such an oeuvre can endure, the answer might be: as long as the dark times last, it too will last. Those who assume that the end of bureaucratically administered socialism also marks the end of dark times, if not of history itself, have already answered the question. But it is also possible to doubt that the disorder of real, existing capitalism constitutes the end of history.

Maybe Brecht can be of help. He, too, has given thought to the question of how long works of art and literature endure. His initial answer was "as long as they demand effort." This might be a satisfactory answer. However, at the end of the long poem, "About the Way to Construct Enduring Works," in which he reflects on this question, Brecht arrives at a different conclusion.

> Why should every wind endure forever?
> A good expression is worth noting
> So long as the occasion can recur
> For which it was good . . .
> . . .
> Therefore the desire to make works of long duration is
> Not always to be welcomed.[1]

Works should endure *so long as there can be a recurrence of the occasion* that gave rise to them. In that there is hope: that the world might someday be changed in such a way that there may never be a recurrence of the events that gave rise to an oeuvre such as that of Peter Weiss.

This might provide consolation for the thought that even the great works may not be forever.

NOTES

1. Bertolt Brecht, "About the Way to Construct Enduring Works," in Brecht, *Poems, 1913–1956*, ed. John Willett and Ralph Manheim, with the cooperation of Erich Fried (New York: Methuen, 1974) 195–96.

BIBLIOGRAPHY

Only those primary and secondary sources used for the present work are listed below. For more general literature and suggestions for further reading, see below, "Bibliographical References." Works by Peter Weiss are listed in the order they were written, with the date of their creation in brackets unless it coincides with the publication date. The editions listed are those used in this book.

WORKS BY PETER WEISS

FICTION

"Die Insel. Eine Art Flugschrift. Vor Augen geführt durch Skruwe. Herausgegeben von Peter Ulrich Weiss mit freundlicher Genehmigung des Bundes-Archives" (1936–37). In *Der Maler Peter Weiss*. Berlin: Frölich and Kaufmann (1982). 126–27.

"Kindheit des Zauberers. Ein autobiographisches Märchen." Handwritten and illustrated by Peter Weiss (1938). In Hermann Hesse, *Kindheit des Zauberers.* Frankfurt/Main: Insel-Verlag, 1974 (with an afterword by Peter Weiss).

"Der verbannte Ehemann oder Anton Schievelbeyn's ohnfreywillige Reisse nacher Ost-Indien." Handwritten and illustrated by Peter Weiss (1938). In Hermann Hesse, *Der verbannte Ehemann oder Anton Schievelbeyn's ohnfreywillige Reisse nacher Ost-Indien.* Frankfurt/Main: Insel-Verlag, 1977.

"Traktat von der ausgestorbenen Welt" (1938–39). In *Der Maler Peter Weiss*. Berlin: Frölich and Kaufmann (1982). 51–61.

Von Insel zu Insel. (1944. Original Swedish title *Från ö till ö.* Stockholm: Bonnier, 1947.) German trans. Heiner Gimmler. Berlin: Frölich and Kaufmann, 1984.

Die Besiegten. (Original Swedish title *De Besegrade.* Stockholm: Bonnier, 1948.) German translation by Beat Mazenauer. Frankfurt/Main: Suhrkamp, 1985.

Der Fremde. (Der Vogelfreie. 1947–48. Swedish version titled *Dokument I.* Published privately by PW in Stockholm in 1949.) German trans. under the author's pseudonym Sinclair, *Der Fremde. Erzählung.* Frankfurt/Main: Suhrkamp, 1980.

Der Turm (1949). In Weiss, *Stücke I.* Frankfurt/Main: Suhrkamp, 1976. 7–33, 453.

Das Duell. (1951. Original Swedish title *Duellen.* Stockholm: Private press, 1953.) German trans. J. C. Görsch in conjunction with Peter Weiss. Frankfurt/Main: Suhrkamp, 4th ed., 1982.

BIBLIOGRAPHY

Der Schatten des Körpers des Kutschers (1952). Frankfurt/Main: Suhrkamp, 1964.

Die Versicherung. Ein Drama (1952). In Weiss, *Stücke I.* 35–87.

Abschied von den Eltern (1959–60). Frankfurt/Main: Suhrkamp, 1980.

Fluchtpunkt (1960–61). Frankfurt/Main: Suhrkamp, 6th ed., 1973.

Das Gespräch der drei Gehenden (1962). Frankfurt/Main: Suhrkamp, 7th ed., 1977.

"Bericht über Einrichtungen und Gebräuche in den Siedlungen der Grauhäute" (1963). In *Peter Weiss. In Gegensätzen denken. Ein Lesebuch.* Selected by Rainer Gerlach and Matthias Richter. Frankfurt/Main: Suhrkamp, 1986. 119–35.

Nacht mit Gästen. Eine Moritat (1963). In Weiss, *Stücke I.* 89–111.

Die Verfolgung und Ermordung Jean Paul Marats dargestellt durch die Schauspielgruppe des Hospizes zu Charenton unter Anleitung des Herrn de Sade. Drama in zwei Akten (1963). Revised by the author 1965. In Weiss, *Stücke I.* 155–255.

Wie dem Herrn Mockinpott das Leiden ausgetrieben wird. Spiel in 11 Bildern (1963; final version 1968). In Weiss, *Stücke I.* 113–53.

Die Ermittlung. Oratorium in 11 Gesängen (1964). In Weiss, *Stücke I.* 257–449.

Gesang vom lusitanischen Popanz. Stück mit Musik in 2 Akten (1967). In Weiss, *Stücke II/1.* 7–71.

Diskurs über die Vorgeschichte und den Verlauf des lang andauernden Befreiungskrieges in Viet Nam als Beispiel für die Notwendigkeit des bewaffneten Kampfes der Unterdrückten gegen ihre Unterdrücker sowie über die Versuche der Vereinigten Staaten von Amerika die Grundlagen der Revolution zu vernichten (1968). In Weiss, *Stücke II/1.* 73–264.

Trotzki im Exil. Stück in 2 Akten (1968–69) In Weiss, *Stücke II/2.* 417–517.

Hölderlin. Stück in zwei Akten (1970, 1971). In Weiss, *Stücke II/2.* 265–416.

Der Prozess. Stück in zwei Akten (1974). In Weiss, *Stücke II/2.* 519–94.

Stücke I. Frankfurt/Main: Suhrkamp, 1976. (Contains *Der Turm, Die Versicherung, Nacht mit Gästen, Wie dem Herrn Mockinpott das Leiden ausgetrieben wird,* Marat/Sade, and *Die Ermittlung.*)

Stücke II/1. Frankfurt/Main: Suhrkamp, 1977. (Contains *Gesang vom lusitanischen Popanz* and *Viet Nam Diskurs.*)

Stücke II/2. Frankfurt/Main: Suhrkamp, 1977. (Contains *Hölderlin, Trotzki im Exil,* and *Der Prozess.*)

Die Ästhetik des Widerstands. Vol. I (1975), vol. II (1978), vol. III (1981). Single volume edition. Frankfurt/Main: Suhrkamp, 2nd ed., 1986.

Notizbücher 1971–1980. 2 vols. Frankfurt/Main: Suhrkamp, 2d ed., 1982.

Notizbücher 1960–1971. 2 vols. Frankfurt/Main: Suhrkamp, 1982.

Der neue Prozess. Frankfurt/Main: Suhrkamp, 1984. In this edition, which is readily available and contains useful additional material, the conclusion of Scene 31 as well as the brief Scenes 32 and 33, which end the play, were omitted. For an adequate evaluation of the play see the first edition: Peter Weiss, *Der neue Prozess. Stück in drei Akten, Spectaculum 35. Sechs moderne Theaterstücke.* Frankfurt/Main: Suhrkamp, 1982. 219–78. The complete text is now also available in *Peter Weiss. Werke in sechs Bänden.*

Peter Weiss. In Gegensätzen denken. Ein Lesebuch. Selected by Rainer Gerlach and Matthias Richter. Frankfurt/Main: Suhrkamp, 1986.
Peter Weiss. Werke in sechs Bänden. Ed. Suhrkamp, in cooperation with Gunilla Palmstierna-Weiss. Frankfurt/Main: Suhrkamp, 1991. (Contains only Weiss's fictional works.)

ESSAYS AND LETTERS

"Aus dem Briefwechsel mit Hermann Hesse" (1937–62). In Raimund Hoffmann, *Peter Weiss. Malerei Zeichnungen Collagen.* Berlin: Henschelverlag, 1984. 162–69.
"Aus dem Briefwechsel mit Hermann Levin Goldschmidt und Robert (Bob) Jungk" (1939–41). In Raimund Hoffmann, *Peter Weiss. Malerei Zeichnungen Collagen.* Berlin: Henschelverlag, 1984. 169–73.
"Sechs Reportagen aus Deutschland für *Stockholms Tidningen*" (June–August 1947). In Weiss, *Die Besiegten.* German trans. Beat Mazenauer. Frankfurt/Main: Suhrkamp, 1985. 123–52.
"Brief an Peter Suhrkamp" (1948). In Siegfried Unseld, *Peter Suhrkamp. Zur Biographie eines Verlegers.* Frankfurt/Main: Suhrkamp, 1975.
"Avantgarde Film." (Translation of several chapters from Weiss's book *Avantgarde Film,* which was published in Swedish in 1956.) In Weiss, *Rapporte.* 7–35.
"Avantgarde Film." (Translation of a short passage from *Avantgarde Film.*) In *Peter Weiss. In Gegensätzen denken. Ein Lesebuch.* Selected by Rainer Gerlach and Matthias Richter. Frankfurt/Main: Suhrkamp, 1986. 66–68. (Not identical with the text with the same name in *Rapporte.*)
"Aus dem Kopenhagener Journal" (1960). In Weiss, *Rapporte.* 51–71.
"Gegen die Gesetze der Normalität" (1962). In Weiss, *Rapporte.* 72–82.
"Aus dem Pariser Journal" (1962). In Weiss, *Rapporte.* 83–112.
"Frankfurter Auszüge" (1964). *Kursbuch* 1 (June 1965): 152–88.
"Meine Ortschaft" (1964). In Weiss, *Rapporte.* 113–24.
"Unter dem Hirseberg" (1965). In Weiss, *Rapporte 2.* 7–13.
"Vorübung zum dreiteiligen Drama divina commedia" (1965). In Weiss, *Rapporte.* 125–41.
"Gespräch über Dante" (1965). In Weiss, *Rapporte.* 142–69.
"Laokoon oder Über die Grenzen der Sprache" (1965). In Weiss, *Rapporte.* 170–87.
"Brief an H. M. Enzensberger" (1965). In Weiss, *Rapporte 2.* 35–44. (Originally published as "Enzensbergers Illusionen," *Kursbuch* 6 [July 1966]: 165–70.)
"10 Arbeitspunkte eines Autors in der geteilten Welt" (1965). In Weiss, *Rapporte 2.* 14–23.
"Antwort auf einen Offenen Brief von Wilhelm Girnus an den Autor in der Zeitung 'Neues Deutschland' " (1965). In Weiss, *Rapporte 2.* 24–34.
"Antwort auf eine Kritik zur Stockholmer Aufführung der 'Ermittlung' " (1966). In Weiss, *Rapporte 2.* 45–50.

"Rede in englischer Sprache gehalten an der Princeton University USA am 25. April 1966, unter dem Titel: 'I Come Out of My Hiding Place.' " In Volker Canaris, ed., *Über Peter Weiss*. Frankfurt/Main: Suhrkamp, 4th ed., 1976. 9–14.

"Vietnam!" (2 August 1966). In Weiss, *Rapporte 2*. 51–62.

"Der Sieg, der sich selbst bedroht" (1967). In Weiss, *Rapporte 2*. 70–72.

"Offener Brief an den Tschechoslowakischen Schriftstellerverband" (10 September 1967). In Weiss, *Rapporte 2*. 73–81.

"Che Guevara!" (1967). In Weiss, *Rapporte 2*. 82–90.

Rapporte (1968). Frankfurt/Main: Suhrkamp, 2d ed., 1981.

"Notizen zum dokumentarischen Theater" (1968). In Weiss, *Rapporte 2*. 91–104.

"Offener Brief an die 'Literaturnaja Gaseta,' Moskau" (Letter to Lew Ginsburg of 4 April 1970). In Weiss, *Rapporte 2*. 141–50.

"Rekonvaleszenz" (1970). In *Peter Weiss. Werke in sechs Bänden*. Ed. Suhrkamp Verlag in cooperation with Gunilla Palmstierna-Weiss. Frankfurt/Main: Suhrkamp, 1991. 2:345–546.

Rapporte 2. Frankfurt/Main: Suhrkamp, 1971.

"Zur Lage in Vietnam." *Deutsche Volkszeitung* 49 (7 December 1978).

"Die Hetze gegen Vietnam geht weiter." *Deutsche Volkszeitung* 50 (14 December 1978).

"Für Max Frisch." In *Begegnungen. Eine Festschrift für Max Frisch*. Frankfurt/Main: Suhrkamp, 1981. 217–18.

"Wurzeln." *die horen* 27, no. 126 (Summer 1982): 185–87.

CONVERSATIONS AND INTERVIEWS

(Conversations contained in Gerlach/Richter are not listed individually.)

Arnold, Heinz Ludwig. " '. . . ein ständiges Auseinandersetzen mit den Fehlern und mit den Missgriffen. . . .' Heinz-Ludwig Arnold im Gespräch mit Peter Weiss (19 Sept. 1981)." In Alexander Stephan, ed., *Die Ästhetik des Widerstands*. Frankfurt/Main: Suhrkamp, 1983. 11–58.

Brundahl, Anita. "3 x Weiss. Ein Gespräch zwischen Peter Weiss, Gunilla Palmstierna-Weiss und Anita Brundahl." In Weiss, *Der neue Prozess*. 109–19.

Clausen, Oliver. "Weiss/Propagandist and Weiss/Playwright." In *The New York Times Magazine* 2 October 1966: 28–29, 124–34.

"Dialog der Literatur- und Theaterwissenschaftler." In Werner Hecht (compiler and editor), *Brecht-Dialog 1968. Politik auf dem Theater*. Munich: Rogner and Bernhard, 1969. 77–109.

Farocki, Harun. " 'Seine Entwicklungsgeschichte in den Rahmen der Weltläufe stellen.' Ein Gespräch mit Peter Weiss über die Motive zu seiner 'Ästhetik des Widerstands.' " *Frankfurter Rundschau* 24 November 1979.

———. "Gespräch mit Peter Weiss." In Rainer Gerlach, ed., *Peter Weiss*. Frankfurt/Main: Suhrkamp, 1984. 119–28.

Gerlach, Rainer, and Matthias Richter, eds. *Peter Weiss im Gespräch*. Frankfurt/Main: Suhrkamp, 1986.

Lodemann, Jürgen. "Jeder Mensch, der denken kann, kann auch weiterdenken. Jürgen Lodemann im Gespräch mit Peter Weiss." *Deutsche Volkszeitung* 38 (17 September 1981).

Roos, Peter. "Der Kampf um meine Existenz als Maler. Peter Weiss im Gespräch mit Peter Roos. Unter Mitarbeit von Sepp Hiekisch und Peter Spielmann." (Stockholm, 19 December 1979). In *Der Maler Peter Weiss*. 11–43.

ENGLISH TRANSLATIONS

The Tower (*Der Turm*, 1948). Trans. Michael Benedikt and Michel Heine. *Postwar German Theatre*. Ed. Michael Benedikt and George E. Wellwarth. New York: Dutton, 1967. 315–48.

The Shadow of the Coachman's Body (*Der Schatten des Körpers des Kutschers*, 1952). Trans. E. B. Garside. In Weiss, *Bodies and Shadows*. New York: Delacorte, 1969. 1–57.

Leavetaking (*Abschied von den Eltern*, 1960). Trans. E. B. Garside, Alastair Hamilton, and Christopher Levenson. Weiss, *Exile*. New York: Delacorte, 1968. 1–88.

Vanishing Point (*Fluchtpunkt*, 1960–61). Trans. E. B. Garside, Alastair Hamilton, and Christopher Levenson. Weiss, *Exile*. New York: Delacorte, 1968. 89–245.

Conversation of the Three Wayfarers (*Das Gespräch der drei Gehenden*, 1962). Trans. Rosemarie Waldrop. In Weiss, *Bodies and Shadows*. New York: Delacorte, 1969. 59–120.

Night with Guests (*Nacht mit Gästen*, 1963). Trans. Laurence Dobie. Stanley Richards, ed. *The Best Short Plays, 1968*. Philadelphia: Chilton, 1968. 131–58.

The Persecution and Assassination of Jean-Paul Marat as Performed by the Inmates of the Asylum of Charenton under the Direction of the Marquis de Sade (*Die Verfolgung und Ermordung Jean Paul Marats dargestellt durch die Schauspielgruppe des Hospizes zu Charenton unter Anleitung des Herrn de Sade*, 1963). Trans. Geoffrey Skelton. New York: Atheneum, 1981.

"My Place" ("Meine Ortschaft," 1964). Trans. Christopher Middleton. In Middleton, ed., *German Writing Today*. Harmondsworth, England: Penguin, 1967. 20–28.

The Investigation (*Die Ermittlung*, 1964). Trans. Jon Swan and Ulu Grosbard. New York: Atheneum, 1966.

"I Come Out of My Hiding Place" (written in English by Peter Weiss). *The Nation* 30 May 1966: 652, 655.

Song of the Lusitanian Bogey (*Gesang vom lusitanischen Popanz*, 1967). Trans. Lee Baxandall. Weiss, *Two Plays*. New York: Atheneum, 1970. 1–63.

"Che Guevara!" ("Che Guevara!" 1967). Trans. Peter Weiss. Weiss, *Notizbücher 1960–1971*. 2 vols. Frankfurt/Main: Suhrkamp, 1982. 555–61.

Discourse on the Progress of the Prolonged War of Liberation in Viet Nam and the Events Leading up to It as Illustration of the Necessity for Armed Resistance against Oppression and on the Attempts of the United States of America to Destroy the Foundations of Revolution (*Diskurs über die Vorgeschichte und den Verlauf des lang andauernden Befreiungskrieges in Viet Nam als Beispiel für die Notwendigkeit des bewaffneten Kampfes der Unterdrückten gegen ihre Unterdrücker sowie über die Versuche der Vereinigten Staaten von Amerika die Grundlagen der Revolution zu vernichten,* 1968). Trans. Geoffrey Skelton. Weiss, *Two Plays.* New York: Atheneum, 1970. 65–249.

"The Material and the Models. Notes Towards a Definition of Documentary Theatre" ("Notizen zum Dokumentarischen Theater," 1968). Trans. Heinz Bernard. *Theatre Quarterly* 1, no. 1 (January–March 1971): 41–43.

How Mr. Mockinpott Was Cured of His Sufferings (*Wie dem Herrn Mockinpott das Leiden ausgetrieben wird,* 1963, 1968). Trans. Christopher Holmes. *The Contemporary German Theater.* Ed. Michael Roloff. New York: Avon, 1972.

Trotsky in Exile (*Trotzki im Exil,* 1968, 1969). Trans. Geoffrey Skelton. New York: Atheneum, 1972.

BIBLIOGRAPHIES

Cohen, Robert. "Kommentierte Bibliographie." In Cohen, *Bio-bibliographisches Handbuch zu Weiss' "Ästhetik des Widerstands."* Berlin: Argument, 1989. 165–86.

———. "Literaturverzeichnis." In Cohen, *Versuche über Weiss' "Ästhetik des Widerstands."* Bern: Peter Lang, 1989. 229–49.

Gerlach, Rainer. "Peter Weiss—Bibliographie. 1959–1981." In Heinz Ludwig Arnold, ed., *Text + Kritik* 37 (Peter Weiss). Completely revised 2d ed., 1982. 115–34.

———. "Bibliographie." "Uraufführung der Theaterstücke." In Gerlach, ed., *Peter Weiss.* Frankfurt/Main: Suhrkamp, 1984. 331–44.

Haiduk, Manfred. "Aufführungsliste." "Peter-Weiss-Verzeichnisse." in Haiduk, *Der Dramatiker Peter Weiss.* East Berlin: Henschelverlag, 1977. 303–34.

Vogt, Jochen. "Bibliographie." In Vogt, *Peter Weiss.* Reinbek b. Hamburg: Rowohlt-Monographie, 1987. 147–54.

SECONDARY SOURCES ON AUTHOR AND WORKS

ANTHOLOGIES AND DOCUMENTATIONS

Ästhetik Revolte Widerstand. Zum literarischen Werk von Peter Weiss. Ed. Jürgen Garbers et al. Lüneburg and Jena: zu Klampen, Universitätsverlag, 1990. Fourteen essays of varying quality presented at a Weiss conference in Hamburg in November

1988. Covers early literary work and plays with emphasis (5 articles) on The Aesthetics of Resistance.

Ästhetik Revolte Widerstand. Ergänzungsband. Ed. Internationale Peter-Weiss-Gesellschaft. Lucerne: 1990. Second volume of the above. Thirty-seven essays covering topics from Weiss as filmmaker to Weiss as playwright, with emphasis on The Aesthetics of Resistance (28 essays).

Arnold, Heinz Ludwig, ed. *Text + Kritik* 37 (Peter Weiss). Completely revised 2d ed., 1982. Contains a previously unpublished short fragment by Weiss on Rimbaud and 10 essays of varying quality. Emphasis is on early literary works and on The Aesthetics of Resistance. Plays not covered.

Beckermann, Thomas, and Volker Canaris, eds. *Der andere Hölderlin. Materialien zum "Hölderlin"-Stück von Peter Weiss.* Frankfurt/Main: Suhrkamp, 1972. Contains useful information on all aspects of the play, including its historical background, Weiss's concept, and the play's critical reception.

Braun, Karlheinz, ed. *Materialien zu Peter Weiss' "Marat/Sade."* Frankfurt/Main: Suhrkamp, 1967. Valuable work containing pertinent information on all aspects of the play, including its historical background, Weiss's concept, and the various versions of the play, as well as examples of its critical reception and three Germanist articles.

Canaris, Volker, ed. *Über Peter Weiss.* Frankfurt/Main: Suhrkamp, 4th ed., 1976. Seventeen essays covering Weiss's major literary works from *The Shadow of the Coachman's Body* to *Trotsky in Exile.* Includes Weiss's important speech, "I Come Out of My Hiding Place" (in German).

Cohen, Robert. *Bio-bibliographisches Handbuch zu Weiss' "Ästhetik des Widerstands."* Berlin: Argument, 1989. Contains information on all aspects of The Aesthetics of Resistance, including an index, a detailed table of contents, short biographies of numerous figures, and an annotated bibliography. A valuable tool in dealing with the 1,000 pages of Weiss's novel.

Der Maler Peter Weiss. Berlin: Frölich and Kaufmann, 1982. Contains numerous plates, many of them in color, of Weiss's paintings, a lengthy and important interview with the artist, a previously unpublished early literary work, and several essays on Weiss as a painter. Very useful.

Gerlach, Rainer, ed. *Peter Weiss.* Frankfurt/Main: Suhrkamp, 1984. Sixteen essays on all aspects of Weiss's work from his paintings and films to his literary work. From early Swedish texts to *Der Neue Prozess* all major works are covered. Useful collection.

Götze, Karl Heinz, and Klaus R. Scherpe, eds. *Die "Ästhetik des Widerstands" lesen. Über Peter Weiss.* Berlin: Argument, 1981. Early and still excellent collection of 15 essays that paved the way for a broad reception of this difficult book.

Hoffmann, Raimund. *Peter Weiss. Malerei Zeichnungen Collagen.* Berlin: Henschelverlag, 1984. Contains numerous plates, many of them in color, of Weiss's paintings, as well as an excellent introduction by Hoffmann and previously unpublished letters from Weiss to Hermann Hesse, Hermann Levin Goldschmidt, and Robert Jungk.

Höller, Hans, ed. *Hinter jedem Wort die Gefahr des Verstummens. Sprachproblematik und literarische Tradition in der 'Ästhetik des Widerstands' von Peter Weiss.* Stuttgart: Akademischer Verlag, 1988. A collection of 11 articles of uneven quality; excellent essay by Karl Heinz Götze on Weiss's childhood in Bremen.

Lange-Fuchs, Hauke. *Peter Weiss und der Film. Materialien zur Retrospektive der Nordischen Filmtage Lübeck 1986.* Lübeck: 1986. Contains an extensive and valuable annotated filmography, as well as an interview with Gunilla Palmstierna-Weiss, and an essay on Weiss as a filmmaker.

Lüdke, Martin, and Delf Schmidt, eds. "Widerstand der Ästhetik? Im Anschluss an Peter Weiss." *Literaturmagazin* 27. Reinbek b. Hamburg: Rowohlt, 1991.

Stephan, Alexander, ed. *Die Ästhetik des Widerstands.* Frankfurt/Main: Suhrkamp, 1983. Fourteen articles on Weiss's novel, with excellent contributions by Jost Hermand, Burkhardt Lindner, Manfred Haiduk, Peter Bürger, and Michael Winkler, among others.

Palmstierna-Weiss, Gunilla, and Jürgen Schutte. eds. *Peter Weiss. Leben und Werk.* Frankfurt/Main: Suhrkamp, 1991. Contains 21 generally useful essays, each in German and Swedish, on various aspects of Weiss's life and work, as well as many previously unpublished photographs. Excellent contributions by Heiner Müller, Heinrich Vormweg, Manfred Haiduk, Klaus Scherpe, and others.

Wolff, Rudolf, ed. *Peter Weiss. Werk und Wirkung.* Bonn: Bouvier, 1987. Uneven collection of 10 articles with topics ranging from Weiss as a socialist to the city in Weiss's work. Excellent essay by Klaus Scherpe on the relationship between The Aesthetics of Resistance and Dante's *Divina Commedia.*

MONOGRAPHS AND ARTICLES

"Avantgarde—Arbeiterklasse—Erbe. Gespräch zu Peter Weiss' 'Die Ästhetik des Widerstands.' " *Sinn und Form* 36, no. 1 (1984): 68–97. Minutes of an important colloquium, in the former GDR, on The Aesthetics of Resistance. Valuable contributions by Thomas Metscher, Silvia Schlenstedt, and others.

Bathrick, David. " 'The Theater of the White Revolution Is Over': The Third World in the Works of Peter Weiss and Heiner Müller." In Reinhold Grimm and Jost Hermand, eds., *Blacks and German Culture.* Madison: University of Wisconsin Press, 1986. 135–49.

Bengtsson, Jan Christer. "Peter Weiss über Film und Filmemachen." In Hauke Lange-Fuchs, *Peter Weiss und der Film. Materialien zur Retrospektive der Nordischen Filmtage Lübeck 1986.* Lübeck: 1986. 13–17.

———. "Peter Weiss, der Film und die Grossstadt." In Rudolf Wolff, ed., *Peter Weiss. Werk und Wirkung.* Bonn: Bouvier, 1987. 129–45.

Berghahn, Klaus L. " 'Wenn ich so singend fiele. . . .' Dichter und Revolutionär, gestern und heute, Hölderlin und Weiss." In Thomas Beckermann and Volker

Canaris, eds., *Der andere Hölderlin. Materialien zum "Hölderlin"-Stück von Peter Weiss.* Frankfurt/Main: Suhrkamp, 1972. 171–90.

Best, Otto F. *Peter Weiss.* Bern: Francke, 1971.

———. "O Marx und Business." In *Basis* 3 (1972): 238–44.

Bohrer, Karl Heinz. "Die Tortur. Peter Weiss' Weg ins Engagement. Die Geschichte des Individualisten" (1970). In Rainer Gerlach, ed., *Peter Weiss.* Frankfurt/Main: Suhrkamp, 1984. 182–207. An essay from 1970 that at the time was quite influential but today seems unconvincing and as confused as its title.

Bommert, Christian. " 'Offene Fragen im phantastischen Tumult.' Die Revolutionsinterpretation in Peter Weiss' 'Marat'—Drama." In Harro Zimmermann, ed., *Schreckensmythen—Hoffnungsbilder. Die Französische Revolution in der deutschen Literatur.* Frankfurt/Main: Atheneum, 1989. 323–45.

Braun, Karlheinz. "Schaubude—Irrenhaus—Auschwitz. Überlegungen zum Theater des Peter Weiss." In Braun, ed., *Materialien zu Peter Weiss' "Marat/Sade."* Frankfurt/Main: Suhrkamp, 1967. 136–55.

Brook, Peter. "Introduction" (1964). In Peter Weiss, *The Persecution and Assassination of Jean-Paul Marat as Performed by the Inmates of the Asylum of Charenton under the Direction of the Marquis de Sade.* New York: Atheneum, 1981. v–vii.

Buch, Hans Christoph. "Seine Rede ist Ja ja, nein nein. Hans Christoph Buch über Peter Weiss' 'Die Ästhetik des Widerstands.' " *Der Spiegel* 47 (20 November 1978).

Cohen, Robert. *Versuche über Weiss' "Ästhetik des Widerstands."* Bern: Peter Lang, 1989. Divided into 3 parts, this book deals with the formal aspects of the novel; with the concept and the figure of the narrator; with the Brecht passages in the novel; and with Weiss's reception of Brecht's work.

———. "Der Gesang von Plötzensee. Zur Darstellung des antifaschistischen Widerstands in Peter Weiss' 'Ästhetik des Widerstands.' " In Helmut Pfanner, ed., *Der Zweite Weltkrieg und die Exilanten.* Bonn: Bouvier, 1991. 197–208. This article also in *Wissenschaftliche Zeitschrift der Wilhelm-Pieck-Universität Rostock* G-Reihe 38 (1989): 13–18.

———. "Versuch über Peter Weiss' 'Gesang vom lusitanischen Popanz': Enzensberger, Fanon, Antilopen-Mann." *literatur für leser* 4 (1991): 225–36.

Durzak, Manfred. *Dürrenmatt Frisch Weiss.* Stuttgart: Philipp Reclam, jr., 2d ed., 1973.

Eklund, Irene. "Frieda Weiss, née Hummel—A Life' " (1979). "Letter" and "Interview." In Åsa Eldh, *The Mother in the Work and Life of Peter Weiss.* Bern: Peter Lang, 1990. 163–98. Weiss's sister's notes and comments about life in the Weiss family paint a very different picture from Weiss's own recollections in his autobiographical novels and interviews.

Enzensberger, Hans Magnus. "Europäische Peripherie." *Kursbuch* 2 (August 1965): 154–73.

———. "Peter Weiss und andere." *Kursbuch* 6 (July 1966): 171–76.

Fischer, Ludwig. "Dokument und Bekenntnis oder Von der Schwierigkeit, durchs Schreiben ein Sozialist zu werden. Erwägungen zum schriftstellerischen Weg des Peter Weiss." *Text und Kontext* 5, no. 1 (1977): 73–124.

Friedrich, Gerhard. "Auf der Suche nach Herakles: Zu Peter Weiss' Romantrilogie 'Die Ästhetik des Widerstands.' " *Monatshefte* 77, no. 2 (Summer 1985): 171–80.

Gerlach, Rainer. "Leben im Exil. Drei Briefe von Peter Weiss." In Gerlach, ed., *Peter Weiss*. Frankfurt/Main: Suhrkamp, 1984. 15–31.

——. "Isolation und Befreiung. Zum literarischen Frühwerk von Peter Weiss." In Gerlach, ed., *Peter Weiss*. Frankfurt/Main: Suhrkamp, 1984. 147–81.

Ginsburg, Lew. " 'Selbstdarstellung' und Selbstentlarvung des Peter Weiss." Trans. from the Russian by Hermann Pörzgen. In Volker Canaris, ed., *Über Peter Weiss*. Frankfurt/Main: Suhrkamp, 4th ed., 1976. 136–41.

Götze, Karl Heinz. "Der Ort der frühen Bilder. Peter Weiss und Bremen. Eine Spurensuche." In Hans Höller, ed., *Hinter jedem Wort die Gefahr des Verstummens. Sprachproblematik und literarische Tradition in der "Ästhetik des Widerstands" von Peter Weiss*. Stuttgart: Akademischer Verlag, 1988. 173–96.

Grimm, Reinhold. "Blanckenburgs 'Fluchtpunkt' oder Peter Weiss und der deutsche Bildungsroman." *Basis* 2 (1971): 234–45.

Haiduk, Manfred. "Peter Weiss' 'Gesang vom lusitanischen Popanz' "(1967). In Peter Weiss, *Gesang vom lusitanischen Popanz. Mit Materialien*. Frankfurt/Main: Suhrkamp, 1974. 77–82.

——. *Der Dramatiker Peter Weiss*. East Berlin: Henschelverlag, 1977. Invaluable book on Weiss's dramatic work. Haiduk, who befriended Weiss for many years, discusses each play in great detail and contributes a wealth of information on all of them.

——. "Summa. Zur Stellung der 'Ästhetik des Widerstands' im Werk von Peter Weiss." In Karl Heinz Götze and Klaus R. Scherpe, eds., *Die "Ästhetik des Widerstands" lesen. Über Peter Weiss*, Berlin: Argument, 1981. 41–56. Also published under the title, "Zur Stellung der 'Ästhetik des Widerstands' im Werk von Peter Weiss.' " In Rainer Gerlach, ed., *Peter Weiss*. Frankfurt/Main: Suhrkamp, 1984. 307–24.

——. "Faschismuskritik als Imperialismuskritik im Werk von Peter Weiss. Thesenhafte Bemerkungen zu einem Forschungsgegenstand." In Jens Peter Lund Nielsen et al., eds., *Antifaschismus in deutscher und skandinavischer Literatur*. Aarhus: Arkona, 1983. 131–40.

——. "Identifikation und Distanz. Aspekte der Kafka-Rezeption bei Peter Weiss." *Weimarer Beiträge* 6 (1984): 916–25.

Hensing, Dieter. "Die Positionen von Peter Weiss in den Jahren 1947–1965 und der Prosatext 'Der Schatten des Körpers des Kutschers.' " In Gerd Labroisse, ed., *Amsterdamer Beiträge zur neueren Germanistik*. Amsterdam: 1973. 137–87.

Hiekisch-Picard, Sepp. "Zwischen surrealistischem Protest und kritischem Engagement. Zu Peter Weiss' früher Prosa." In Heinz Ludwig Arnold, ed., *Text + Kritik* 37 (Peter Weiss). Completely revised 2d ed., 1982. 22–38.

———. " 'In den Vorräumen eines Gesamtkunstwerks.' Anmerkungen zum Zusammenhang zwischen schriftstellerischem, filmischem und bildkünstlerischem Werk bei Peter Weiss." *Kürbiskern* 2 (April 1985): 116–27. Hiekisch-Picard specializes in Weiss as filmmaker and painter, and this essay, like his other articles, contains useful insights.

Hilzinger, Klaus Harro. *Die Dramaturgie des dokumentarischen Theaters.* Tübingen: Niemeyer, 1976.

Jahnke, Manfred. "Von der Revolte zur Revolution. Zum dramatischen Werk von Peter Weiss." In Heinz Ludwig Arnold, ed., *Text + Kritik* 37 (Peter Weiss). Completely revised 2d ed., 1982. 58–65.

Karnick, Manfred. "Peter Weiss' dramatische Collagen. Vom Traumspiel zur Agitation." In Rainer Gerlach, ed., *Peter Weiss.* Frankfurt/Main: Suhrkamp, 1984. 208–48.

Köppen, Manuel. "Die halluzinierende Stadt. Strukturen räumlicher Wahrnehmung im malerischen und frühen erzählerischen Werk von Peter Weiss." In Rudolf Wolff, ed., *Peter Weiss. Werk und Wirkung.* Bonn: Bouvier, 1987. 9–26.

Krause, Rolf D. *Faschismus als Theorie und Erfahrung: "Die Ermittlung" und ihr Autor Peter Weiss.* Frankfurt/Main: Peter Lang, 1982. Exhaustive and painstakingly researched thesis that contains a wealth of information on all aspects of *The Investigation.*

———. "Peter Weiss in Schweden. Verortungsprobleme eines Weltbürgers." In Rainer Gerlach, ed., *Peter Weiss.* Frankfurt/Main: Suhrkamp, 1984. 57–90.

Levin Goldschmidt, Hermann. "Von Zürich nach Zürich. Peter Weiss, 1938–1978." In Raimund Hoffmann, *Peter Weiss. Malerei Zeichnungen Collagen.* Berlin: Henschelverlag, 1984. 173–74.

Lindner, Burkhardt. "Entzifferung Kafkas auf der Schaubühne" (1982). In Rainer Gerlach, ed., *Peter Weiss.* Frankfurt/Main: Suhrkamp, 1984. 294–301.

———. "Halluzinatorischer Realismus. Die 'Ästhetik des Widerstands,' die 'Notizbücher' und die Todeszonen der Kunst." In Alexander Stephan, ed., *Die Ästhetik des Widerstands.* Frankfurt/Main: Suhrkamp, 1983. 164–204. Perceptive study of *The Aesthetics of Resistance* and of Weiss's concept of art.

———. *Im Inferno. "Die Ermittlung" von Peter Weiss.* Badenweiler: Oase-Verlag, 1988.

Mandel, Ernest. "Trotzki im Exil" (1970). In Volker Canaris, ed., *Über Peter Weiss.* Frankfurt/Main: Suhrkamp, 4th ed., 1976. 131–35.

Marcuse, Ludwig. "Was ermittelte Peter Weiss?" *Kürbiskern* 2 (1966): 84–89.

Nägele, Rainer. "Zum Gleichgewicht der Positionen. Reflexionen zu 'Marat/Sade' von Peter Weiss." In Reinhold Grimm and Jost Hermand, eds., *Basis. Jahrbuch für deutsche Gegenwartsliteratur* 5. Frankfurt/Main: Suhrkamp, 1975. 150–65.

Nemes, Endre "Endre Nemes über Peter Weiss." In *Der Maler Peter Weiss.* Berlin: Frölich and Kaufmann, 1982. 45–50.

Oesterle, Kurt. "Dante und das Mega-Ich. Literarische Formen politischer und ästhetischer Subjektivität bei Peter Weiss." In Martin Lüdke and Delf Schmidt, eds., *Literaturmagazin* 27. Reinbek b. Hamburg: Rowohlt, 1991. 45–72.

Palmstierna-Weiss, Gunilla. "Vorwort." In Peter Weiss, *Von Insel zu Insel* (1947). German trans. Heiner Gimmler. Berlin: Frölich and Kaufmann, 1984.

———. "Nachwort." In Peter Weiss, *Die Besiegten.* Frankfurt/Main: Suhrkamp, 1985. 153–57.

———. "Eigentlich haben wir die meisten Filme gemeinsam gemacht." Interview with Gunilla Palmstierna-Weiss by Christine Fischer-Defoy. In Hauke Lange-Fuchs, *Peter Weiss und der Film. Materialien zur Retrospektive der Nordischen Filmtage Lübeck 1986.* Lübeck: 1986. 10–12.

Peitsch, Helmut. "Wo ist die Freiheit? Peter Weiss und das Berlin des Kalten Krieges." In Jürgen Garbers et al., eds., *Ästhetik Revolte Widerstand. Zum literarischen Werk von Peter Weiss* 34–56. Insightful essay on the way in which Weiss, in his postwar journalistic reports from Berlin, deals with postwar Germany.

Pietzcker, Carl. "Individualistische Befreiung als Kunstprinzip. 'Das Duell' von Peter Weiss." In Johannes Cremerius, ed., *Psychoanalytische Textinterpretationen.* Hamburg: Hoffmann and Campe, 1979. 208–46.

Raddatz, Fritz J. "Abschied von den Söhnen? Kein Fresko, sondern ein Flickerlteppich: Zum Abschluss der Roman-Trilogie. Peter Weiss 'Ästhetik des Widerstands.' " *Die Zeit* 8 May 1981.

Reich-Ranicki, Marcel. "Die zerredete Revolution. Peter Weiss 'Trotzki im Exil.' " In Reich-Ranicki, *Lauter Verrisse.* Munich: Piper, 1970. 147–51.

———. "Peter Weiss. Poet und Ermittler 1916–1982." In Rainer Gerlach, ed., *Peter Weiss.* Frankfurt/Main: Suhrkamp, 1984. 7–11.

Richter, Matthias. " 'Bis zum heutigen Tag habe ich Ihre Bücher bei mir getragen.' Über die Beziehung zwischen Peter Weiss und Hermann Hesse." In Rainer Gerlach, ed., *Peter Weiss.* Frankfurt/Main: Suhrkamp, 1984. 32–56.

Rischbieter, Henning. "Swinarskis Inszenierung in Berlin." In Karlheinz Braun, ed., *Materialien zu Peter Weiss' "Marat/Sade."* Frankfurt/Main: Suhrkamp, 1967. 74–80.

———." 'Gesang vom lusitanischen Popanz' " (1967). In Volker Canaris, ed., *Über Peter Weiss.* Frankfurt/Main: Suhrkamp, 4th ed., 1976. 97–105.

———. "Peter Weiss. 'Wie dem Herrn Mockinpott das Leiden ausgetrieben wird.' " In Peter Weiss, *Wie dem Herrn Mockinpott das Leiden ausgetrieben wird.* Stuttgart: Ernst Klett, 1983. 78–83.

Sareika, Rüdiger. "Peter Weiss' Engagement für die 'Dritte Welt.' 'Lusitanischer Popanz' und 'Viet Nam Diskurs.' " In Rainer Gerlach, ed., *Peter Weiss.* Frankfurt/Main: Suhrkamp, 1984. 249–67. Insightful and informative study on Weiss and the Third World.

Schlunk, Jürgen E. "Auschwitz and Its Function in Peter Weiss's Search for Identity." *German Studies Review* 10, no. 1 (February 1987): 11–30.

Schmidt-Henkel, Gerhard. "Die Wortgraphik des Peter Weiss." In Volker Canaris, ed., *Über Peter Weiss*. Frankfurt/Main: Suhrkamp, 4th ed., 1976. 15–24.

Schneider, Helmut J. "Der verlorene Sohn und die Sprache." In Volker Canaris, ed., *Über Peter Weiss*. Frankfurt/Main: Suhrkamp, 4th ed., 1976. 28–46.

Schneider, Peter. "Über das Marat-Stück von Peter Weiss" (1964). In Karlheinz Braun, ed., *Materialien zu Peter Weiss' "Marat/Sade."* Frankfurt/Main: Suhrkamp, 1967. 125–36.

Schonauer, Franz. "Heldenlegende vor düsterem Hintergrund. Zur Fortsetzung von Peter Weiss' Roman 'Die Ästhetik des Widerstands.' " *Der Tagesspiegel* (Berlin) 25 March 1979.

Sebald, W. G. "Die Zerknirschung des Herzens. Über Erinnerung und Grausamkeit im Werk von Peter Weiss." *Orbis Litterarum* 41, no. 1 (1986): 265–78.

Söllner, Alfons. *Peter Weiss und die Deutschen*. Opladen: Westdeutscher Verlag, 1988.

Sontag, Susan. "Marat/Sade/Artaud." *Partisan Review* 32, no. 2 (Spring 1965): 210–19. Important but one-sided interpretation of *Marat/Sade* that was very influential in the reception of Weiss's play in the United States.

Spielmann, Peter. "Das grosse Welttheater. Bemerkungen zum Maler Peter Weiss." In *Der Maler Peter Weiss*. Berlin: Frölich and Kaufmann, 1982. 65–74.

Steinlein, Rüdiger. "Ein surrealistischer 'Bilddichter.' Visualität als Darstellungsprinzip im erzählerischen Frühwerk von Peter Weiss." In Rudolf Wolff, ed., *Peter Weiss. Werk und Wirkung*. Bonn: Bouvier, 1987. 60–87.

Töteberg, Michael. "Späte Rückkehr nach Bremen. Peter Weiss und die Stadt seiner Kindheit." *die horen* 27 no. 125 (Spring 1982): 113–22.

Vegesack, Thomas von. "Dokumentation zur 'Ermittlung.' " *Kürbiskern* 2 (1966): 83. Useful documentation on the reception of *The Investigation*.

Vogt, Jochen. *Peter Weiss*. Reinbek b. Hamburg: Rowohlt-Monographie, 1987. A limited but useful introduction to Weiss's life and work.

―――. " 'Ich tötete und ich wurde getötet.' Zughörigkeitsprobleme bei Peter Weiss." In Jost Hermand and Gert Mattenklott, eds., *Jüdische Intelligenz in Deutschland*. Berlin: Argument, 1988. 126–38.

―――. " 'Er projizierte die inneren Bilder auf Tafeln. . . .' Sprachkrise, Exilerfahrung und Filmarbeit bei Peter Weiss." In Alexander Stephan, ed., *Exil. Literatur und Künste nach 1933*. Bonn: Bouvier, 1990. 189–204.

Vormweg, Heinrich. "Ein grosser Entwurf gegen den Zeitgeist. Peter Weiss hat 'Die Ästhetik des Widerstands' abgeschlossen." *Süddeutsche Zeitung* 20 May 1981.

―――. *Peter Weiss*. Munich: Beck, 1981. Short, insightful book on Weiss's life and literary work, but does not discuss Weiss's work as a painter or filmmaker or his early Swedish writings and his plays *Trotsky in Exile* and *Hölderlin*.

―――. "Der Schriftsteller als junger Künstler." In Gunilla Palmstierna-Weiss and Jürgen Schutte, eds., *Peter Weiss. Leben und Werk*. Frankfurt/Main: Suhrkamp, 1991. 24–38.

Walberg, Ernst J. "Die Ästhetik der Imagination. Peter Weiss' Frühwerk 'Von Insel zu Insel.' " *die horen* 4 (1984): 137–39.

Warneken, Bernd Jürgen. "Kritik am 'Viet Nam Diskurs' " (1970). In Volker Canaris, ed., *Über Peter Weiss*. Frankfurt/Main: Suhrkamp, 4th ed., 1976. 112–30.

Wendt, Ernst. "Brooks Inszenierung in London." In Karlheinz Braun, ed., *Materialien zu Peter Weiss' "Marat/Sade."* Frankfurt/Main: Suhrkamp, 1967. 83–86.

Wiese, Benno von. "Peter Weiss' 'Hölderlin.' Ein kritisches Essay." In Thomas Beckermann and Volker Canaris, eds., *Der andere Hölderlin. Materialien zum "Hölderlin"-Stück von Peter Weiss*. Frankfurt/Main: Suhrkamp, 1972. 217–46.

Witting, Gunther. "Bericht von der hohen Warte. Zu Peter Weiss' 'Der Schatten des Körpers des Kutschers.' " *Der Deutschunterricht* 37, no. 3 (1985): 55–64.

Wolf, Ror. "Die Poesie der kleinsten Stücke." In Volker Canaris, ed., *Über Peter Weiss*. Frankfurt/Main: Suhrkamp, 4th ed., 1976. 25–27.

Zimmermann, Ulrike. *Die dramatische Bearbeitung von Kafkas "Prozess" durch Peter Weiss*. Frankfurt/Main: Peter Lang, 1990. First monograph on Weiss and Kafka. Contains useful information but uses an incomplete edition(!) of *Der neue Prozess* and thus remains limited in its insights.

ADDITIONAL WORKS CITED

Adorno, Theodor W. "Kulturkritik und Gesellschaft" (1949). In Adorno, *Prismen*. Frankfurt/Main: Suhrkamp, 3d ed., 1987. 7–26.

———. "Aufzeichnungen zu Kafka" (1942–53). In Adorno, *Prismen*. 250–83.

———. "Versuch, das Endspiel zu verstehen" (1961). In Adorno, *Noten zur Literatur*. Frankfurt/Main: Suhrkamp, 1981. 281–321.

———. "Engagement" (1962). In Adorno, *Noten zur Literatur*. 409–30.

———. *Negative Dialektik*. Frankfurt/Main: Suhrkamp, 1970.

Anders, Günther. "Kafka, pro und contra. 'Die Prozess-Unterlagen' " (1951). In Anders, *Mensch ohne Welt. Schriften zur Kunst und Literatur*. Munich: Beck, 1984. 45–131.

———. "Auschwitz 1966." In Anders, *Besuch im Hades*. Munich: Beck, 2nd ed., 1985. 7–36.

Arendt, Hannah. "Das Bild der Hölle" ("The Image of Hell," 1946). Trans. Eike Geisel. In Arendt, *Nach Auschwitz. Essays und Kommentare 1*. Berlin: Tiamat 1989. 49–62.

———. *Eichmann in Jerusalem. Ein Bericht von der Banalität des Bösen* (*Eichmann in Jerusalem: A Report on the Banality of Evil,* 1963). Trans. Brigitte Granzow. Munich: Piper, 6th ed., 1987.

———. "Was heisst persönliche Verantwortung unter einer Diktatur?" ("Personal Responsibility under Dictatorship," 1964). Trans. Eike Geisel. In Arendt, *Nach Auschwitz*. 81–97.

Artaud, Antonin. *Das Theater und sein Double* (*Le Théâtre et son double,* 1938). Trans. Gerd Heninnger. Frankfurt/Main: Fischer, 1989.

Bertaux, Pierre. *Hölderlin und die Französische Revolution* (1969). Frankfurt/Main: Suhrkamp, 5th ed., 1980.

Brecht, Bertolt. "Herr Puntila und sein Knecht Matti" (1940). In Brecht, *Werke*. Annotated Berlin and Frankfurt edition. Frankfurt/Main: Suhrkamp, 1989. Vol. 6.

———. "Über die Bauart langdauernder Werke." In Brecht, *Gesammelte Werke in acht Bänden*. Ed. Suhrkamp in cooperation with Elisabeth Hauptmann. Frankfurt/Main: Suhrkamp, 1967. 4:387–90.

———. "About the Way to Construct Enduring Works." In Brecht, *Poems 1913–1956*. Ed. John Willett and Ralph Manheim, with the cooperation of Erich Fried. New York: Methuen, 1974.

———. "Der Schuh des Empedokles." *Werke* 12 (1988): 30–32.

Bürger, Peter. *Theory of the Avant-Garde* (*Theorie der Avantgarde*, 1974). Trans. Michael Shaw. Minneapolis: University of Minnesota Press, 1984.

Claussen, Detlev. "Nach Auschwitz. Ein Essay über die Aktualität Adornos." In Dan Diner, ed., *Zivilisationsbruch. Denken nach Auschwitz*. Frankfurt/Main: Fischer, 1988. 54–68.

Deutscher, Isaac. *The Prophet Outcast*. (Vol. 3 of Deutscher's biography of Trotsky.) London: Oxford University Press, 1963.

Diner, Dan, ed. *Zivilisationsbruch. Denken nach Auschwitz*. Frankfurt/Main: Fischer, 1988.

Duffett, John, ed. *Against the Crime of Silence. Proceedings of the Russell International War Crimes Tribunal*. New York: O'Hare Books, 1968.

Engels, Friedrich. *Der Deutsche Bauernkrieg* (1850). East Berlin: Dietz, 1974.

Fanon, Frantz. *Die Verdammten dieser Erde* (*Les damnés de la terre*, 1961). Trans. Traugott König. Frankfurt/Main: Suhrkamp, 1981.

Fischer, Ernst. "Franz Kafka." In Fischer, *Von Grillparzer zu Kafka*. Frankfurt/Main: Suhrkamp, 1975. 325–83.

Grass, Günter. *Schreiben nach Auschwitz. Frankfurter Poetik-Vorlesung*. Frankfurt/Main: Luchterhand, 1991.

Haug, Wolfgang Fritz, and Kaspar Maase. "Vorwort." In Haug and Maase, eds., *Materialistische Kulturtheorie und Alltagskultur*, Berlin: Argument, 1980. 4–5.

Hofer, Walther, ed. *Der Nationalsozialismus. Dokumente 1933–1945*. Frankfurt/Main: Fischer, 1957.

Hölderlin, Friedrich. "Der Tod des Empedokles. Erste Fassung." In Hölderlin, *Werke. Briefe. Dokumente*. Based on the text established by Friedrich Beissner for the smaller Stuttgart Hölderlin edition. Selected, annotated, and with an afterword by Pierre Bertaux. Munich: Winkler, 1977. 381–442.

Kafka, Franz. *Das Schloss*. Novel in the version of the hand-written manuscript. Ed. Malcolm Pasley. Frankfurt/Main: Fischer, 1982.

———. *Der Process*. Ed. Malcolm Pasley. Frankfurt/Main: Fischer, 1990.

Kofler, Leo. "Beckett, Warten auf Godot" (1975). In Kofler, *Avantgardismus als Entfremdung. Ästhetik und Ideologiekritik*. Frankfurt/Main: Sendler, 1987. 203–6.

Lenin, V. I. *Ausgewählte Werke*. 6 vols. East Berlin: Dietz, 1970 onward.

Limqueco, Peter, and Peter Weiss, eds. *Prevent the Crime of Silence. Reports from the sessions of the International War Crimes Tribunal founded by Bertrand Russell*, London: 1971.

Lukács, Georg. "Hölderlins Hyperion" (1934). In Lukács, *Deutsche Literatur in zwei Jahrhunderten. Werke* 7. Neuwied: Luchterhand, 1964. 164–84.

———. "Franz Kafka oder Thomas Mann" (1957). In Lukács, *Essays über Realismus. Werke* 4. Neuwied: Luchterhand, 1971. 500–550.

———. "Vorwort zu Band 6" (1964). In Lukács, *Der historische Roman. Werke* 6. Neuwied: Luchterhand, 1965. 7–13.

Mann, Heinrich. *Der Untertan*. Munich: dtv, 20th ed., 1980.

Markov, Walter, and Albert Soboul. *1789. Die Grosse Revolution der Franzosen*. Cologne: Pahl-Rugenstein, 2d ed., 1980.

Marx, Karl. "Thesen über Feuerbach" (1845). In *Marx Engels Werke*. Berlin: Dietz, 1956–. 3:5–7.

———. "Zur Kritik der politischen Ökonomie. Vorwort." In *Marx Engels Werke*. Berlin: Dietz, 1956–. 13:7–9.

Meyer, Raimund. *Dada in Zürich. Die Akteure, die Schauplätze*. Frankfurt/Main: Luchterhand, 1990.

Müssener, Helmut. *Exil in Schweden*. Munich: Hanser, 1974.

Olson, James S., and Randy Roberts. *Where the Domino Fell. America and Vietnam, 1945 to 1990*. New York: St. Martin's, 1991.

Papcke, Sven G. "Che Guevara und die Neue Linke in der Bundesrepublik—Chronik einer psycho-politischen Jüngerschaft." In Heinz Rudolf Sonntag, ed., *Che Guevara und die Revolution*. Frankfurt/Main: Fischer, 1968. 99–124.

Sadoul, Georges. *Histoire du Cinéma*. Paris: Flammarion, 1962.

Seghers, Anna. Correspondence with Georg Lukács (1938–39). In Georg Lukács, *Essays über Realismus. Werke* 4. Neuwied: Luchterhand, 1971. 345–76.

Soboul, Albert. *Kurze Geschichte der Französischen Revolution* (1965). Trans. Bernd Schwibs and Joachim Heilmann. Berlin: Wagenbach, 1980.

Sonntag, Heinz Rudolf, ed. *Che Guevara und die Revolution*. Frankfurt/Main: Fischer, 1968.

Valentin, Veit. *Geschichte der Deutschen*. With a digest of German history from 1945 to the present by Erhard Klöss. Cologne: Kiepenheuer and Witsch, 1979.

Walser, Martin. "Unser Auschwitz." *Kursbuch* 1 (June 1965): 189–200.

Weber, Hermann. *Lenin* (1970). Reinbek b. Hamburg: Rowohlt-Bildmonographie, 1978.

Wilde, Harry. *Trotzki* (1969). Reinbek b. Hamburg: Rowohlt-Bildmonographie, 1979.

Ziegler, Jean. "Staatslogik gegen Klassenlogik." In Ziegler, *Gegen die Ordnung der Welt. Befreiungsbewegungen in Afrika und Lateinamerika (Les Rebelles / Contre l'ordre du monde*, 1983). Trans. Elke Hammer. Wuppertal: Hammer, 2d ed., 1986. 263–322.

INDEX

In many of his works of fiction Weiss used the names of actual persons. The names in the index, however, refer only to the real historical individuals, not to Weiss's fictionalized characters—a distinction that is not always easy to make. The index does not include references to material in the notes.